J. Haythornthwr

Physics for All
Second Edition

J J Wellington, BSc., M.A., C.Phys., M.Inst.P.
University of Sheffield
(formerly Head of Physics, Daneford Comprehensive School, Bethnal Green, London)

Stanley Thornes (Publishers) Ltd.

Text © J J Wellington 1982, 1988
Illustrations © Stanley Thornes (Publishers) 1982, 1988

All rights reserved. No part of this publication may be reproduced, stored in a retrieval system, or transmitted in any form or by any means, electronic, mechanical, photocopying, recording or otherwise, without the prior permission of the copyright holder. Requests for such permission should be addressed to the publishers:

First published in 1982 by Stanley Thornes (Publishers) Ltd.
Old Station Drive, Leckhampton
CHELTENHAM, GL53 0DN

Reprinted 1983 twice
2nd Edition 1988

British Cataloguing in Publication Data

Wellington, J. J. (Jerry J.)
   Physics for all.—GCSE ed.
   1. Physics. For schools
   I. Title
   530

   ISBN 0 85950 819 6

Text typeset by Promenade Graphics Ltd., Cheltenham.
Printed and bound in Great Britain at The Bath Press, Avon.

Contents

PREFACE	v
ACKNOWLEDGEMENTS	vi
INTRODUCTION	1

Part 1

IMPORTANT IDEAS IN PHYSICS

1. Different kinds of energy	8
2. Molecules	14

Part 2

FORCES AND MOVEMENT

3. Different types of forces	24
4. Forces and moving objects	29
5. Forces and machines	36
6. Forces and balance	42
7. Forces in liquids and gases	48
8. Pressure	52

Part 3

HEAT ENERGY

9. Temperature and thermometers	62
10. Measuring heat energy	66
11. Expansion of solids, liquids and gases	70
12. The way that heat travels	75
13. Melting, boiling and evaporation	82
14. Using heat energy	88

Part 4

LIGHT AND SOUND ENERGY: WAVES

15.	How does light travel?	96
16.	Reflecting light	99
17.	Refraction of light	104
18.	Optical instruments	110
19.	Colours of light and the spectrum	116
20.	Waves	120
21.	Sound waves and sound energy	128

Part 5

ELECTRICAL ENERGY

22.	Making electricity	140
23.	Electric circuits	145
24.	Magnetism	154
25.	Electricity and magnetism	161
26.	Using electrical energy	167

Part 6

ATOMIC PHYSICS

27.	The atom and radiation	180
28.	Using radioactivity and atomic energy	186
29.	Electrons and electronics	192

Appendixes

1.	Measurements in physics	202
2.	Triangles used for calculations	204
3.	Meters used in physics	205
4.	Famous names in physics	206
5.	Drawing electric circuits	208

INDEX 209

Preface to the Second Edition

Physics for All sets out to provide a brief, readable summary of the important facts and principles in basic physics. It covers the key areas common to most GCSE syllabuses without attempting to deal with all the subject matter needed for GCSE examinations.

The language is kept as simple and readable as possible throughout and the book is highly illustrated — the simple, small black square (■) leads the reader on to the appropriate figure.

All calculations use straightforward numbers. No practical work is described in detail — the book is designed for revision and consolidation to follow up practical work.

At the end of each chapter there is a good supply of graded questions to test both knowledge and understanding.

Each section ends with a crossword, closely related to the text leading up to it.

A number of photographs have been included to show the applications of physics and its uses in society.

SI units have been used throughout. The plural of a unit written *in full* has been given an 's' (e.g. 5 newtons, 4 joules, 2 kilograms) in line with everyday usage.

J J Wellington
1988

Acknowledgements

■ ■ ■ ■ ■ ■ ■ ■ ■ ■ ■ ■ ■ ■ ■ ■

I should like to thank: Mr J C Siddons, for carefully checking the original typescript and for making many suggestions for improvement; Mr D F Manley, for providing the crosswords and wordfinder; my brother, Simon, for helping to sketch the original diagrams; Ethan Danielson, for turning the sketches into artistic drawings; and especially my wife, Wendy, for long hours spent reading and checking the manuscript and proofs.

I am also grateful to the following examination boards who kindly gave permission for their questions to be reproduced:

East Midland Regional Examination Board (EMREB)
London Regional Examining Board (LREB)
South Western Examination Board (SWEB)
West Yorkshire and Lindsey Regional Examining Board
    (WY and LREB)
Yorkshire Regional Examinations Board (YREB)

The cover photograph shows white light being dispersed by a prism, courtesy of the Paul Brierley Photo Library, Harlow, Essex.

Finally I should like to thank Faber and Faber Ltd. for permission to use the extract from *Lord of the Flies* by William Golding on p. 115.

The author and publishers are also grateful to the following who provided photographs and gave permission for reproduction:

> All-Sport Photographic Agency Ltd. (p. 22 middle); J. Allan Cash Ltd. (pp. 59 top left, 59 bottom, 60 bottom left, 93 top right, 93 middle, 137 top left, 137 top right, 138 bottom left, 200 top right, 200 middle and 200 bottom); Bruce Coleman Ltd. (pp. 21 top, 21 bottom, 59 top right, 60 middle, 137 middle, 138 top left, 138 top right, 138 bottom right, 177 bottom and 178 top left); Andrew Lambert (pp. 93 top left, 94 bottom and 178 bottom); Alan Rutherford (p. 22 bottom right); Science Photo Library (pp. 22 top, 59 middle, 60 bottom right, 93 bottom, 94 top, 94 middle, 137 bottom, 177 middle, 200 top left, 201 top left, 201 top right, 201 bottom left and 201 bottom right).

J J Wellington

Introduction

Introduction

What is physics?

This is a difficult question to answer. It is easy to make a list of the different parts of physics — the main subjects are forces and movement, heat energy, optics, sound and waves, electricity and magnetism, and atomic physics.

Physics is the part of science which studies the way that objects and things 'behave' — ranging from very small things (like atoms and molecules) to much larger objects like the moon, the planets and the sun. Physics is made up of many laws and theories which come from experiments and discoveries made as long as 2000 years ago. Some famous experiments were done by Archimedes, one of the ancient Greeks, Galileo (in Italy) and Sir Isaac Newton (in England), and these led to laws of physics that we still use today. The most famous are called *Newton's Laws of Motion*.

Some of the discoveries in physics have led to a lot of the machines and inventions we use today: radar control, computers, colour television, microscopes and periscopes are just a few examples. Another discovery, the splitting of the atom, has led to the nuclear reactor and the atomic bomb.

Measurement and 'units' in physics

Physics is sometimes called 'the science of measurement'. Nearly all experiments in physics involve measuring something. Length, time, speed, acceleration, weight, force, energy and power are a few examples. Each of these things is measured in its own 'units' in physics. Length is measured in metres, time is measured in seconds, speed is measured in metres per second, and so on. On the page opposite is a table of the measurements and units that will be used in this book.

Measurement	Unit	Symbol
length	metre	m
time	second	s
mass	kilogram	kg
weight	newton	N
speed	metre per second	m/s
acceleration	metre per second per second	m/s^2
force	newton	N
energy	joule	J
power	watt	W
area	square metre	m^2
volume	cubic metre	m^3
density	kilogram per cubic metre	kg/m^3
frequency	hertz	Hz
pressure	newton per square metre (pascal)	N/m^2
electric current	ampere	A
temperature	kelvin	K

These are called SI units.

Mass and weight

Mass has a special meaning in physics. It is sometimes called 'a measure of the amount of stuff in an object'. Large objects, like the Earth or the Sun, have a large mass. Smaller objects, like a book or an apple, have a smaller mass. Large masses need a large force to get them moving, or to slow them down. This means that the mass of an object can be explained by its resistance to being moved. (The word for this is *inertia*, as we shall discover in Chapters 3 and 4.)

The mass of an object is *always* the same. A kilogram of sugar will contain the same number of spoonfuls on the Earth, or on the Moon. But the weight of an object can *change.* A man may weigh 600 N on Earth, only 100 N on the moon, and can even weigh nothing in outer space. The weight of an object is the pull of gravity on it.

This table shows the differences between weight and mass:

The *weight* of an object ...	The *mass* of an object ...
... changes	... is always the same
... is the pull of gravity on it	... is the amount of 'stuff' in the object
... is a force	... is its resistance to being moved
... is measured in newtons	... is measured in kilograms

A mass of one kilogram has a weight of about ten newtons on Earth, though its weight on the moon is about six times less. (An 'average-sized' apple weighs about one newton on Earth.)

A mass of one kilogram weighs about 10 newtons on Earth.

Ten apples weigh about 10 newtons

Other units in physics

Some of the units shown in the table on p.3 are sometimes too big and clumsy to measure certain things, and so smaller units have to be used. A metre, which is slightly longer than a man's arm, can be split into 100 parts called centimetres (cm), or 1000 parts called millimetres (mm):

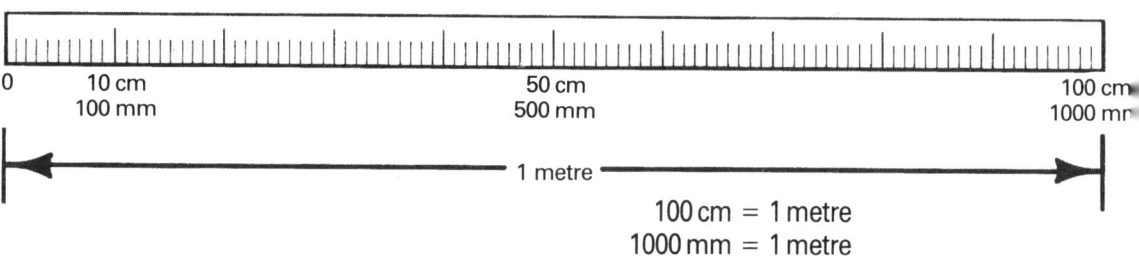

(not life size!)

0
10 cm / 100 mm
50 cm / 500 mm
100 cm / 1000 mm

1 metre

100 cm = 1 metre
1000 mm = 1 metre

Larger distances and lengths can be measured in kilometres. A kilometre is 1000 metres:

1000 metres = 1 kilometre

A kilogram, which is quite a large mass, can be divided into 1000 parts to make one gram (1g):

1000 grams = 1 kilogram

Grams are often more useful for measuring mass than kilograms.

Questions.......... Introduction

1. What would the weight of each of these masses be on Earth:
   (a) 6 kg   (b) 8 kg   (c) 12 kg   (d) 50 kg?
2. What would they weigh on the moon (roughly)?
3. How many metres are there in:
   (a) 2 kilometres   (b) ½ kilometre
   (c) 4½ kilometres   (d) 12½ kilometres?
4. How many grams in:
   (a) 2 kg   (b) 4½ kg   (c) 11½ kg?
5. Find out the names of six famous physicists and the discoveries they are famous for.
6. Try to explain the difference between mass and weight, in your own words.
7. The diagrams below show four different *measuring instruments* used in physics. Draw each instrument and write underneath it:
   – the name of the instrument
   – its use
   – the units it measures in.
   (You will need to look through the rest of the book to answer this).

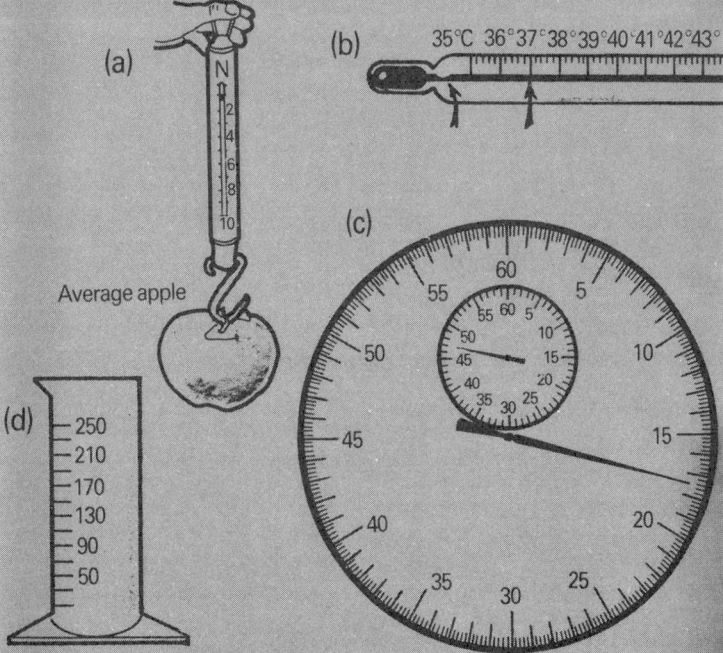

What are the readings shown on the instruments in (a) and (c)?

WORDFINDER

32 answers are hidden in the grid above (one of them has two words). They go in straight lines in any direction including diagonally. Copy out the grid and put a ring around each of the words. One of the words already has a ring to give you a start.

The 32 answers include:

- 11 measurements and their units, one of which occurs twice (look at the table on p. 3)
- 3 heavenly bodies
- a Greek and an Italian who did experiments (see p. 2)
- something to measure one of the measurements
- something which has been split to give energy (see p. 180)
- the unit of electrical resistance (see p. 148)
- 2 units which are not used very much in physics—one for mass and one for length

Part 1
Important Ideas in Physics

Chapter 1

Different kinds of energy

The forms of energy

There are at least seven different kinds of energy which are all very important in physics, and each of these will be looked at in different parts of this book.

Heat energy and *light* energy both come from the sun. Both can be used to make electricity, or *electrical* energy. *Potential* energy is the name of energy which is stored up, ready to be used.

Chemical energy in things like coal and wood or a man's muscles, is one special type of potential energy. *Sound* energy, carried in sound waves, is another type of energy. Finally, when something is moving, like a car or a train, we say it has *kinetic* energy.

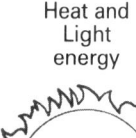
Heat and Light energy

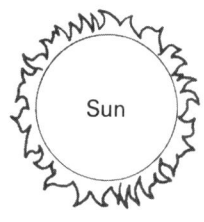

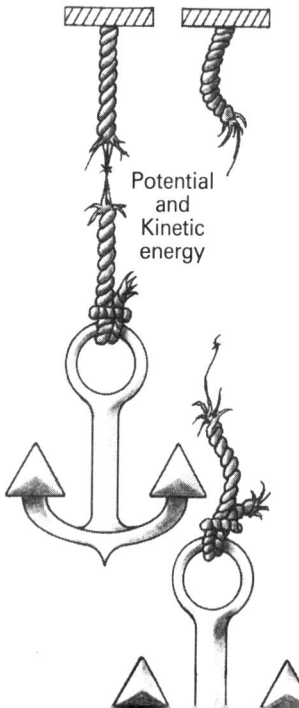
Potential and Kinetic energy

Chemical energy

Coal

Sound energy

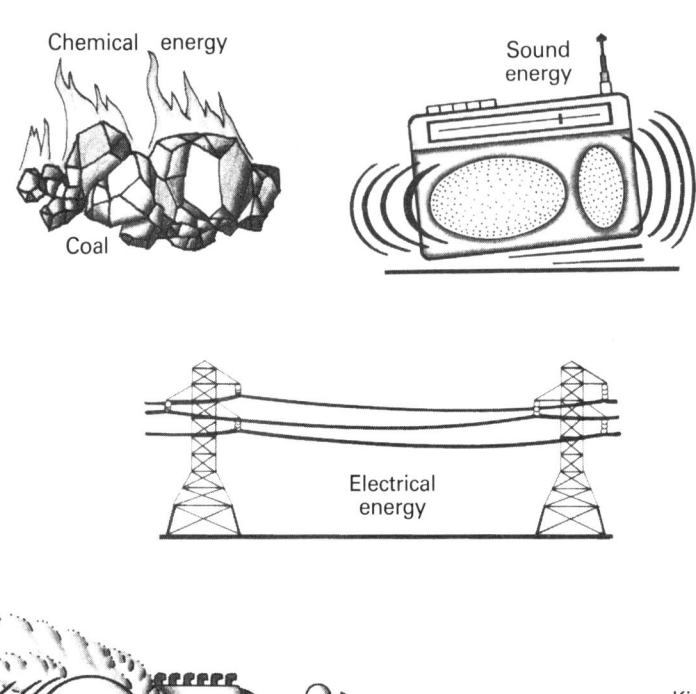

Electrical energy

Kinetic energy

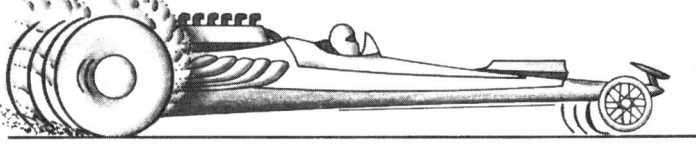

In other words, the seven different 'forms' of energy are: heat, light, sound, electrical, chemical, potential and kinetic energy.

Nuclear energy is another form of energy, which will be described later in the book. It is the energy that can be released from the very centre of an atom: the nucleus.

Changing energy from one form into another

Electrical energy is changed into light energy by an electric light bulb.

Chemical energy is changed into electrical energy by a torch battery.

Kinetic energy is changed into heat energy when you rub your hand up and down on your sleeve.

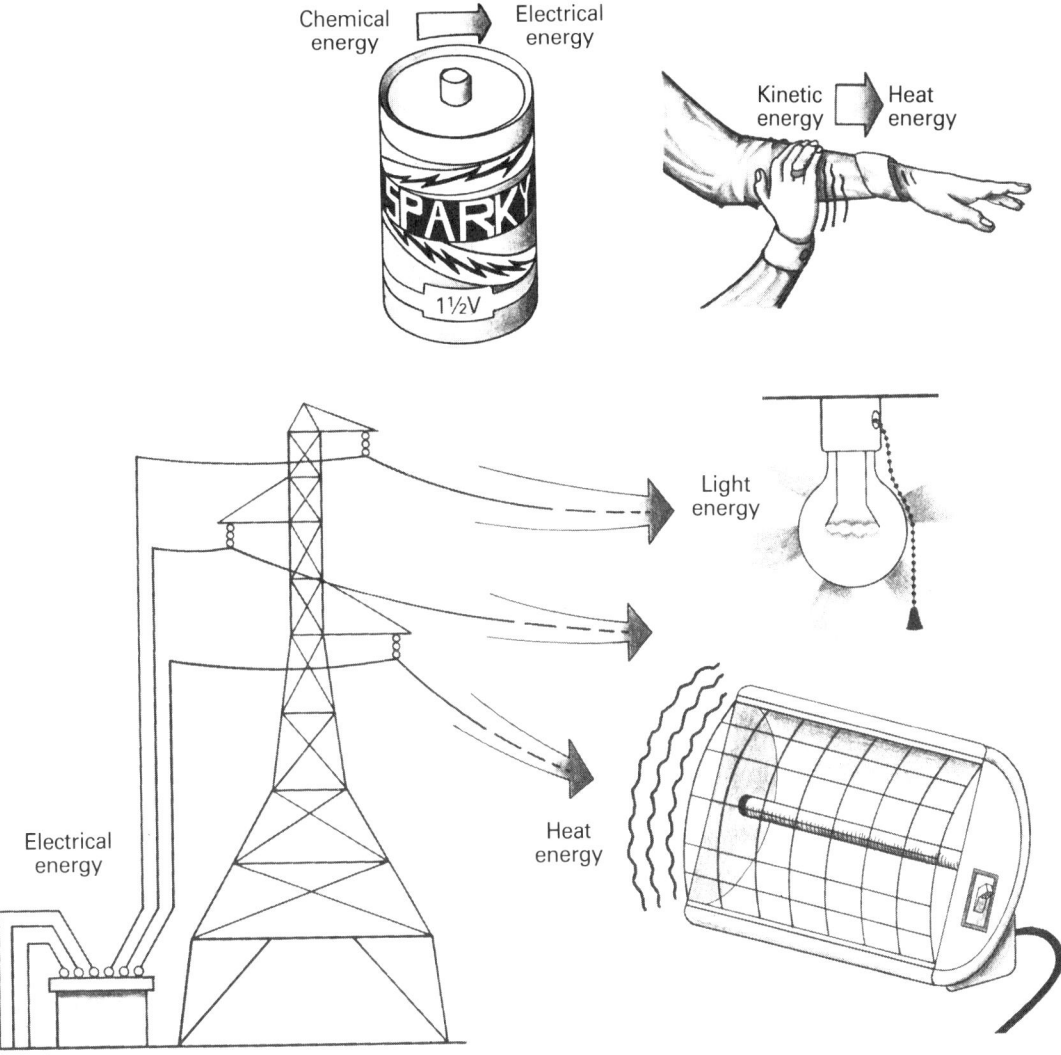

In fact, all forms of energy can be changed into another form. As the diagram shows, electrical energy is probably the most useful.

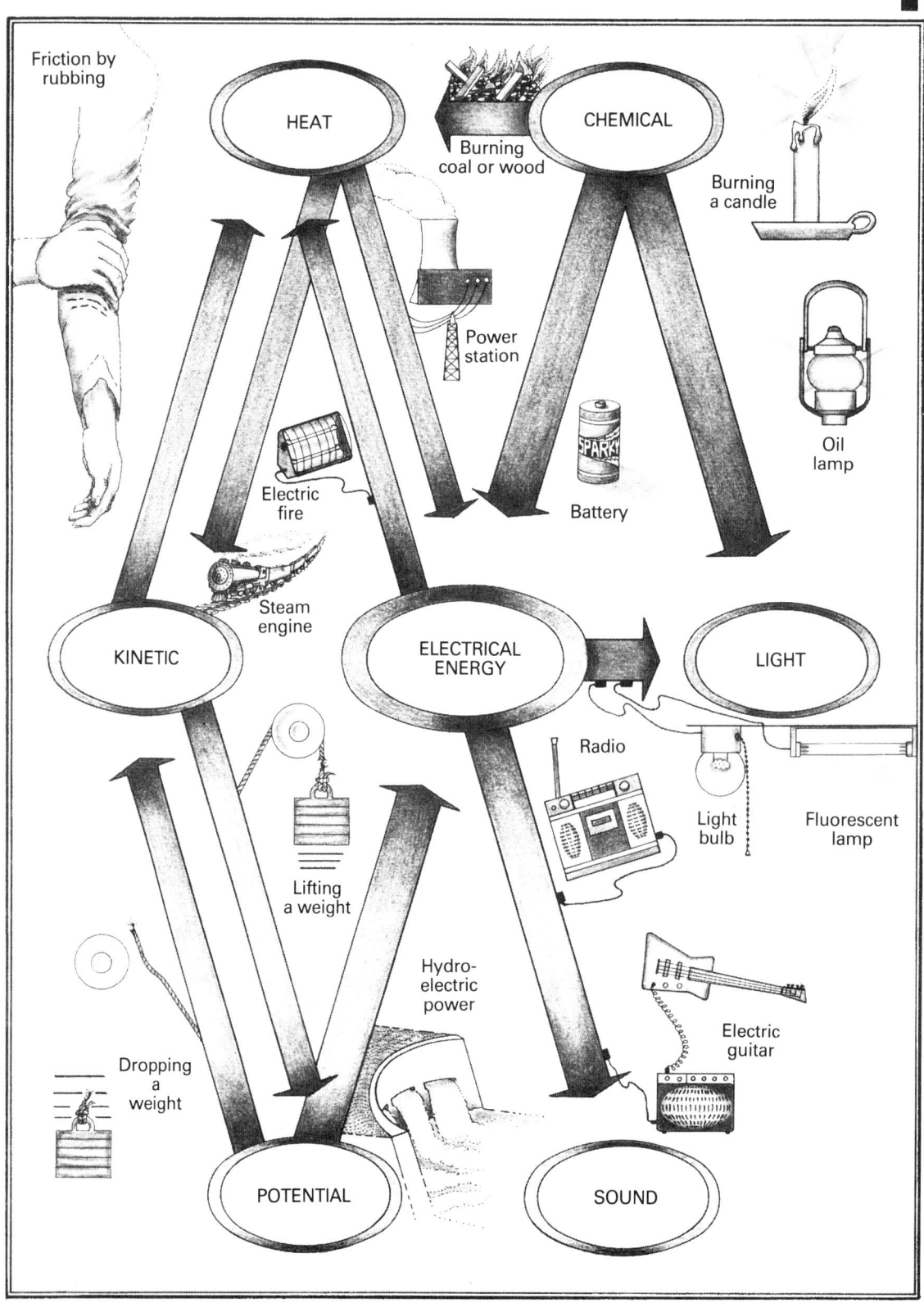

When energy is changed from one form into another, none of it is actually 'lost' or destroyed. This is one of the most important laws in physics called *The Law of Conservation of Energy*.

Energy chains

Energy changing from one form into another can be shown as a kind of 'chain': an *energy chain*. For example, a battery used to light a torch bulb has the energy chain shown below.

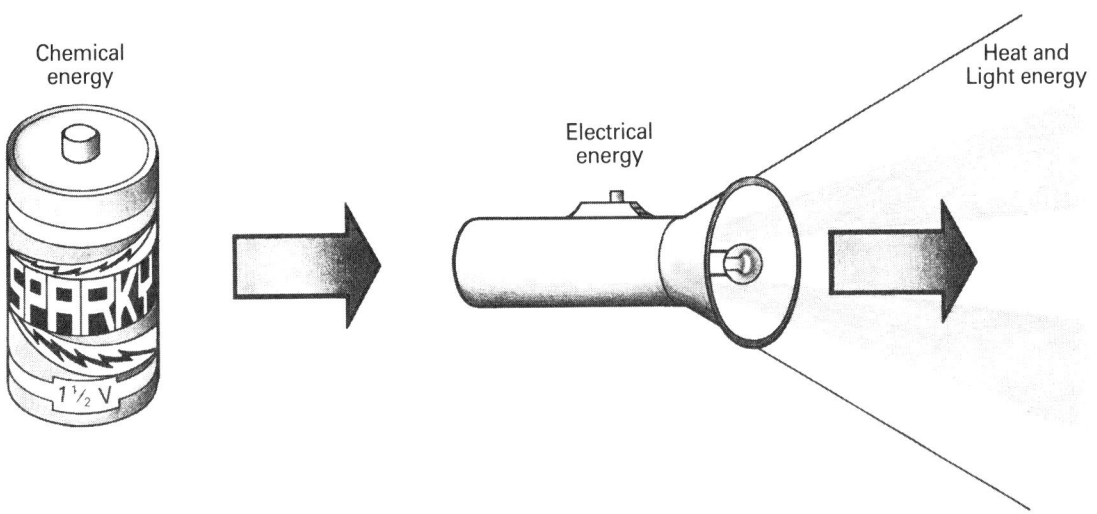

Plants get their energy from the Sun's light and heat. People often eat plants to supply them with energy. They can use this energy to run about or do some work. These changes can be shown with an energy chain.

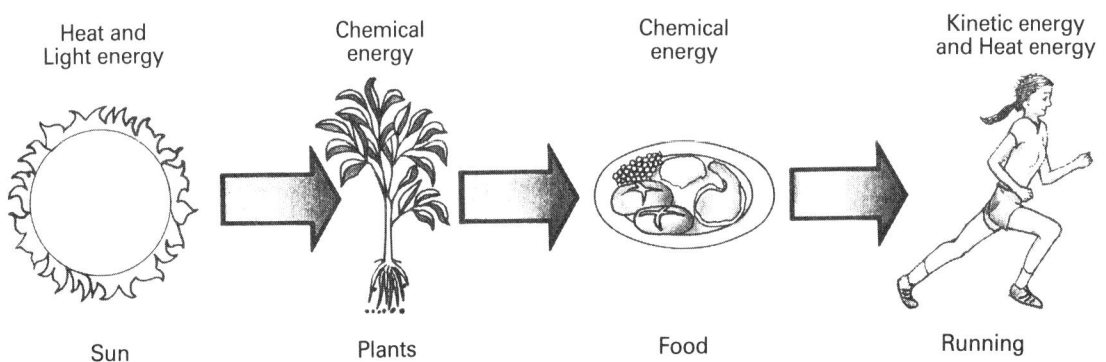

Energy chains like these can be useful for seeing how energy changes from one form to another. Most energy chains end with heat *energy*. None of the energy along the chain is actually destroyed — but heat energy is often wasted as it escapes into the air around us.

Measuring energy and power

Energy is measured in units called *joules* (or J, in short). These units are named after a man called J P Joule of Manchester who found that heat was a form of energy.

If a man in the diagram lifts the heavy weight above his head he uses about 1000 J of chemical energy from his body.

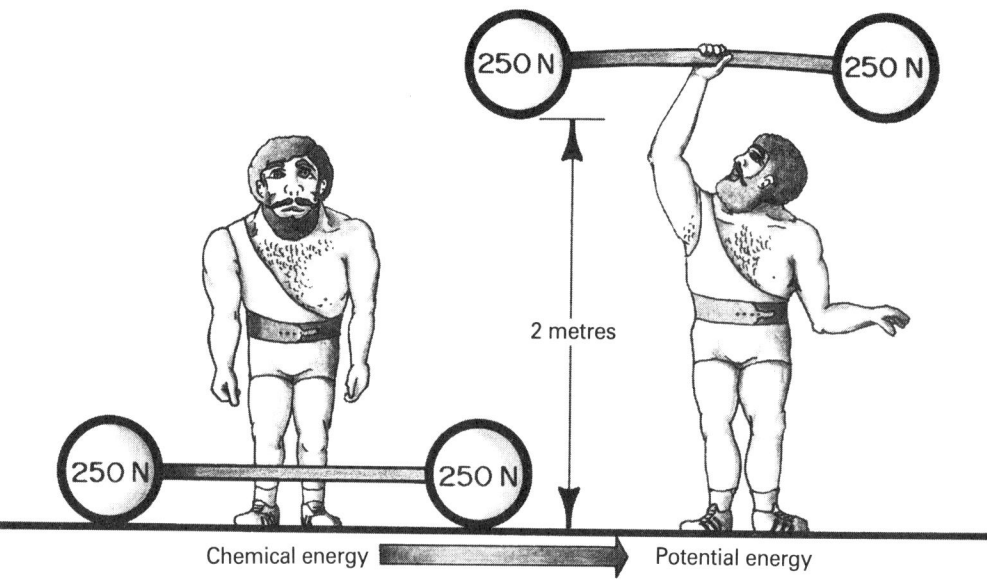

This energy is changed to the potential energy stored by the weight at this height. No energy is lost or destroyed. The man has to do work to raise the weight, and this work, as you will see in Chapter 5, is also measured in joules.

The man's power is measured by seeing how much work he can do every second. The more joules of work he can do in every second, the more powerful he is, and the more energy he uses up from his body. Power is measured in *watts* (or W, in short). These units are named after James Watt, a man who helped to improve the early steam engines.

So, Power in watts = Number of joules used every second

Questions 1

1. Write down the seven different types of energy studied in physics. Which type, do you think, is most useful?
2. How is electrical energy changed into heat energy in our homes? Give some examples.
3. This diagram shows how coal is burnt in a power station to drive a turbine and then generate electricity for house lighting and heating.

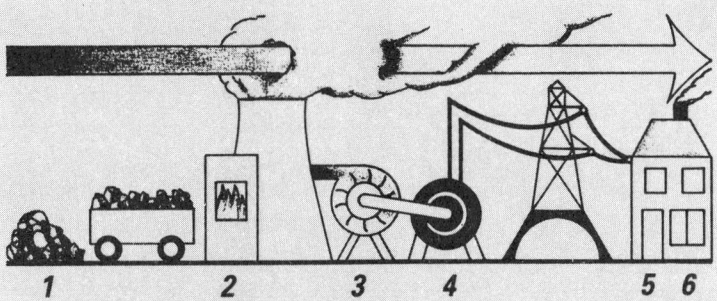

Write down the forms of energy involved at each stage, to complete the 'energy chain'.

4. Where does a human being get his or her energy from?
5. Draw an energy chain for each of these changes. The first one is done for you.
    (a) A light bulb.

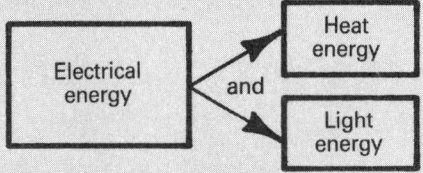

   (b) A burning match.
   (c) A loudspeaker.
   (d) A stone falling off a cliff.
   (e) The engine of a car.
   (f) A meat-eating human being who runs a lot.
6. Calculate the power (in watts) in these examples. The first one is done for you.
    (a) A man using 90 joules of energy for 3 seconds:
        Power = $^{90}/_{3}$ = 30 joules per second or 30 watts.
    (b) A light bulb using 3600 joules every minute.
    (c) A machine using 4000 joules every 10 seconds.
    (d) A girl doing 1200 J of work in 6 seconds.
    (e) A boy using 1200 J of energy in 10 seconds.
7. Find out why James Joule and James Watt became famous.

Chapter 2

Molecules

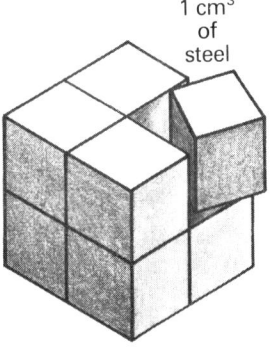

1 cm³ of steel

contains about 100 000 million million million molecules

What are molecules?

Everything in the world is made up of tiny particles called *molecules*. These molecules are too small to be seen even with the strongest microscope. If 500 million oil molecules could be laid side by side they would not even stretch for one metre. All substances are made up of millions and millions of molecules. In 1cm³ of steel there are about 100 000 million million million molecules.

There are two important things to remember about these molecules:
(a) They are continually moving, backwards and forwards and in every direction. Whenever something gets warmer and its temperature goes up, its molecules move faster and faster.
(b) The molecules in solids and liquids hold each other together. They attract each other.

Solids, liquids and gases

Every substance is either a *solid*, a *liquid* or a *gas*. The molecules in a gas move around freely in all directions, so gases must be completely enclosed in a container. In liquids, the molecules are not as free to move around as they are in a gas. But liquids still have to be kept in containers. The molecules in solids are held in position and cannot move around freely. This means that solids have their own shape and do not need to be kept in containers.

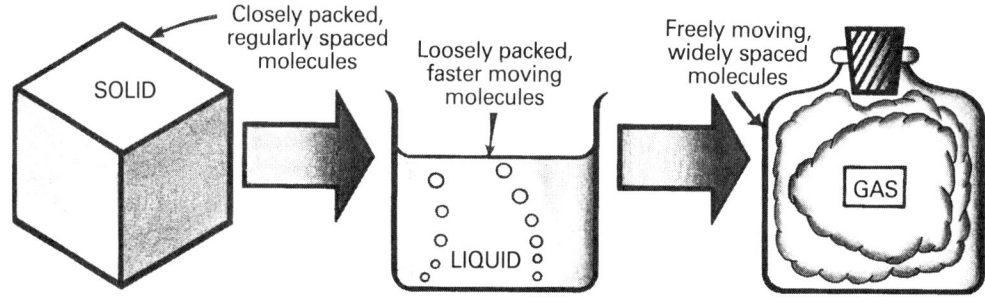

If a solid, like ice, is heated its molecules move faster and faster. When they move fast enough the ice melts and becomes water. If water is heated its molecules move faster and faster until they break away. The water boils and steam is made. Steam is a gas and its molecules spread out in every direction. ■

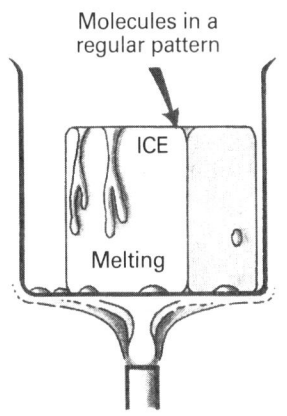

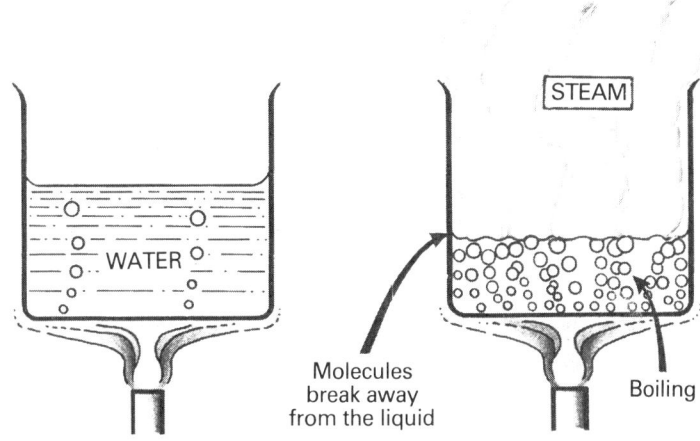

Stretching and squeezing

In a solid the molecules hold each other in position. If they are pulled apart, they attract each other together. But if they are pushed too close together, they repel each other away again. Molecules have a 'natural' distance apart which means that any piece of solid has its own 'natural' size.

When a steel wire is stretched its molecules are pulled slightly apart. If the wire is released these molecules attract each other and pull the wire back to its natural length.

The steel wire is elastic. ■

Molecules in solids and liquids don't 'like' to be too far apart. But they don't 'like' to be too close together either. When you squeeze a spring you are forcing its molecules too close together. They push against you. Liquids cannot be squeezed, or compressed, at all. Only gases can be compressed easily. ■

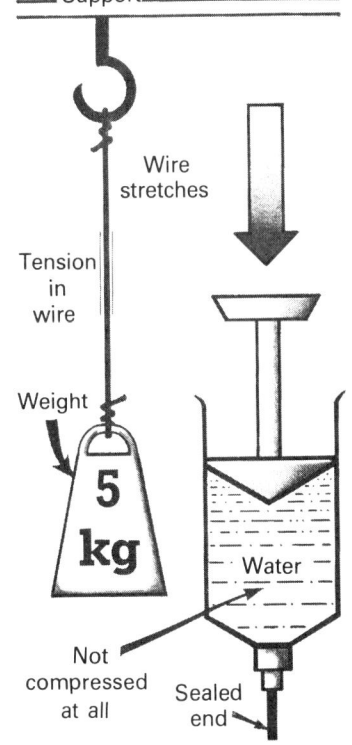

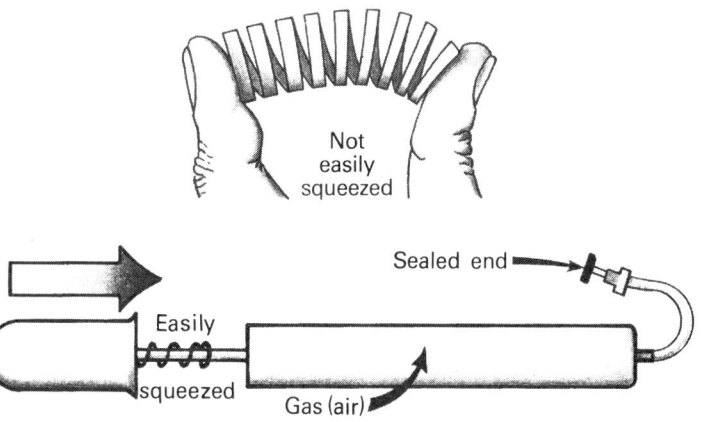

Liquids

When a liquid is put into a container, the top, or surface, of the liquid forms a kind of skin, where the liquid molecules meet the air molecules. A razor blade, or a needle, will rest on this skin. ■

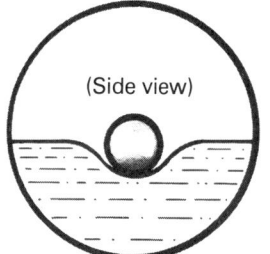
(Side view)

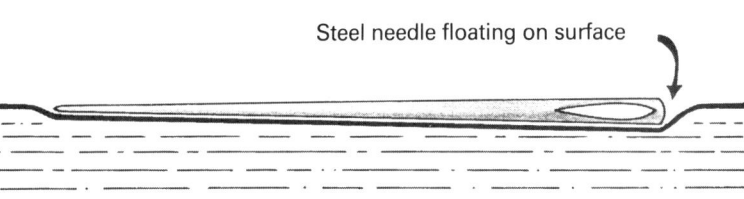
Steel needle floating on surface

This 'skin' on the surface of water is caused by *surface tension*. Insects can walk on the surface of ponds and lakes because of surface tension. Surface tension makes water dripping from a tap form into droplets. ■

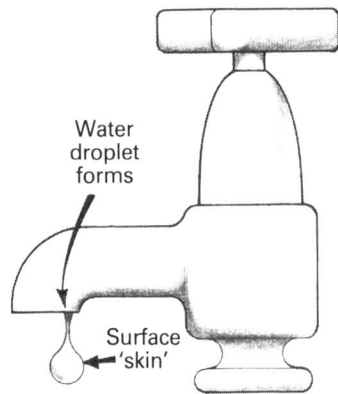
Water droplet forms
Surface 'skin'

Pond skater

This skin on the surface of liquids is made because liquid molecules attract each other. You can see this attraction after a paintbrush has been dipped into water. The bristles are pulled together by the water molecules when the brush is taken out. ■

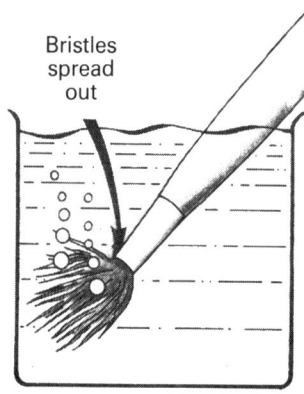
Bristles spread out

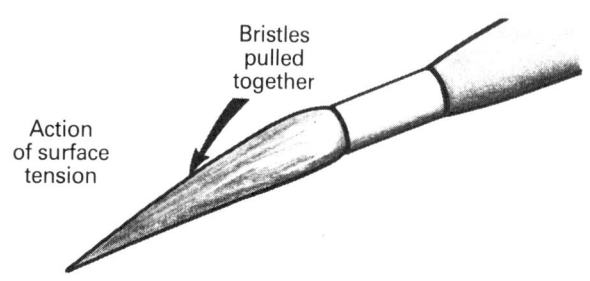
Action of surface tension
Bristles pulled together

Whenever water is put into a glass container it clings to the sides. The water 'wets' the glass. Water molecules are attracted by glass molecules more than by other water molecules. This makes the water surface curve upwards where it meets the glass. ■

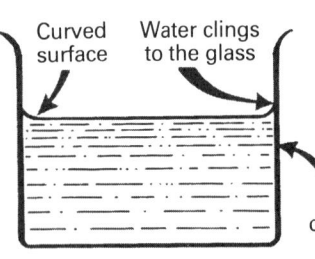
Curved surface
Water clings to the glass
Glass container

A narrow tube made of glass actually pulls water up inside it — the glass molecules attract water molecules and pull them upwards.

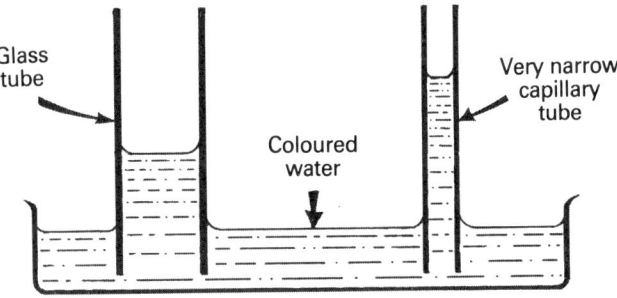

Materials like blotting paper, cotton wool and tissue 'soak up' water in the same way. These materials are full of tiny *capillary* tubes which pull the liquid upwards. Bricks are full of air spaces that soak up water in the same way. When a house is built a waterproof layer is placed between two layers of brick just above the ground to stop rising damp.

The liquid with the strongest surface tension is mercury (the only metal which is a liquid at ordinary temperatures). When mercury is spilled onto a bench it will not spread or 'wet' the bench like water does. Instead, it makes round drops which cling tightly together.

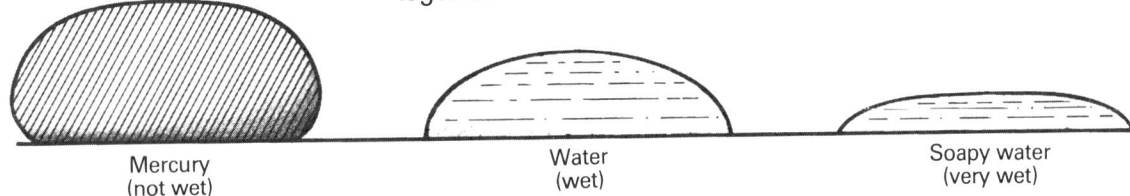

Mercury (not wet)   Water (wet)   Soapy water (very wet)

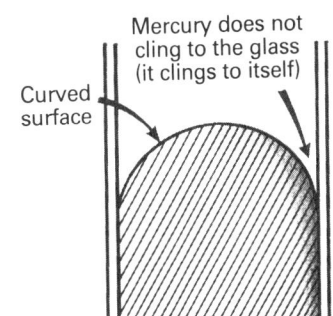

Mercury molecules attract each other more strongly than they are attracted by other molecules.

When mercury is contained in a glass tube its surface curves downwards. The mercury does not wet the glass.

Detergents and soaps are used with water to make its surface tension less. Soapy water is much better for washing because it makes things much 'wetter' than ordinary water.

17

Density

Some materials, like polystyrene or balsa wood, are very light for their size. Other materials, like lead or steel, are very heavy for their size. They are very *dense*. If a material is very heavy for its size we say that it has a *high density*:

High density	*Low density*
Lead Stone	Air Cork
Gold Steel	Wool Foam
Mercury	Polystyrene

The density of a material depends partly on how closely packed together its molecules are. In some solids the molecules are closely packed and so these solids (like lead, steel and stone) are quite dense. The molecules in gases are very spread out, and so gases have a very *low density*.

To compare the density of different materials we compare the mass of a certain size or volume of the materials. We can choose a volume of one cubic metre ($1m^3$) of the material and measure its mass in kilograms.

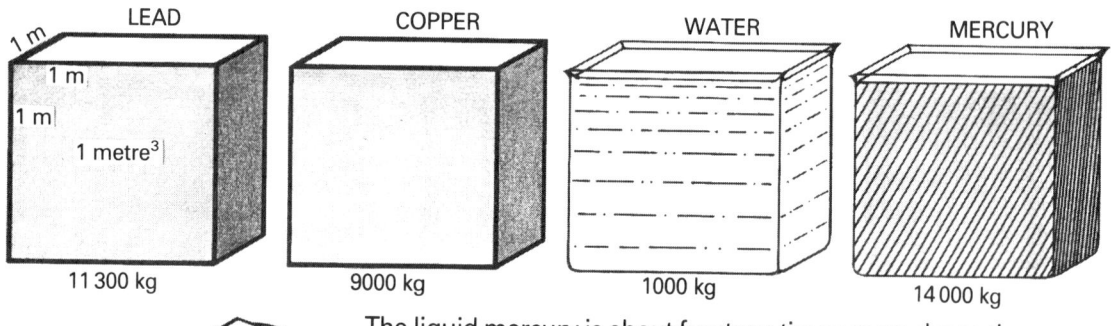

The liquid mercury is about fourteen times more dense than water. Copper is about nine times denser than water.

The mass of $1m^3$ of a material is called its density. Density is measured in kilograms per cubic metre, kg/m^3. But $1m^3$ is a very large volume. We can also measure density in grams per cubic centimetre, g/cm^3. This is done by finding the mass in grams of an object made of the material.

Then its volume, in cm^3, is found.

For example, if its mass = 81 grams, and its volume = $27cm^3$, then each cm^3 has a mass of $81/27$ = 3 grams.
Its density = $3 g/cm^3$.

To calculate density use this formula:

$$\text{Density} = \frac{\text{Mass}}{\text{Volume}}$$

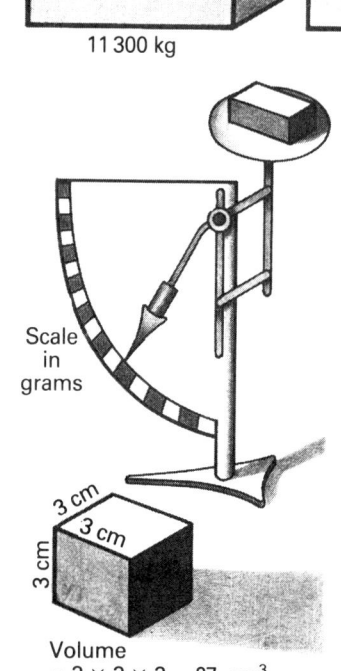

Volume
= $3 \times 3 \times 3 = 27$ cm^3

(There will be more on density in Chapter 7.)

Questions........................... 2

1. This diagram shows how molecules are arranged in a solid and in a liquid.

   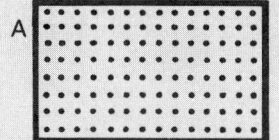 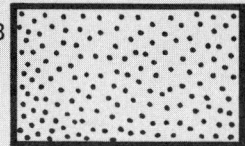

   (a) Which one shows the solid, and which the liquid?
   (b) Explain why.
   (c) Draw a similar diagram to show how the molecules in a gas might look.   (LREB)

2. What happens to the molecules of a gas when it is heated?

3. This diagram shows two clear glass tubes, one containing water, the other mercury:

   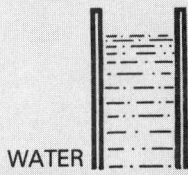 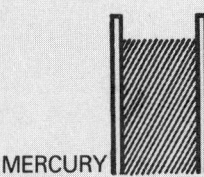

   (a) Draw the shape of the surface of each liquid inside the tube.
   (b) Try to explain why the surfaces are shaped like this.
                                                                  (LREB)

4. Find the density of each of these blocks, in g/cm^3.

   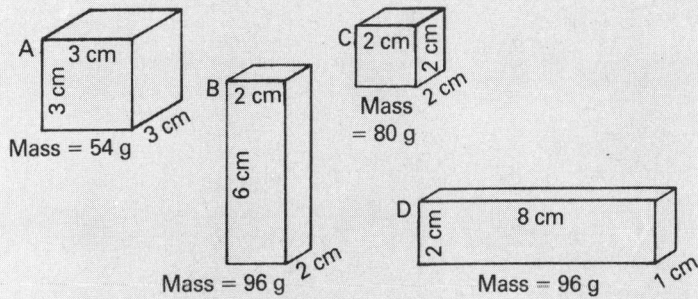

   Which block is the most dense?
   Which is the least dense?

5. Work out the density of each of these materials in kg/m^3:
   (a) 2m^3 of liquid, with a mass of 1600 kg
   (b) 3m^3 of brass, with a mass of 24 000 kg
   (c) 2m^3 of wood, with a mass of 1200 kg

6. Try to explain why:
   (a) It is best to wash in warm soapy water.
   (b) Houses have a damp course.
   (c) Some insects can walk on water.
   (d) Blotting paper soaks up ink.

Trace this grid on to a piece of paper before working out the answers.

Across
1. 2000 grams is equal to 2 —— (9)
6. Cork has a —— density (3)
7. The mass of an object is the —— of stuff in it (6)
10. Liquids seem to have a —— on their surface (4)
12. Sir Issac —— suggested some famous laws (6)
15. The abbreviation for centimetres (2)
16. An object weighs about six times as much on the —— as it does on the moon (5)
18. A narrow glass —— pulls water up inside (4)
19. Abbreviation for 1 across (2)
20. A tiny particle (8)

Down
1. The SI unit of temperature (6)
2. 12 across is famous because of his '—— of motion' (4)
3. A unit with the abbreviation g (4)
4. They have been 'split' to make bombs (5)
5. Our most important source of energy (3)
8. A mass of one kilogram has a weight of about —— newtons on 16 across (3)
9. Large objects in space (5)
11. and 13 When something is moving we say it has —— (7, 6)
13. See 11 down
14. The unit of electric current (6)
17. The abbreviation for hertz (2)

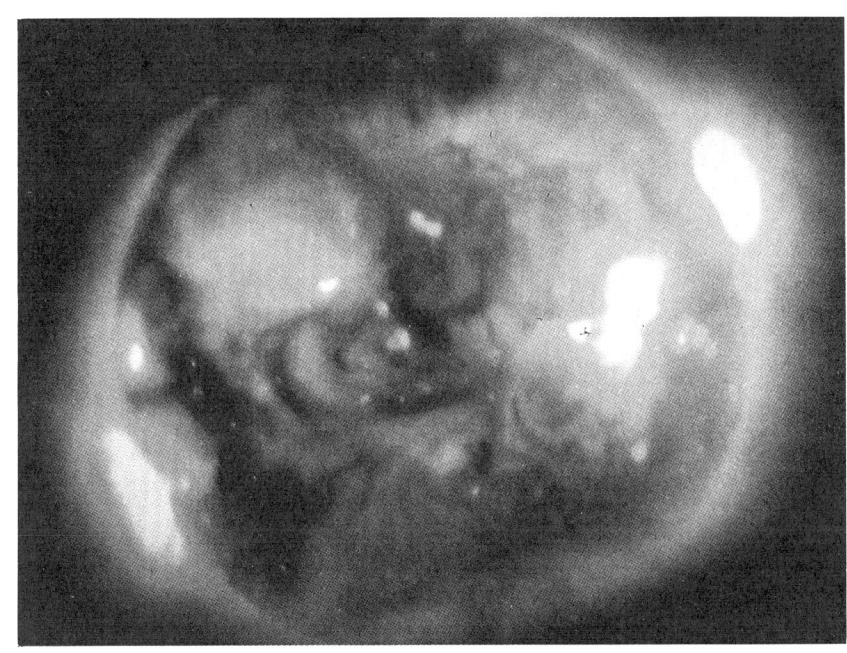

That old energy source the sun, showing its corona and hotspots. (see page 8)

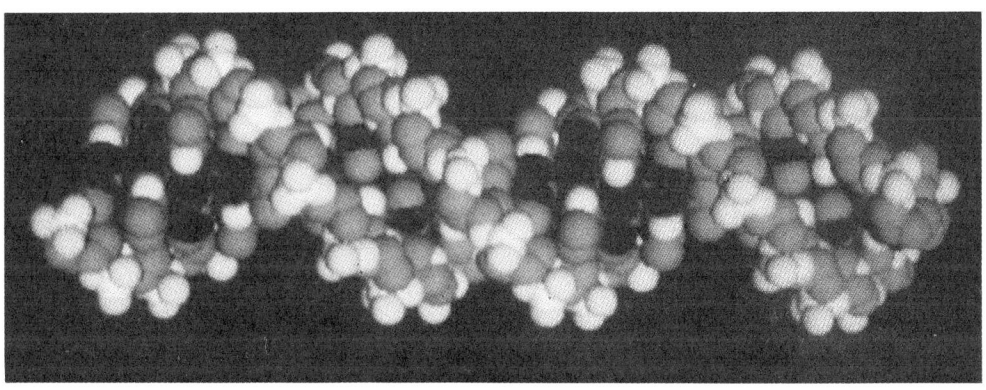

A computer graphic picture of a DNA molecule (see page 14) showing its special structure.

Wind turbines in Palm Springs, USA, used to generate electricity (see page 9 and 10).

A geothermal power station at "The Geysers", the world's largest geothermal field, in California. (see page 9 and 10)

These hurdlers are turning chemical energy into kinetic energy and heat energy. (see page 11)

This plastic sheet stops rising damp caused by capillarity. (see page 17)

The droplets of water are held together by surface tension. (see page 17)

Part 2
Forces & Movement

Chapter 3
Different types of forces

Different forces

Every force is either a push or a pull. When a porter pushes a trolley he uses a force. When a tug is used to pull a ship the *tension* in the rope is another type of force.

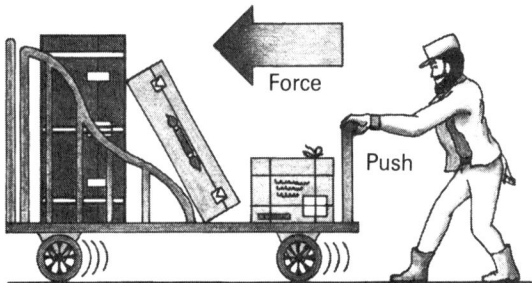
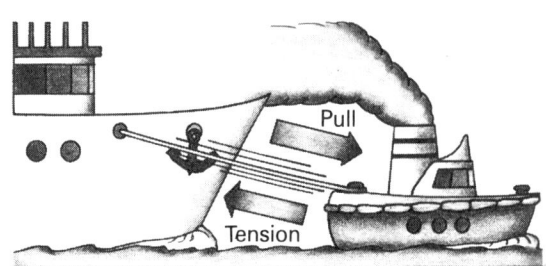

The most common pulling force we know is the pull of *gravity*. The Earth's gravity pulls all objects towards it, including the Moon and the satellites which orbit the Earth.

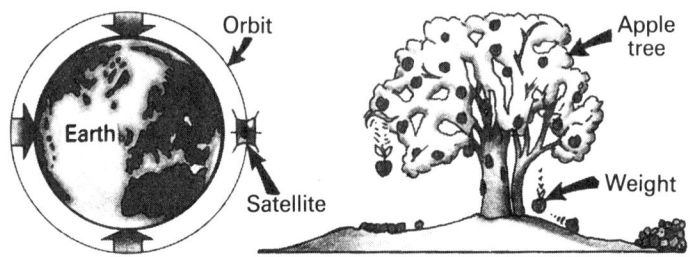

Another common force is *friction,* which occurs whenever two things rub together. One special type of friction is the friction inside some liquids, like engine oil or treacle, which makes them seem sticky and difficult to pour. These liquids are called *viscous liquids*— this type of liquid friction is called *viscosity*.

24

A special type of push and pull can be seen when two magnets are close together. Magnets can be made to attract each other or push each other apart.

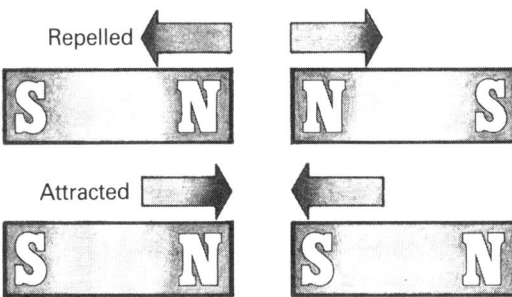

Finally another type of force is seen when certain objects are rubbed together — this is called *electrostatic* force, and can be seen when a plastic pen is rubbed on someone's sleeve and used to pick up a small piece of paper.

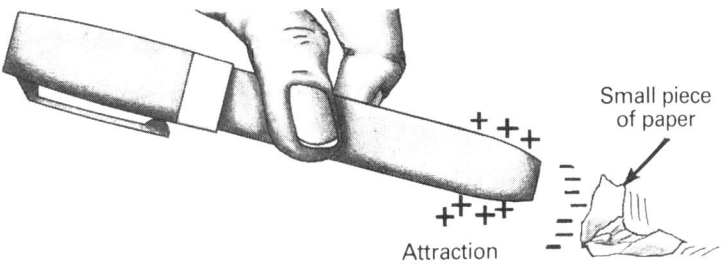

Measuring forces

The best way of measuring force is to use it to stretch a spring. The bigger the force, the more the spring is stretched. This can be proved by hanging weights on the end of a spring and gradually stretching it more and more.

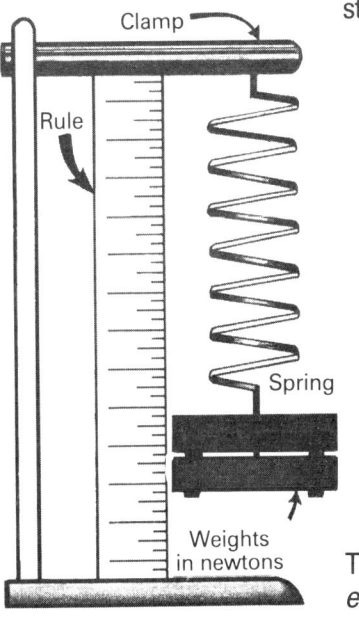
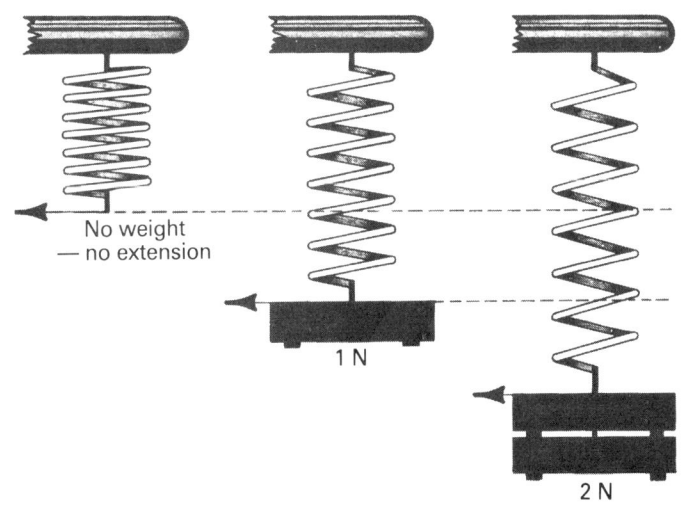

The spring is extended — the larger the weight, **the more the** *extension*.

25

Double the weight produces double the extension — three times the weight makes it extend three times as much, and so on. This rule is called *Hooke's Law*: the extension of a spring is proportional to the force extending it, as long as the spring is not stretched too far.

If a graph is drawn showing the length of a spring compared with the force extending it the graph should be a straight line:

The graph is straight as long as the spring is not stretched too far. The limit of a spring is called its *elastic limit*. If it is stretched beyond this limit it will not spring back to its first, or original, length.

Forces are measured in *newtons*. A special instrument is used to measure forces called a *newton-meter*.

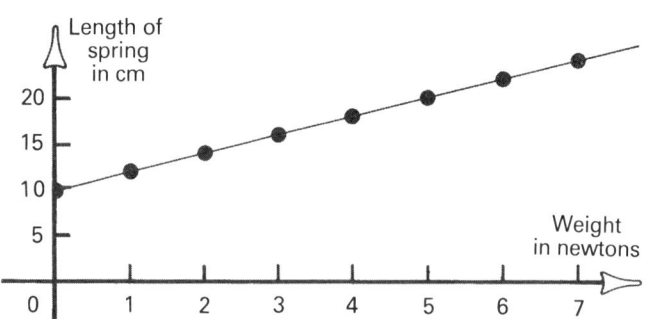

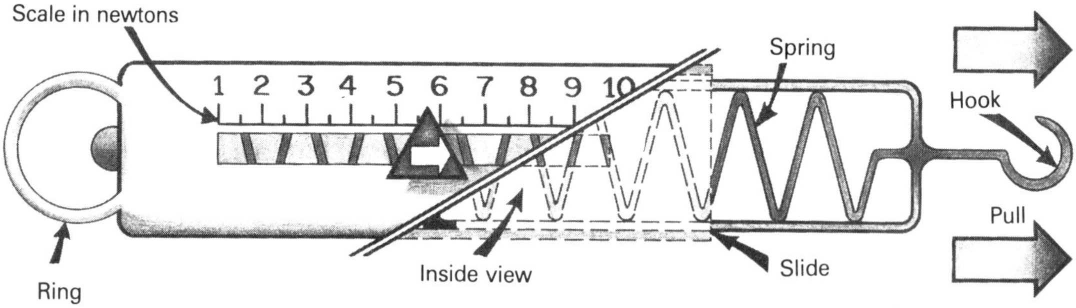

A spring is attached to a small pointer which moves along a scale with numbers of newtons on it. As the spring is pulled by a force the pointer moves along the scale and measures the force in newtons (abbreviated as N). This is just like the spring balance used to weigh a fish. A fish with a mass of 1 kilogram would weigh about 10 newtons.

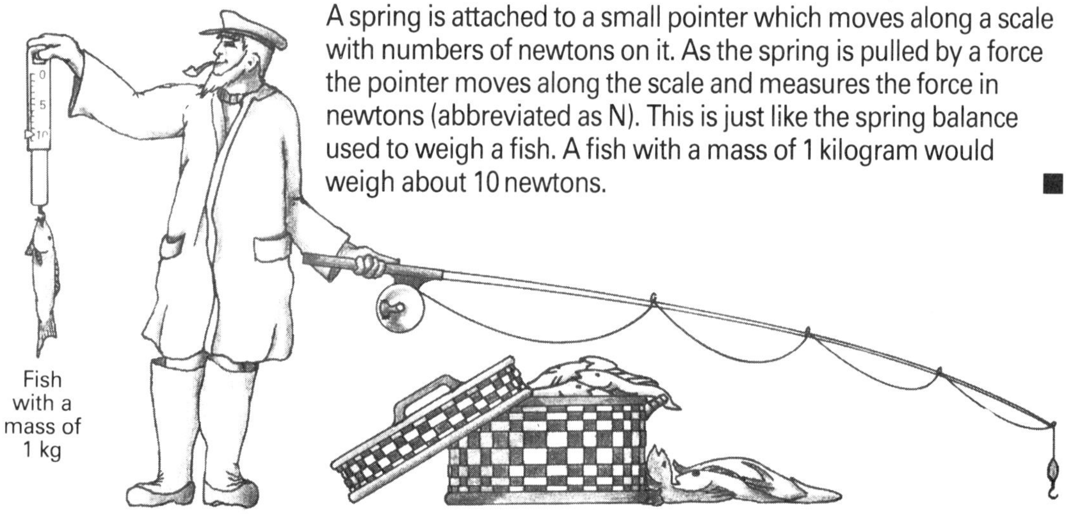

Fish with a mass of 1 kg

26

Vectors

Pushes and pulls, or forces, always act in a definite direction. They have to be represented by a line showing their direction and their size in newtons:

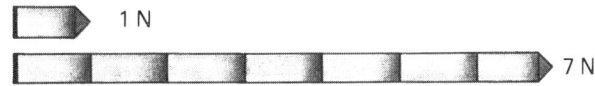

In physics, things like forces which have both a size and a definite direction are called *vectors.* Other examples of vectors are velocity and acceleration, described in the next chapter.

Vectors cannot be added easily because their direction is so important. Two forces of 5 N and 3 N can add up to make either 8 N or 2 N:

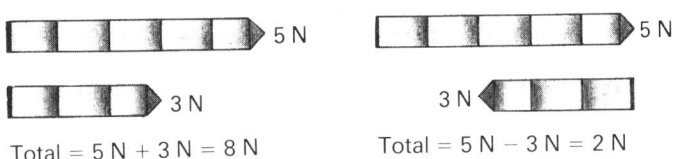

Total = 5 N + 3 N = 8 N   Total = 5 N − 3 N = 2 N

If two vectors, or two forces, are at an angle to each other the result, or *'resultant'*, of the two forces can be found by a *scale drawing*:

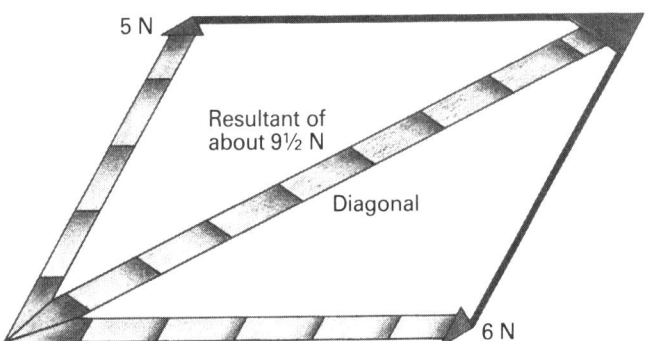

All vectors must be added in this way. The shape drawn in the diagram is called a *parallelogram* and the resultant of two forces is the line going across the parallelogram, called the *diagonal*.

Questions 3

1. Write down four different types of force.
2. What instrument is used to measure forces? Draw a diagram of it.
3. Complete this table.

Mass	Weight (roughly)
1 kg	10 N
2 kg	_ N
_ kg	30 N
4 kg	_ N
_ kg	75 N

4. Give an example to explain Hooke's Law in everyday life. What is meant by the elastic limit of a spring or a rubber band?
5. What is meant by a vector? Give three examples of vectors.
6. If two forces of 9 N and 6 N act in the same direction, what is their sum, or resultant? What is their resultant if they act in opposite directions?
7.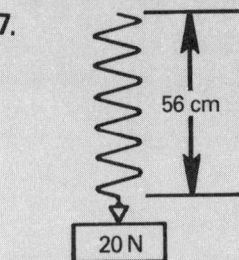

   A spring has a natural length of 50 cm and its elastic limit is reached when a load of 100 newton is applied.
   A load of 20 N on the spring makes its new length 56 cm.
   A load of 40 N makes its new length 62 cm.

   (a) (i) What is the length of the spring when a load of 70 N is applied?
   (ii) What load, in newtons, would cause the new length of the spring to be 77 cm?
   (b) (i) What do you understand by the term *elastic limit*?
   (ii) Describe the extension of the spring when a load of 150 N is added and then removed.
   (c) (i) If a solid wire were used instead of a spring, and loaded with a load of 20 N, how would you expect its extension to compare with that produced in the spring?
   (ii) Explain what is meant by the term *elasticity* in terms of the molecular nature of matter. (LREB)

Chapter 4

Forces and moving objects

■■■■■■■■■■■■■■

Speed, velocity and acceleration

When we measure the speed of a moving object we do not mention its direction — we just say how many metres it travels in one second, e.g. a person walks at about 2 metres per second, a cyclist might travel at 12 metres per second. The speed of a moving object can be found by dividing the distance it travels (in metres) by the time taken (in seconds):

Speed = Distance travelled ÷ Time taken

If a car travels 200 metres in 10 seconds, its speed = 200 ÷ 10 = 20 metres per second (20 m/s). ■

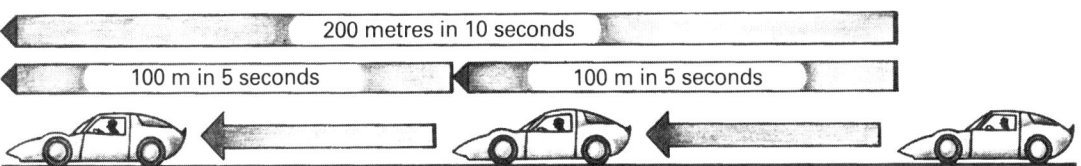

When the *velocity* of an object is measured its *direction* as well as its speed must be found. Velocity means 'speed in a certain direction'. Two boats travelling in the same part of the sea must always know their velocity — in other words both their speed and direction — so that they do not collide: ■

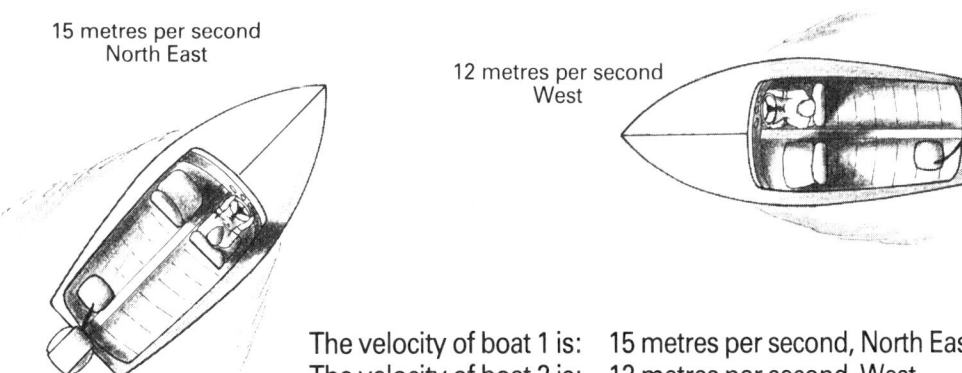

The velocity of boat 1 is: 15 metres per second, North East
The velocity of boat 2 is: 12 metres per second, West

Velocity, like force, is a *vector* because it has both size and direction.

29

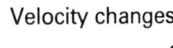

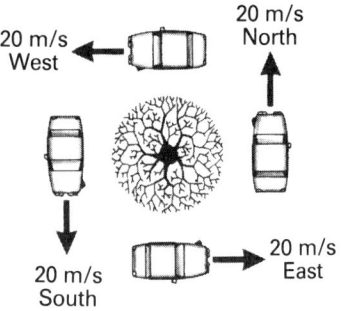

Same speed, different directions

When something travels in a straight line at a steady speed it has *uniform velocity*. If it speeds up its velocity is increasing — it is *accelerating*. When something slows down its velocity is decreasing — it is *decelerating*. But velocity also changes when a moving object changes its direction. A car can move around in a circle at a steady speed. But its *velocity* is always changing because its direction changes. ∎

A car pulling away from traffic lights and gaining velocity is accelerating. If it gains velocity quickly it has a large *acceleration*. Acceleration measures how quickly things gain velocity.

For example, if a car takes 5 seconds to reach a velocity of 20 metres per second its acceleration is 20 ÷ 5 = 4 metres per second per second.

Acceleration is measured in *metres per second per second* or m/s^2 for short:

Acceleration = Velocity gained ÷ Time taken

Connecting forces and acceleration

To make something accelerate a force is always needed. Nothing will speed up, slow down or change direction unless a force is applied to it. Sir Isaac Newton first realised this in 1686 — it is still an important law today. Cars and motor bikes need the force of their engines to make them accelerate. They need the force of friction (usually from their brakes) to make them slow down.

If a trolley is pulled along by a falling weight it *accelerates*. The force making it accelerate is the pull, or *tension,* in the string. If the tension is increased by using more weight then the trolley accelerates more. The larger the force, the larger the *acceleration*. ∎

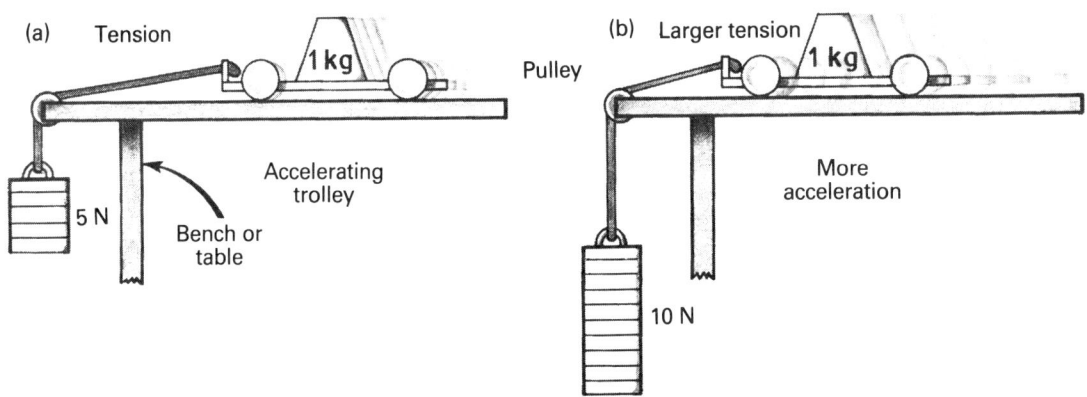

Suppose the mass of the trolley is increased, from 1 kg to 2 kg. Now there is twice as much mass to be accelerated. The trolley does not accelerate as much. The larger the *mass,* the smaller the acceleration. ■

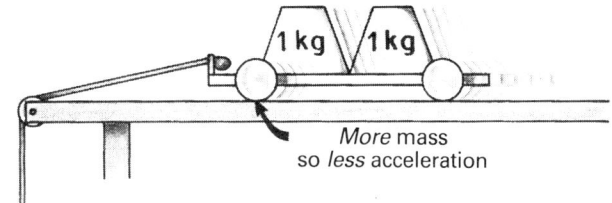

More mass so *less* acceleration

These discoveries about motion were made by Isaac Newton. They are called *Newton's Second Law.* This law tells you how force, mass and acceleration are connected:

(a) for the same mass: the larger the force used, the larger the acceleration will be;

(b) for the same force: the larger the mass, the smaller the acceleration will be;

(c) to get the same acceleration: the larger the mass, the larger the force needed.

Putting these three parts together leads to this formula:

Force   =   Mass   ×   Acceleration
(in newtons)   (in kg)   (in m/s^2)

This formula can be put into a triangle. ■

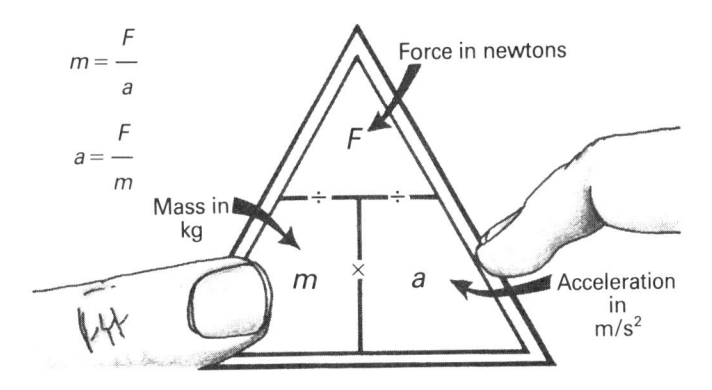

$m = \dfrac{F}{a}$

$a = \dfrac{F}{m}$

To use the triangle just place your finger over the quantity you want to find. For example, to find the acceleration of a moving object place your finger over the *a*. The acceleration is $F \div m$. Here are three examples:

if: Mass = 1 kg and force = 5 N,
        Acceleration = 5/1 = 5 m/s^2

if: Mass = 1 kg and force = 10 N,
        Acceleration = 10/1 = 10 m/s^2

and if: Mass = 2 kg and force = 10 N,
        Acceleration = 10/2 = 5 m/s^2

Graphs of moving objects

Imagine that a car pulls away from traffic lights, accelerates until it reaches a steady speed, then cruises at this speed for a while until it suddenly brakes and then stops. Its journey can be shown on a *speed–time graph*.

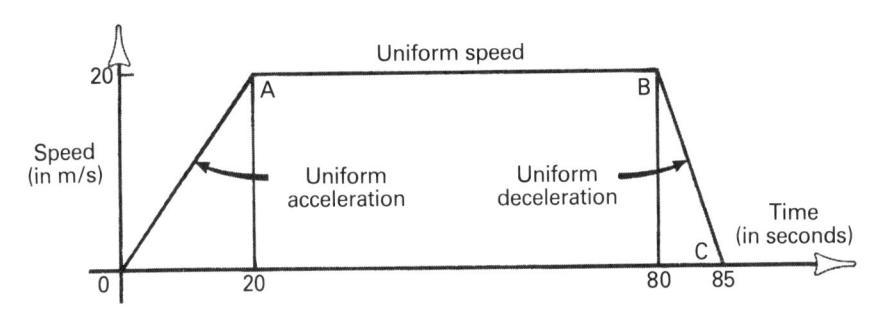

On the graph from 0 to A the car accelerates steadily until it reaches a speed of 20 metres per second — this is called *uniform acceleration*. From A to B it travels at a steady speed, until it suddenly slows down or *decelerates* from B to C.

Another graph that can be drawn is a *distance–time* graph. This shows the distance of a moving object from its starting position compared with time. This could be a graph of a man walking away from a starting position (from 0 to D) then stopping for a few seconds (D to E), then walking back to the start again (E to F).

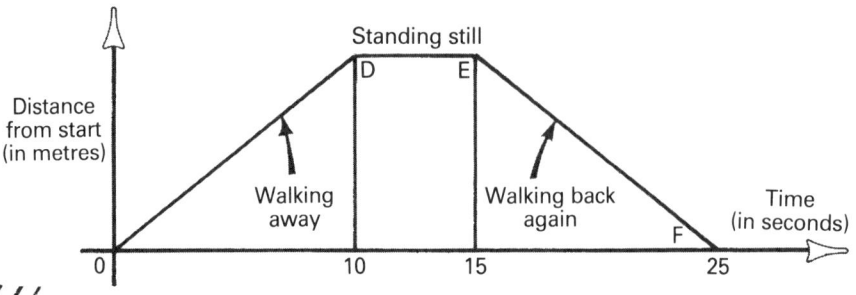

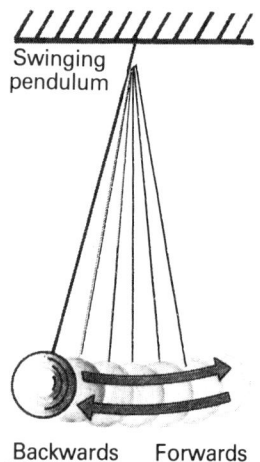

Speed–time and distance–time graphs are both useful in physics for picturing or describing the way things move. For example, the swinging pendulum of a clock which moves backwards and forwards (to and fro) has a distance–time graph like a wave.

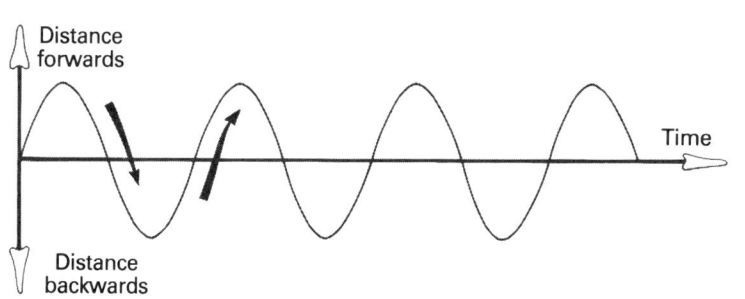

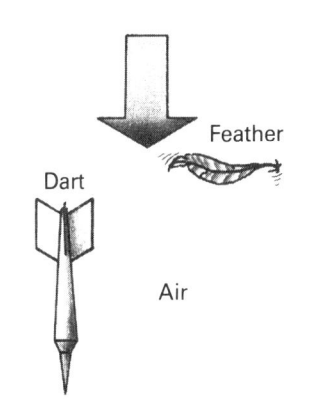

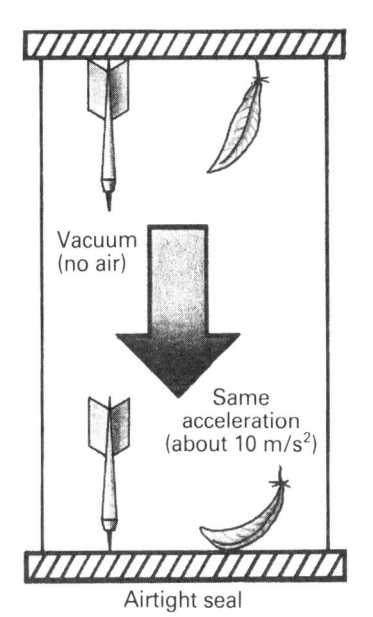

Movement caused by gravity

Whenever something is dropped, gravity pulls it towards the Earth until it hits the ground. In everyday life falling objects are slowed down by air resistance.

In a vacuum, where there are no air molecules, all objects fall with the same *acceleration*. This is called *free fall under gravity*. The acceleration of a freely falling object is 9.81 metres per second per second. This is called g.

(Usually, the value of g is given as 10 m/s^2, to make calculations simpler).

Before anything (like a rocket for example) can escape from Earth's gravity it has to reach a very high velocity. This is called *escape velocity*.

A satellite or spaceship that orbits the Earth has not escaped from the pull of the Earth's gravity. It is gravity that keeps the satellite moving in a circle around the Earth. Without gravity it would fly off in a straight line into outer space.

An astronaut inside a spacecraft orbiting the Earth has a feeling called *weightlessness*. The astronaut and his spacecraft are both kept in a circular path by the force of gravity. This means that the astronaut is not pulled to the floor of the craft — he just floats around unless he is strapped to his seat.

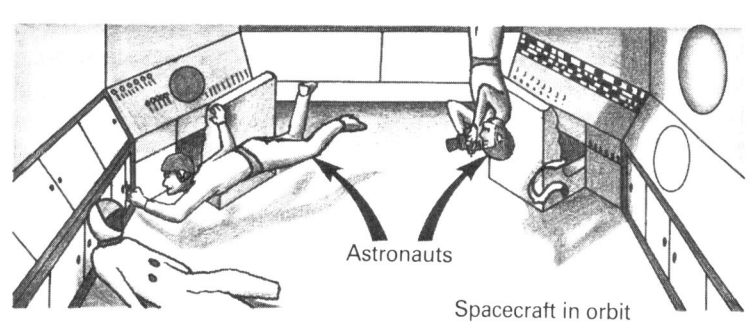

In the Solar System the planets are kept in their orbits by the pull of the Sun's gravity. Without it they would fly off in a straight line.

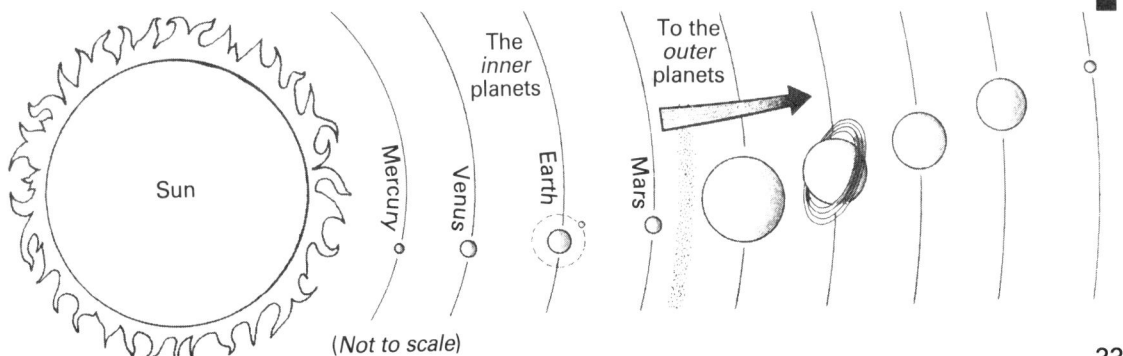

Questions............................ 4

1. What is the average speed of a car if it travels:
   (a) 100 metres in 5 seconds
   (b) 300 m in 20 seconds
   (c) 500 metres in 25 seconds
   (d) 2 km in 100 seconds?

2. Suppose a car travels at a steady speed of 30 m/s.
   (a) How far will it travel in:
   (i) 2 seconds
   (ii) 20 seconds
   (iii) one minute
   (iv) one hour?
   (b) How long will it take to travel:
   (i) 60 metres
   (ii) 1200 m
   (iii) 3 km
   (iv) 60 km?

3. Try to explain the difference between *speed* and *velocity*. What does *acceleration* mean?

4. This graph shows how the speed of a car changes over a period of 30 seconds:

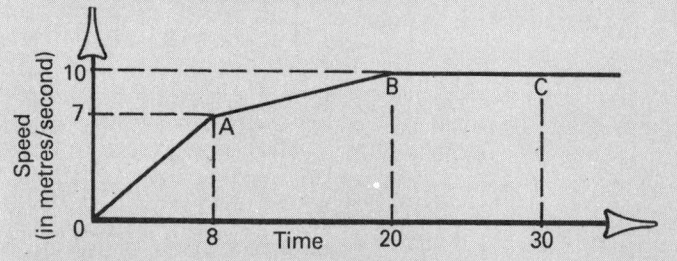

   (a) What is its speed at point A?
   (b) Where is its acceleration greatest?
   (c) How far does the car travel in the last 10 seconds?
   (LREB)

5. What is the acceleration of a car if it gains a velocity of:
   (a) 20 m/s in 5 seconds
   (b) 10 m/s in 2 seconds
   (c) 30 m/s in 6 seconds
   (d) 42 m/s in 7 seconds?

6. A car pulls away from traffic lights, accelerates for 10 seconds until it reaches a speed of 20 m/s, travels at this speed for 20 seconds, and then suddenly brakes and stops within two seconds.
   (a) What is the car's acceleration in the first ten seconds?
   (b) Draw a speed–time graph for the car's movement.

7. Using this triangle, calculate: 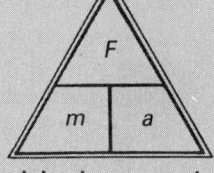
   (a) the force needed to give a mass of 5 kg an acceleration of 2 m/s^2;
   (b) the force needed to give a mass of 20 kg an acceleration of 3 m/s^2;
   (c) the acceleration of a 5 kg mass when it is given a push of 80 N;
   (d) the acceleration of a 200 kg mass given a 600 newton push.

8. This diagram shows a ball A being projected horizontally from a table, and another ball B being dropped from the same height.

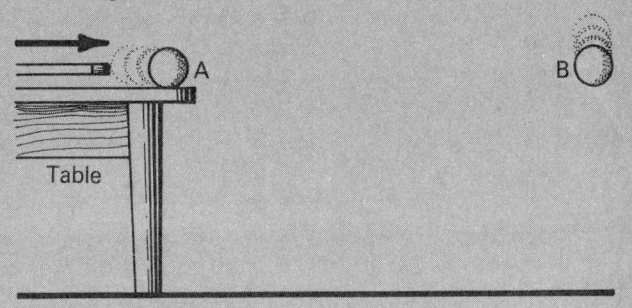

(a) Draw the paths that each ball will take.
(b) Which ball reaches the ground first?
(c) What force accelerates the balls?
(d) What force slows down, or opposes the motion, of each ball? (LREB)

9. A spaceship is travelling in deep space (away from stars and planets) with its rocket engines turned off.
   (a) What will happen to the spaceship if its engines are not re-started?
   (b) What will happen if the rocket engines are fired in the normal way?
   (c) How could the crew of the spaceship slow it down? (LREB)

10. A car engine is leaking oil. The oil drops hit the ground at regular time intervals, one every 2.0 seconds. The diagram below shows the pattern of the drops that the car leaves on part of its journey.

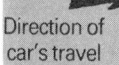

    (a) What can you say about the speed of the car before it reaches the signs?
    (b) Calculate the distance between the drops on the road before it reaches the signs if the car is travelling at 10 m/s.
    (c) After the car passes the signs, what happens to the gaps between the drops of oil? What does this tell you about the motion of the car?
    (d) Further down the road it is found that the distance between the drops on the road has become 30 m. What is the speed of the car at this point?

(Reproduced from LEAG GCSE Physics Specimen Paper 2)

Chapter 5

Forces and machines

Force, work, energy and power

If a person uses the energy in his body to lift a heavy load on to a shelf he has to do *work*. Chemical energy in his body is changed to the potential energy of the load, held at this height.

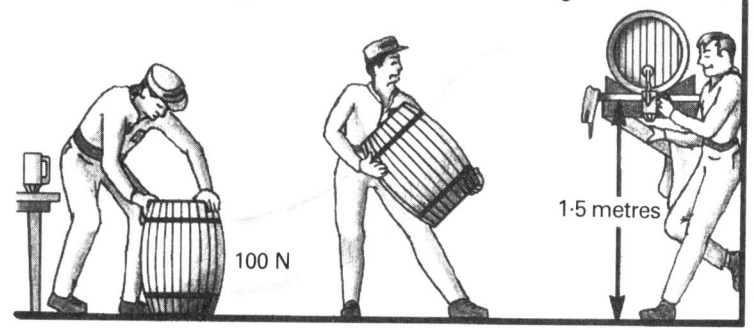

Energy is changed from one form to another, and work is being done. If the load weighs 100 N and it is raised by 1·5 m, the work done = 100 N × 1·5 m = 150 J. The formula used is:

Work done = Force used × Distance moved
(in J)   (in N)   (in m)

Many machines (like cars, lorries or cranes) get their energy from *fuel*. They use the chemical energy from their fuel (like petrol or oil) to do work. These machines can do much more work than men. They are also much more *powerful* — this means they can work more quickly.

The faster a machine can do work the more powerful it is. So the power of a machine (or a person) is the number of joules of work it can do in *one second* (1 s). Power is measured in *watts* (abbreviated as W) and it can be calculated from this formula:

Power = Work done ÷ Time taken
(in W)   (in J)   (in s)

If a machine does 5000 J of work in 10 s, its power is 5000 ÷ 10 or 500 W.

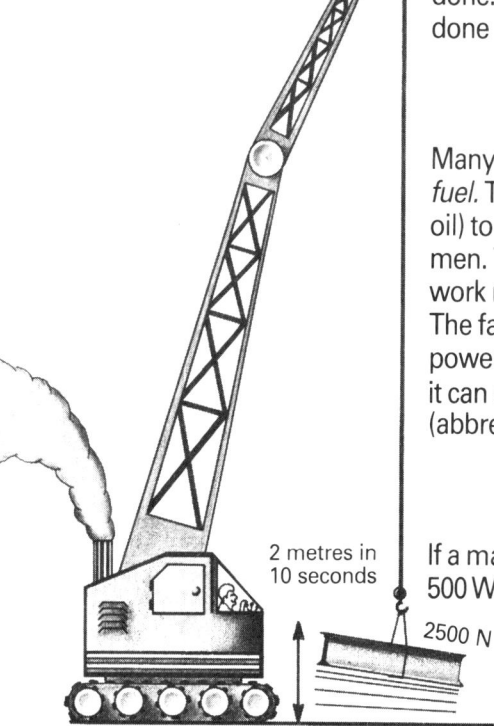

Simple machines

Some simple machines do not use fuel — they are operated by a person. The *lever* and the *inclined plane* are two examples.

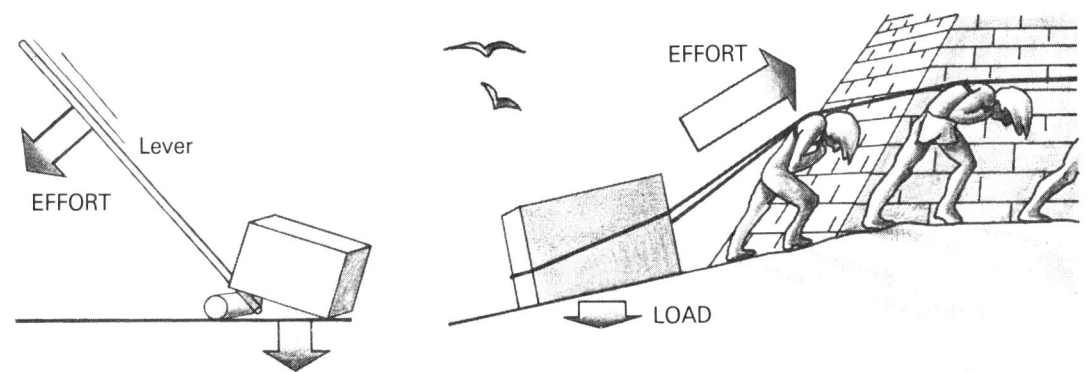

These simple machines have been used for hundreds of years — they were probably both used to build Stonehenge.

There are three important types of simple machine:
(a) *Force multipliers.* A lever is a good example of this type. It can turn a small force into a large one. A small *effort* can be used to lift a large *load.*
(b) *Distance multipliers.* A long pair of scissors is one example — a small movement is turned into a larger movement. Another example is a broom — a small movement at the top of the handle becomes a larger movement of the brush at the bottom. A bike is a third example.
(c) *Direction changers.* A pulley is a direction changer. If a person pulls down on one side, the load moves up on the other.

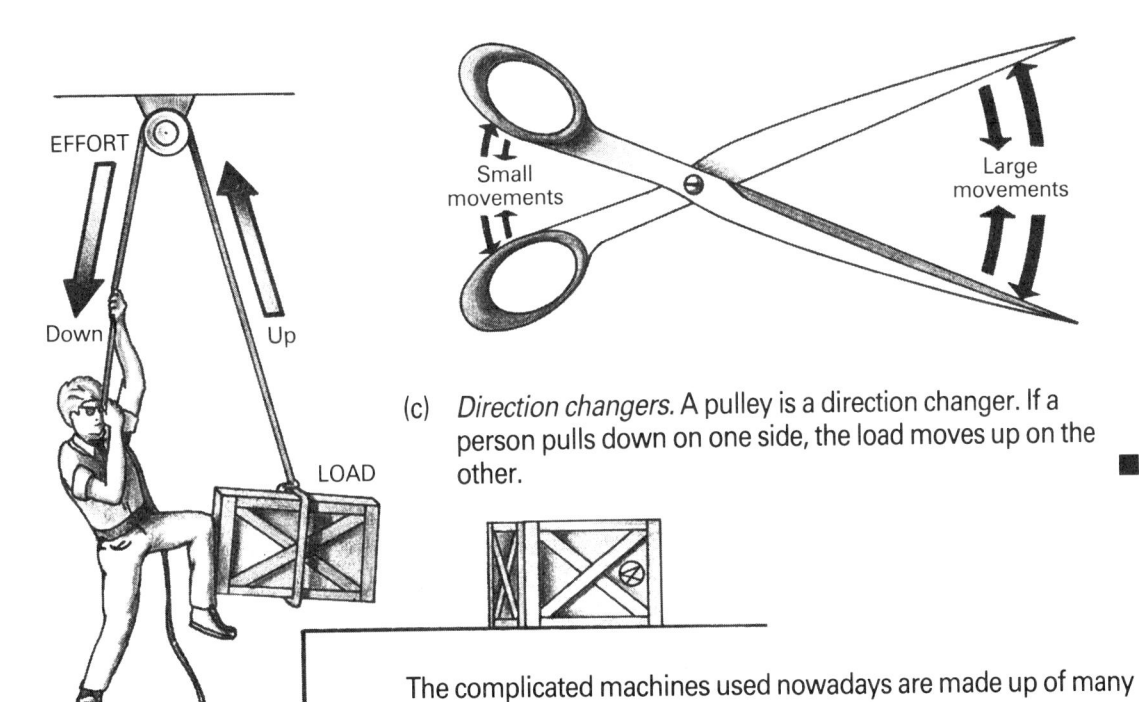

The complicated machines used nowadays are made up of many simple machines like these.

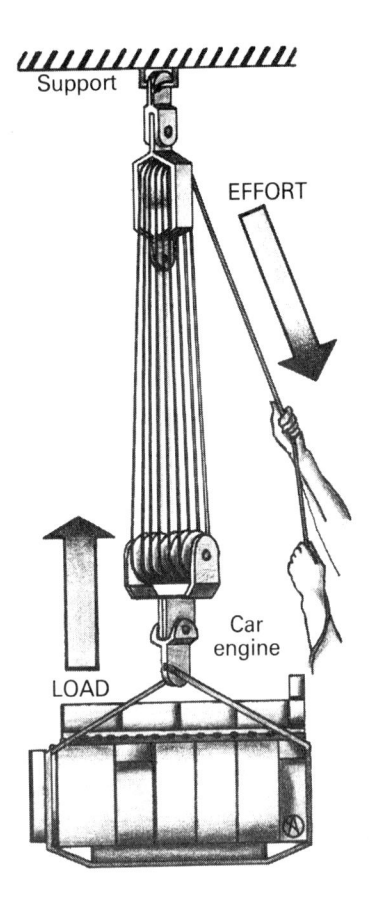

Force multipliers

Two machines which only need a small effort to raise a large load are the *block and tackle* and the *screw-jack*.

A block and tackle is made by connecting several pulleys together with ropes or chains. It is still used in garages to raise car engines. It is also used in cranes and lifts.

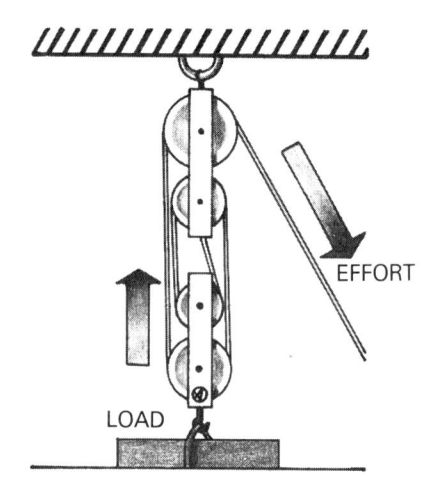

A screw-jack is used like an inclined plane to raise heavy loads, without using too much effort.

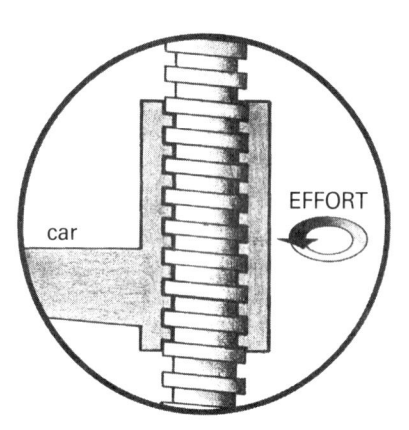

In fact a screw is just an inclined plane wrapped around in a spiral.

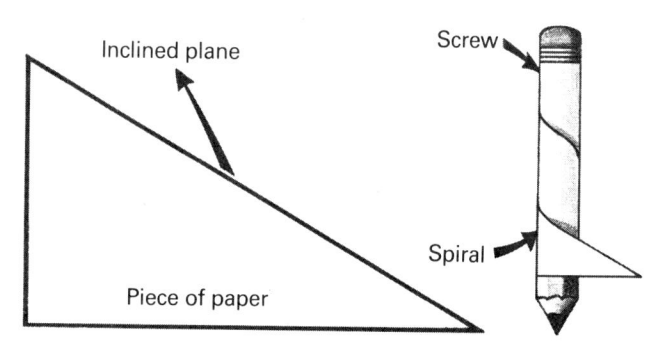

Advantages of machines

When a block and tackle is used to raise a car engine the effort, needed to lift it is much less than the weight of the itself, or the load. The machine gives us a *mechanical advantage*. A simple lever used to raise a load also gives us a mechanical advantage.

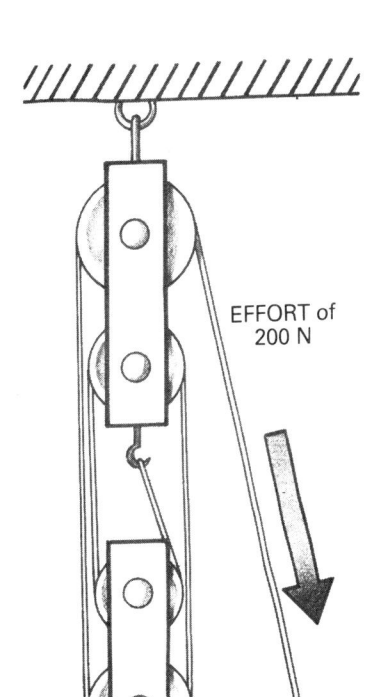

EFFORT = 20 N

LOAD = 80 N

If a force, or effort, of 20 N raises a load of 80 N the mechanical advantage = 80 ÷ 20, or 4. In other words:

Mechanical advantage = Load ÷ Effort

Suppose a block and tackle is used to raise a load of 600 N, with an effort of 200 N. The mechanical advantage = 600 ÷ 200 = 3.

EFFORT of 200 N

LOAD of 600 N

Because this system has so many pulleys the effort has to move through quite a large distance to raise the load by a small distance. In fact with four pulleys the effort has to move a distance of four metres to raise the load by one metre. This 'four to one' ratio is called the *velocity ratio* of the machine.

The velocity ratio of any machine can be found from this formula:

Velocity ratio = Distance moved by the effort ÷ Distance moved by the load

No machine can ever be a force multiplier and a distance multiplier. A screw-jack for example needs only a small effort to raise a large load, like a car. It has a large mechanical advantage. But this effort has to move quite a long way just to raise a car by a few centimetres — the screw-jack also has a large velocity ratio.

Efficiency

A man-operated machine can never do more work than the person using it. In fact all machines waste some of the energy or work put into them. Most of the energy wasted is changed into heat energy by friction inside the machine. For hundreds of years people have tried to make a machine which will run for ever: a perpetual-motion machine. But no machine is ever completely, or 100% *efficient*. There is always some friction.

The efficiency of a machine can be calculated by comparing the energy or work supplied to it, with the work actually done by the machine:

$$\text{Efficiency} = \frac{\text{Work done BY the machine}}{} \div \frac{\text{Work done ON the machine}}{}$$

For example, if you supply 100 J of energy or work to a machine and it does 90 J of work, the efficiency is 90 ÷ 100 or 90%. 10 J of energy are wasted.

The efficiency of a machine can also be found if you know its mechanical advantage and its velocity ratio. In fact:

$$\text{Efficiency} = \text{Mechanical advantage} \div \text{Velocity ratio}$$

For example, a block and tackle with a mechanical advantage of 3 and a velocity ratio of 4 has an efficiency of 3 ÷ 4 — that is, three-quarters or 75%.

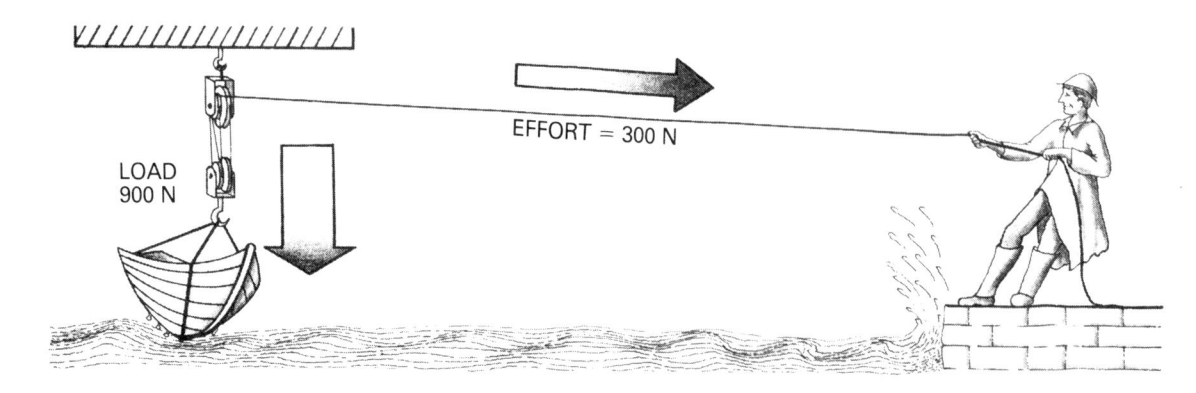

The velocity ratio of a machine must always be bigger than the mechanical advantage — otherwise its efficiency would be more than 100%! Remember that:
some simple machines change a small force moving through a large distance into a larger force moving through a smaller distance (force multipliers)...

...whereas others change a large force moving through a small distance, into a small force moving through a larger distance (distance multipliers).

But no machine can do both!

Questions

1. A person lifts a weight of 250 newtons to a height of ... metres. How much work is done?
   How much work is done in each of these examples:
   (a) a weight of 300 N being lifted to a height of 2 m;
   (b) a load of 620 N being lifted to a height of 3 m;
   (c) a box weighing 400 N being lifted to a height of 4 m.
   (Give each answer in *joules.*)

2. If each of these jobs took 10 seconds what is the power (in watts) in each example?

3. This diagram shows two girls walking up stairs. Both reach a height of 5 m.
   (a) How much work does each one do against the pull of gravity?
   (b) Where does the energy for this work come from?
   (c) What happens to this energy?
   (d) If they both take 5 seconds to reach the top, what is the power of each girl?

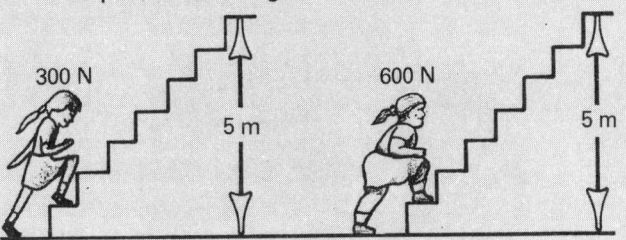

4. Write down one example each of a machine that is:
   (a) a force multiplier;
   (b) a direction changer;
   (c) a distance multiplier.
   Why can't a machine be both a force multiplier and a distance multiplier?

5. This diagram shows a block and tackle. 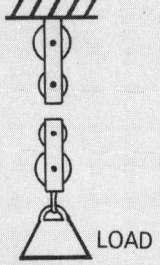
   (a) Draw the pulleys and put in one rope or chain linking all of them.
   (b) What is the velocity ratio of this machine?
   (c) If the load is 60 N and the effort needed is 20 N, what is its mechanical advantage?
   (d) What is the efficiency of the machine?

Chapter 6
Forces and balance

Forces and moments

When two children, one heavy and one light, sit on a see-saw they can balance each other if the heavier child is nearer to the pivot or *fulcrum*.

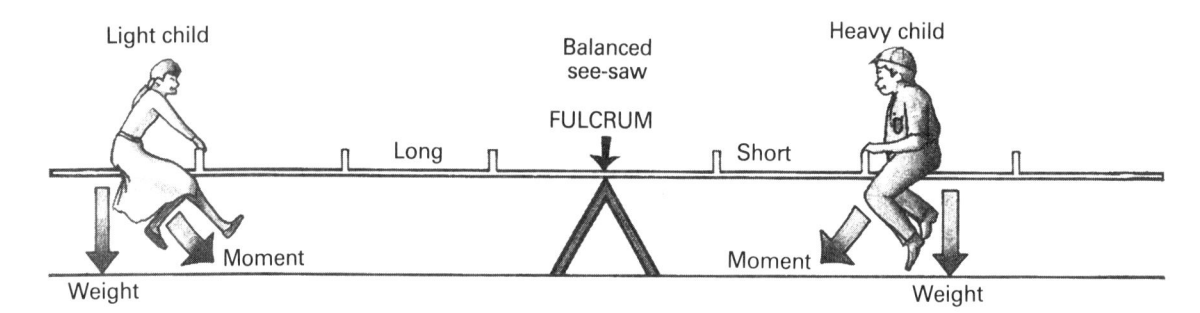

The two children are balanced because in these positions they both have the same *turning effect*. The turning effect of a force is called its *moment*. The moment of a force depends on how far away it is from the fulcrum or pivot, and so a light girl can balance a heavy boy because she is further from the fulcrum. The children have different weights but both have the same turning effect.

The turning effect or moment of a force is used when opening a door, riding a bicycle, or using a crow-bar.

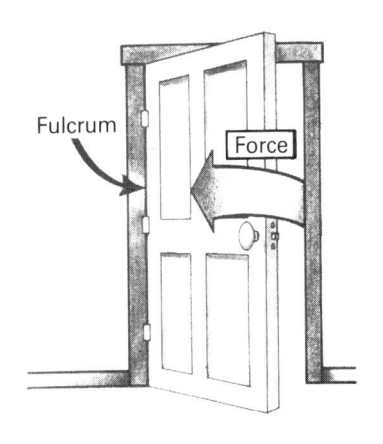

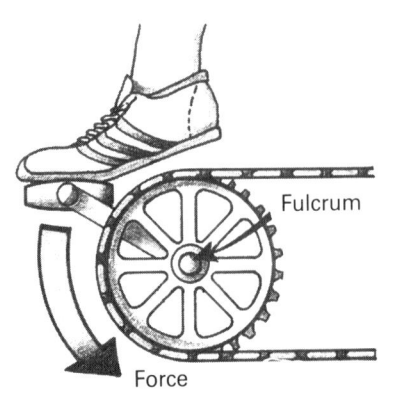

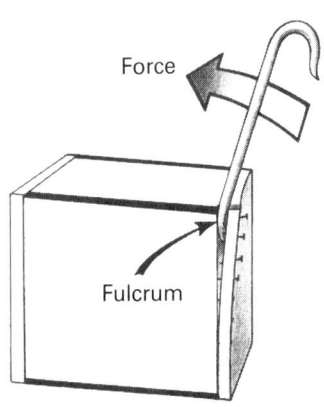

The moment of a force can be calculated by using this formula:

Moment   =   Force used × Nearest distance
(in newton metres)   (in N)   from the fulcrum
or N m)   (in m)

For example, the moment or turning effect of the force below is 100 N × 2 m = 200 newton metres or 200 N m ■

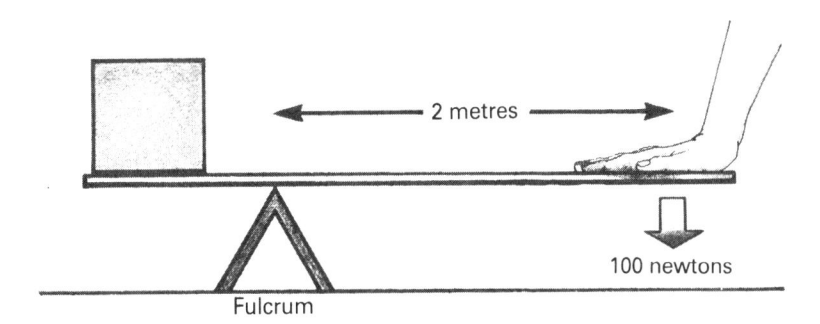

Balancing and centre of gravity

Two weights, one large and one small, can balance one another on a see-saw if they are placed at different distances from the pivot or fulcrum. ■

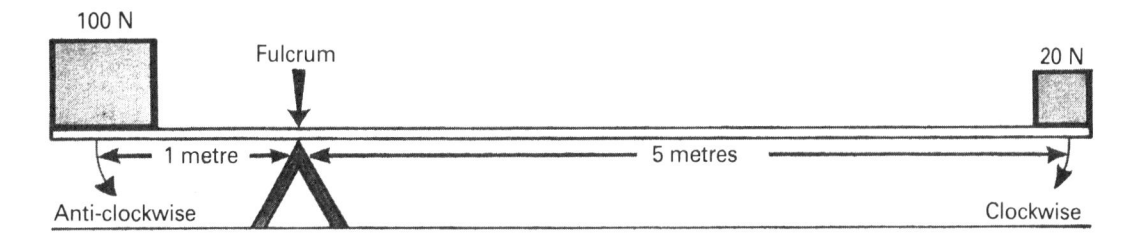

The heavy weight on the left tries to turn the see-saw anti-clockwise, and its moment is 100 N × 1 m or 100 N m. The lighter weight on the right tries to turn the see-saw in a clockwise direction, and this time the moment is 20 × 5 or 100 N m. In other words, both the moments are the same (100 N m) and so the see-saw is balanced.

Here are some more examples of a 'balance'. In both examples the moments on the left and on the right side are equal, and so they balance. ■

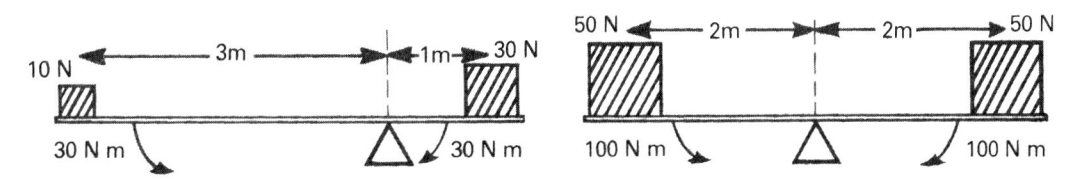

Another way of balancing an object is to support it under its *centre of gravity.* A ladder is easiest to carry when it is supported underneath its centre of gravity — this is the point where the weight of the ladder, or the force of gravity, appears to act. ■

The weight of many objects seems to act through their centre and so their centre of gravity is actually in the middle of the object. ■

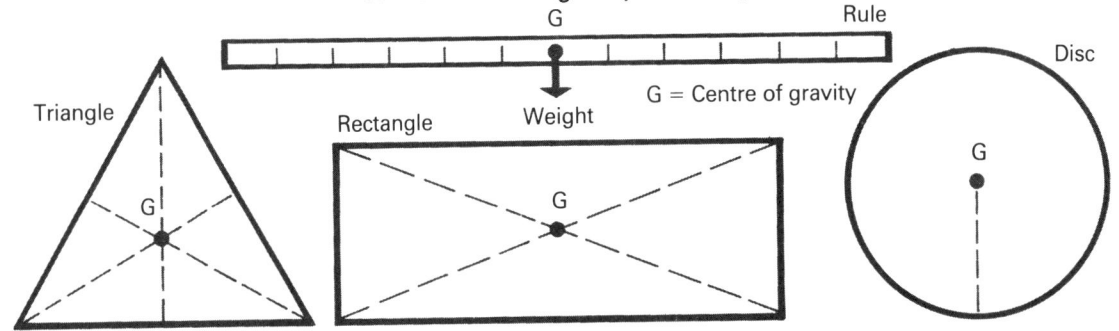

G = Centre of gravity

The centres of gravity of flat objects like these are easy to find, and so they can be balanced by supporting them under their middle point.

With an unusual shape the centre of gravity can be found by suspending it from a needle fixed to a clamp, then hanging a weight on a thread (a plumb line) from the needle. A line is drawn along the plumb line, and then the same is done for different places on the shape. The point where all the lines meet is the centre of gravity. ■

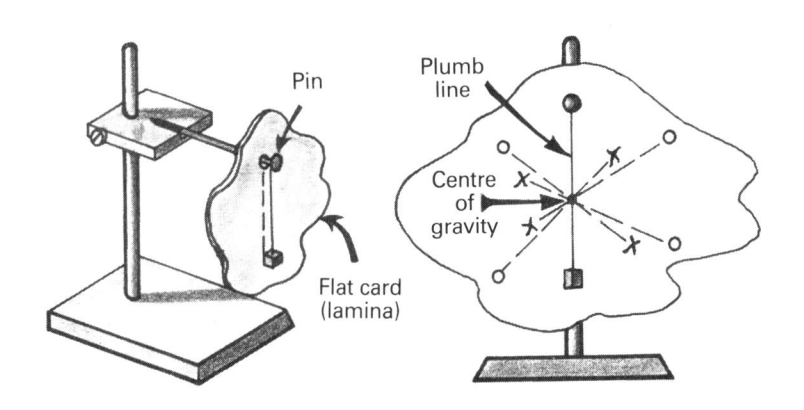

Centre of gravity and 'stability'

It is important to know the centre of gravity of a car when it is being designed. A racing-car is designed with a low centre of gravity and very widely spaced wheels so that it will not overturn, or 'topple', when it takes a corner at high speed. The racing car is said to be very *stable*. Most ordinary cars cannot go round corners at such high speeds. They have a slightly higher centre of gravity, and a narrower 'wheel base' than racing cars.

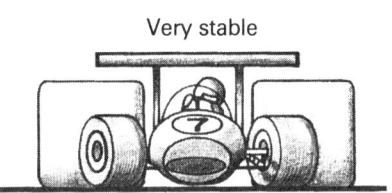

High c.g.

Not so stable

Very stable

Another stable object is a doll with a very heavy base. This heavy base means that its centre of gravity is very low, and the doll will not topple over. Every time the doll is pushed over, its weight will pull it back up again.

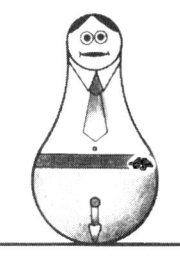

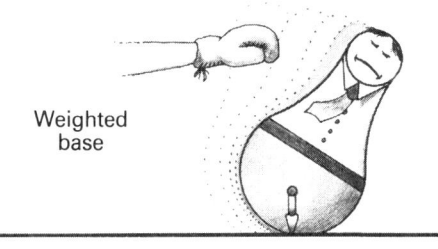

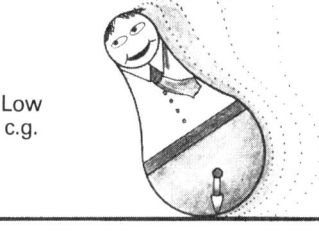

Weighted base

Low c.g.

When an object is balanced it is said to be in *equilibrium*. There are three types of equilibrium: *stable, unstable* and *neutral*. A bunsen burner is in stable equilibrium when its heavy base rests on a bench. The centre of gravity is then as low as possible and if the bunsen is pulled to one side it does not topple. However, if a bunsen stands on the bench the wrong way up it is in *unstable equilibrium* — if it is pushed to one side it topples. Finally, if a bunsen rests on its side it is in *neutral* equilibrium. When it is pushed aside it stays in its new position.

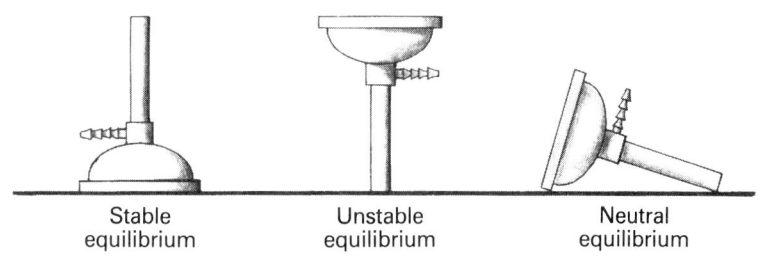

Stable equilibrium

Unstable equilibrium

Neutral equilibrium

Most objects, like a double-decker bus or a metal stand in a lab, are designed so they are in *stable* equilibrium — their centre of gravity is made as low as possible.

Questions 6

1. Write down the force needed to balance each of these see-saws.

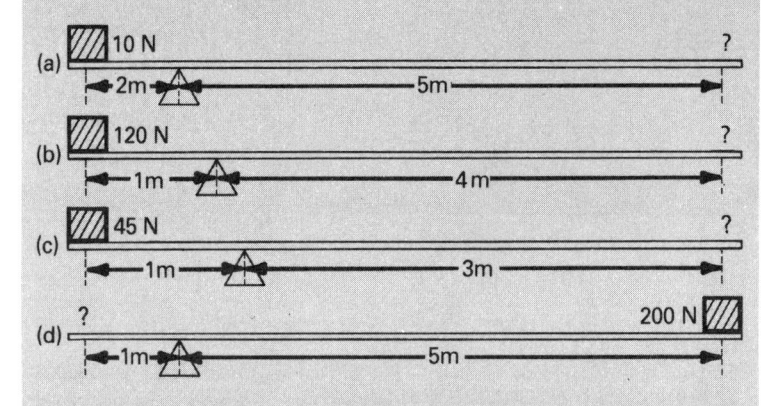

   (a) 10 N, 2m from fulcrum; ? at 5m
   (b) 120 N, 1m from fulcrum; ? at 4m
   (c) 45 N, 1m from fulcrum; ? at 3m
   (d) ? at 1m from fulcrum; 200 N at 5m

2. This diagram shows a spade being used to lift soil weighing 15 newtons.

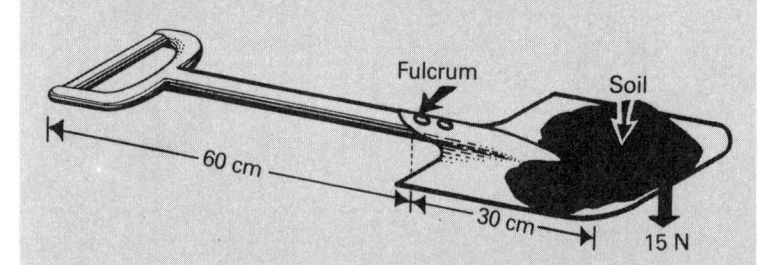

   (Fulcrum shown; handle 60 cm from fulcrum; soil 30 cm from fulcrum on other side; soil weight 15 N)

   (a) Mark in the direction of the smallest force needed to balance the spade.
   (b) How big is this force (roughly)?

3. Draw these objects and mark in roughly where the centre of gravity of each one is.

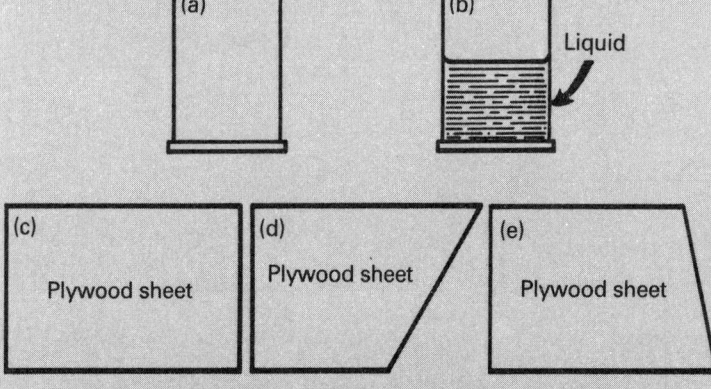

   (a) (swing)
   (b) (container with Liquid)
   (c) Plywood sheet
   (d) Plywood sheet
   (e) Plywood sheet

   Explain why a knowledge of 'centre of gravity' is important in designing cars, buses and lorries.

4. This diagram shows a milk bottle in stable equilibrium. Draw two more diagrams showing a bottle in unstable, and then neutral equilibrium.

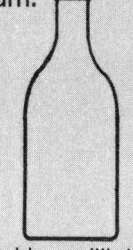

Stable equilibrium

5. Mark with a cross where the centre of gravity of these lamps might be.

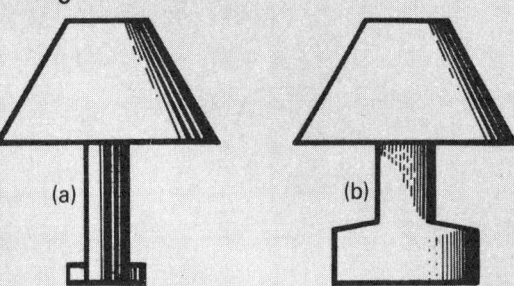

(a) (b)

Which one is likely to be most stable? Give two reasons.

6. This diagram shows the jib of a crane.

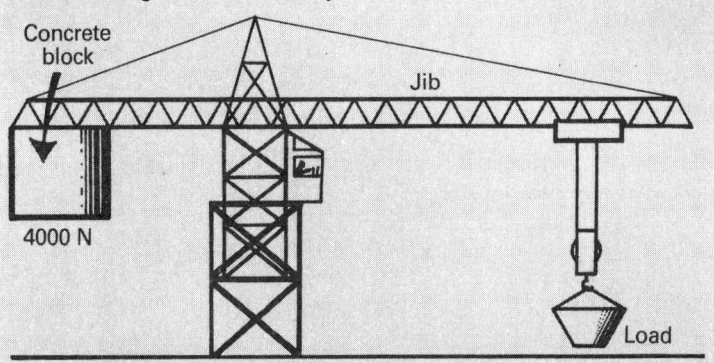

(a) Why is a concrete block placed at one end of the jib?
(b) If the block weighs 4000 newtons, what is the heaviest possible load in its present position (roughly)?

7. Why are people not allowed to stand on the top deck of a double-decker bus?

Chapter 7

Forces in liquids and gases

Floating and sinking

Whenever an object is placed in water, or any other liquid, a force pushes upwards on it — this is called an *upthrust*. The upthrust depends on how much liquid the object pushes aside or *displaces*.

If the weight of the object is bigger than the upthrust on it, the object *sinks*. If the upthrust of the liquid is enough to balance the weight, then the object *floats*.

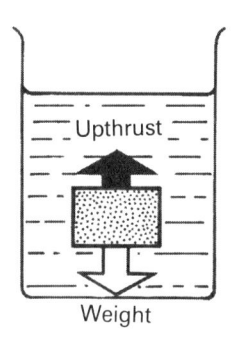

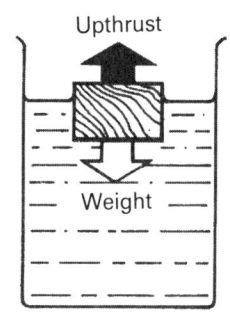

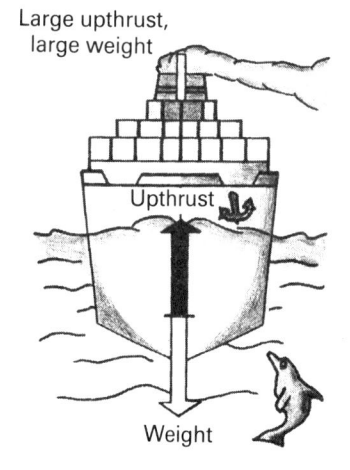

A heavy ship needs a very large upthrust on it to make it float. Ships are designed so that they push aside, or *displace*, a large amount of water — this means that a large upthrust acts on the ship.

An ancient Greek called Archimedes first realised that the more water pushed aside the greater the upthrust. By displacing as much water as possible a person can just float in water.

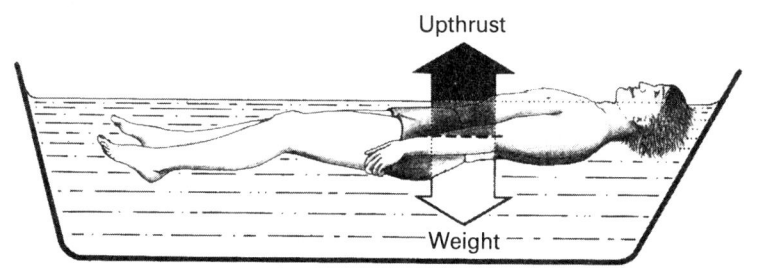

Tropical Fresh, least dense water on this scale

TF
F
T
S
W
WNA

Winter North Atlantic, most dense water

The upthrust also depends on the density of the fluid. It is easier to float in sea water than in fresh water. Sea water is more dense and gives a larger upthrust. A person can float easily in the Dead Sea, a lake between Israel and Jordan, which is full of salt dissolved in the water.

All ships have special lines drawn on them called *Plimsoll lines*. These lines show the level that the water should reach when the ship is fully loaded. There are different levels for tropical water(T), summer(S), winter(W), fresh water(FW), and so on.

Most people think of things floating and sinking in water. But balloons and airships can float in the *air* if they are filled with a 'light' gas, such as hydrogen or helium.

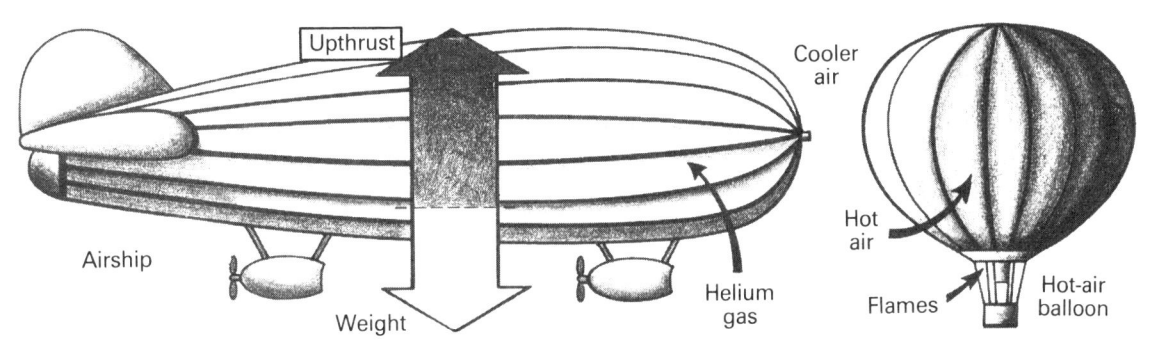

Airship — Upthrust, Weight, Helium gas
Hot-air balloon — Cooler air, Hot air, Flames

The balloon displaces air. This *displaced air* pushes the balloon upwards, making it float. But the gas inside the balloon must be lighter or less dense than the air it displaces. Hot-air balloons float because hot air is less dense than cold air.

Density

Floating and sinking are closely connected with density. If an object is more dense than water it *sinks,* if it is less dense it *floats.* The density of water is almost exactly one gram per cm^3 (1 g/cm^3) So if an object's density is above 1 g/cm^3 it sinks in water — if it is less than 1 g/cm^3 it floats.

An object's density is sometimes given a number called its *relative density.* This means its density compared with water. For example, one kind of wood is about half as dense as water so its relative density is one half, or 0.5, and it floats. Brass is more than 8 times as dense as water. Its relative density is 8.5, and it sinks.

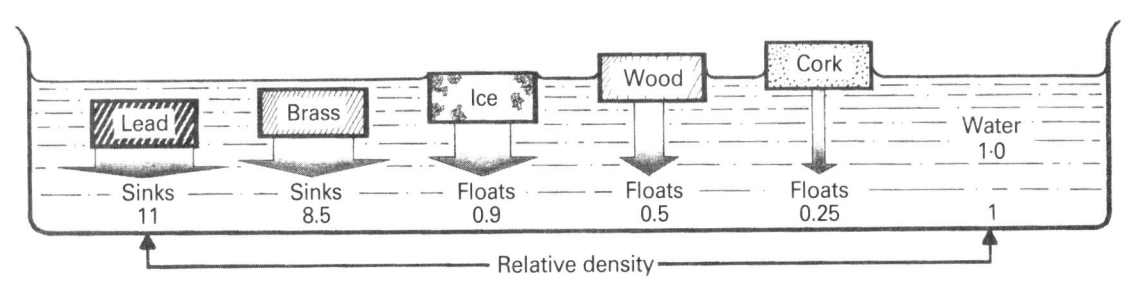

Lead	Brass	Ice	Wood	Cork	Water
Sinks 11	Sinks 8.5	Floats 0.9	Floats 0.5	Floats 0.25	1.0

Relative density

The density of a material that sinks, such as stone or brick, can be found by using a special can called an *Archimedes' Can*. The object is lowered into a full can of water. It pushes water aside and this overflows into a measuring cylinder — the volume of water that overflows is the same as the volume of the object. ∎

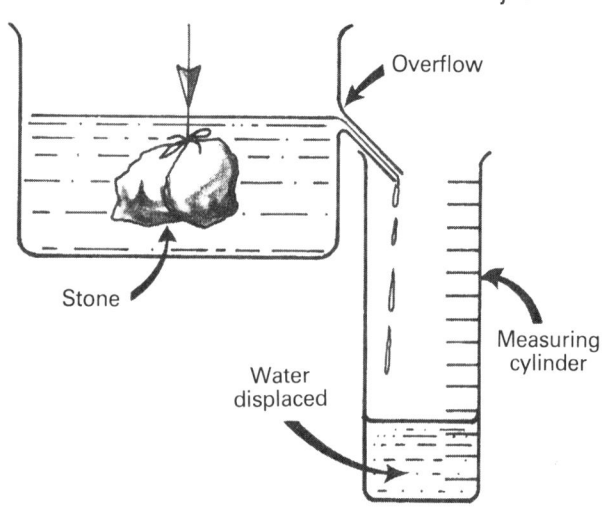

The object's mass can be found by placing it on a balance. Its density can then be found from the formula:

$$\text{Density} = \frac{\text{Mass}}{\text{Volume}}$$

Finding a liquid's density

Some liquids, such as sea water or sulphuric acid, are more dense than water and so their relative density is larger than 1. Other liquids, like meths or paraffin, are less dense than water, therefore their relative density is below 1.

The density of liquids is measured by a *hydrometer* which looks similar to a fishing float. If the hydrometer sinks deeply into a liquid then the liquid is less dense than water. If the hydrometer is pushed out of the liquid by a large upthrust then the liquid is denser than water. So the scale on a hydrometer has low readings at the top and higher readings of density further down. ∎

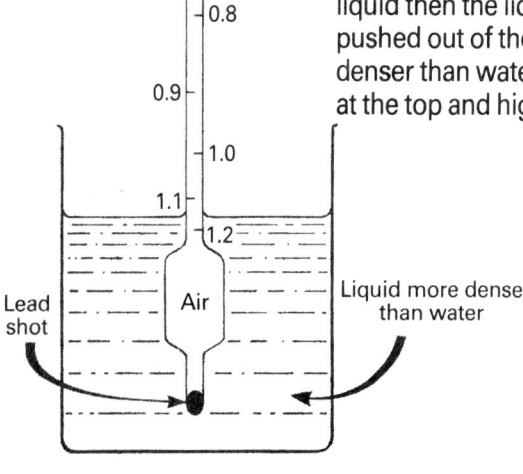

Questions 7

1. This diagram shows three objects which are at rest in water. How does the density of each object compare with that of water — is it more dense, less dense or the same density as water?

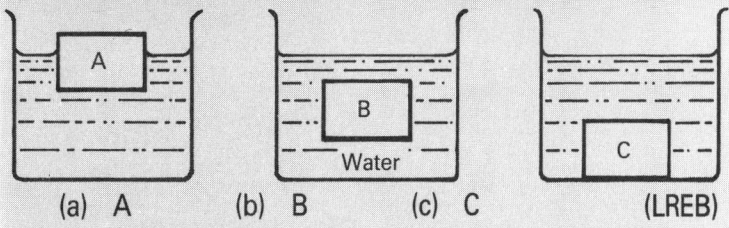

   (a) A   (b) B   (c) C   (LREB)

2. Why do all ships have Plimsoll lines on the side? Explain why there are several loading marks on a ship and not just one Plimsoll line.

3. This diagram shows a block of wood with a mass of 120 g.
   (a) Work out its volume, in cm^3.
   (b) Calculate its density, in g/cm^3.
   (c) Would it float or sink in water? Explain why.

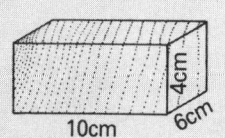

4. Why does an airship filled with helium gas float in the air?

5. Draw three simple diagrams of a hydrometer floating in three different liquids — one being water, one less dense than water, one more dense than water. Explain why the hydrometer floats at different levels in each liquid.

6. An object was weighed on a spring balance, first of all in air and then in water. The results are written by the side of each diagram.

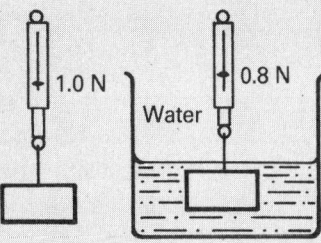

   (a) What is the upthrust on the object when it is placed in water?
   (b) What is the downward force on the object when in the water?
   (c) What upward force, other than upthrust, acts on the object when in the water?
   (d) Explain why the object would sink in water if it were released from the spring balance.
   (e) What would the upthrust be if the object were placed in a liquid of twice the density of water? What would then be the reading of the spring balance? (LREB)

51

Chapter 8 Pressure

What is pressure?

The pressure due to a force depends on the area which the force is acting over. A woman wearing very narrow, pointed heels places much more pressure on the floor than if she wears flat shoes. With the flat shoes, the woman's weight is spread over a much larger area.

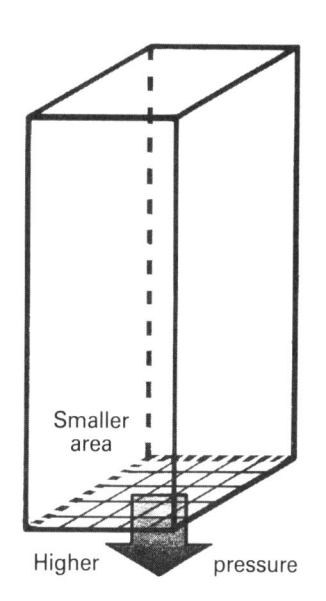

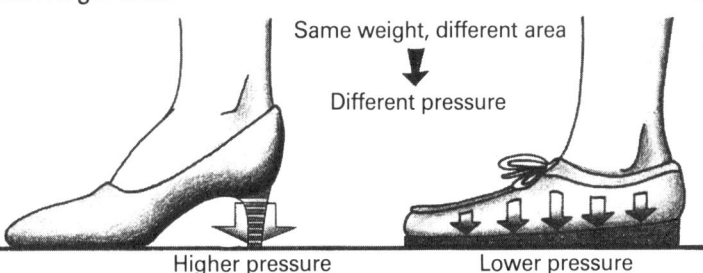

Same weight, different area
Different pressure
Higher pressure   Lower pressure

The same block of wood places a larger pressure on a bench when it stands 'on end' than it does when it is 'laid flat'.

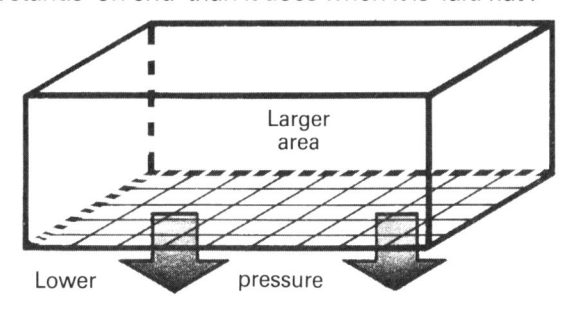

Smaller area
Higher pressure

Larger area
Lower pressure

Pressure depends on both the force acting and the area it acts over. The smaller the area, the larger the pressure:

$$\text{Pressure (in newtons per square metre or N/m}^2\text{)} = \frac{\text{Force (in N)}}{\text{Area (in m}^2\text{)}}$$

This formula can be put into a triangle.

To calculate pressure put your finger over P:

$$\text{Pressure} = \text{Force} \div \text{Area}$$

For example, if a force of 500 N is spread over an area of 2 m^2:

$$\text{Pressure} = {}^{500}\!/\!_2 = 250 \text{ N/m}^2$$

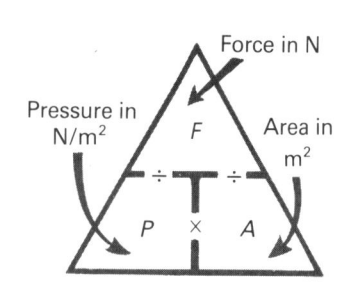

Pressure in liquids

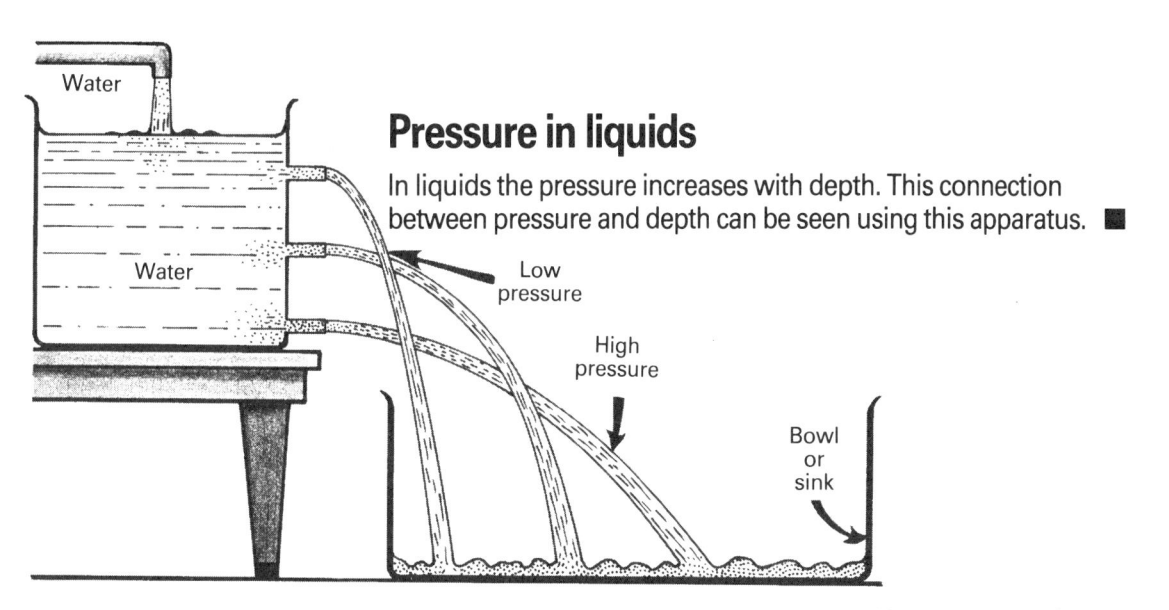

In liquids the pressure increases with depth. This connection between pressure and depth can be seen using this apparatus. ■

A deep-sea diver needs a protective suit and helmet to stand up to the pressure underwater. Also, the wall of a dam is built much thicker at the bottom than at the top. ■

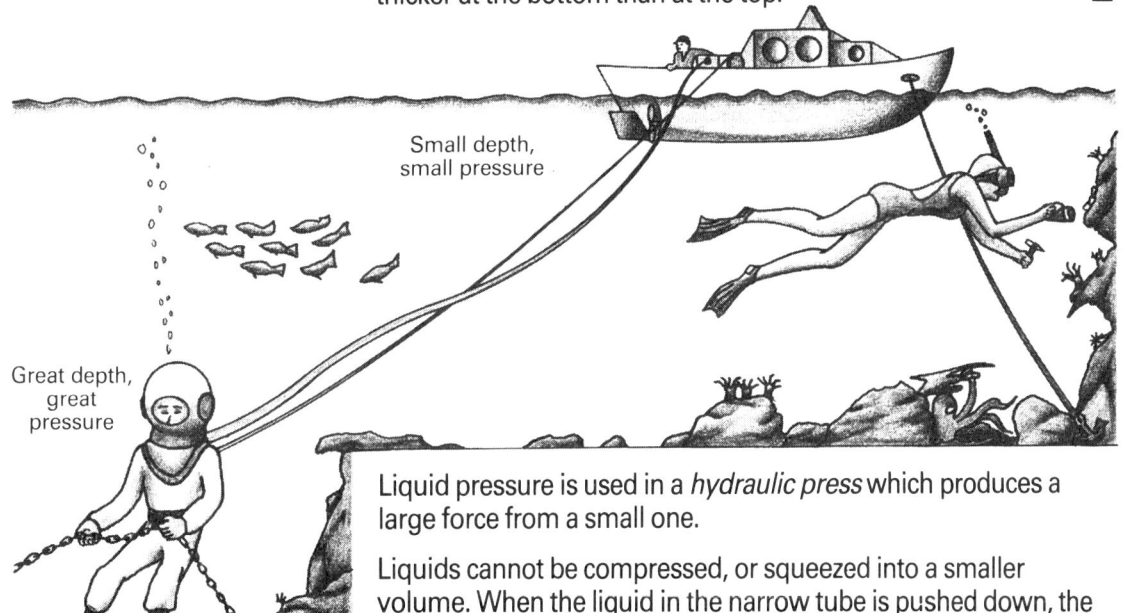

Liquid pressure is used in a *hydraulic press* which produces a large force from a small one.

Liquids cannot be compressed, or squeezed into a smaller volume. When the liquid in the narrow tube is pushed down, the liquid in the wide tube is forced up. A small force in the narrow tube makes quite a high pressure. This pressure is carried through to the wider tube. ■

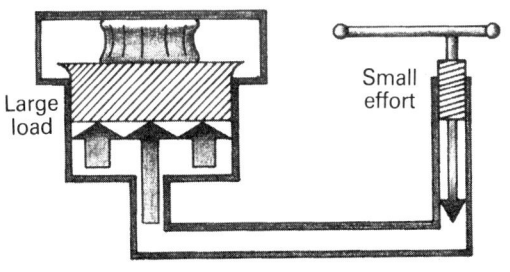

A hydraulic press like this is a force multiplier. It can be used for lifting heavy loads, or in car brakes.

Pressure in gases

All gases produce pressure by the non-stop movement of their molecules. Fast-moving gas molecules collide with the walls of their containers, pressing against them.

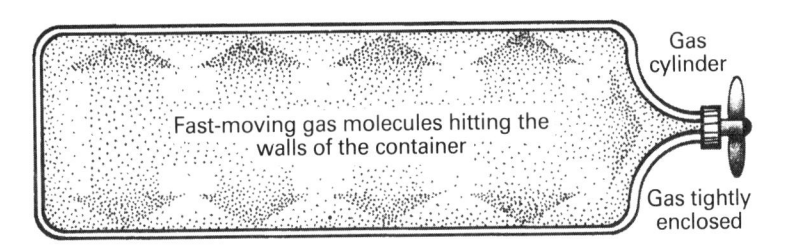

If the gas becomes hotter, its molecules move faster and faster. They press harder against the walls and the gas pressure increases.

The pressure of a gas supply is easily measured by balancing it against a column of liquid. The stronger the gas pressure, the more the liquid moves round the tube. This is called a *manometer*.

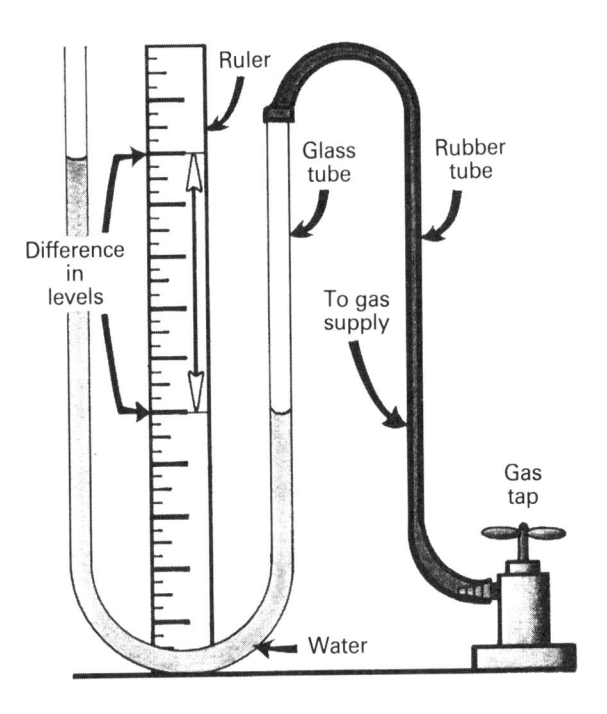

If the manometer is filled with *water,* there is a big difference in levels between the sides of the manometer. The larger the difference in levels, the larger the gas pressure.

But if the manometer is filled with a more dense liquid, such as mercury, the difference in levels is much smaller. So a mercury manometer is more suitable for measuring higher gas pressures.

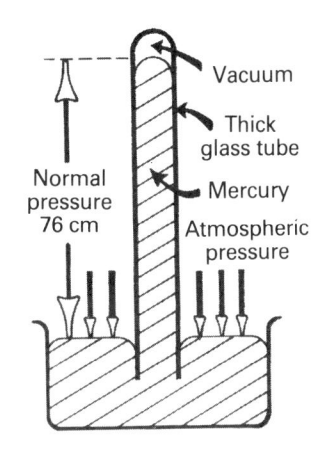

Atmospheric pressure

The air or atmosphere around us is always pressing on every object, although this pressure is not always obvious. It is called *atmospheric pressure,* and can be measured by a *barometer.* One type of barometer, the mercury barometer, consists of a long column of mercury in a glass tube with an empty space, or vacuum, above it. The mercury column is held up by the pressure of the atmosphere. At normal atmospheric pressure the column is 76 centimetres (cm) high, at low pressure only about 74 cm, and at high pressure the atmosphere supports a mercury column of about 77 cm or higher.

Another instrument for measuring air pressure is the *aneroid barometer,* which is also used in planes for finding their height, or altitude. It is made from a metal tin which contains a partial vacuum. When atmospheric pressure is high the tin is pushed inwards and moves a pointer on a scale to show high pressure — when the air pressure drops, the tin expands and the pointer moves the other way.

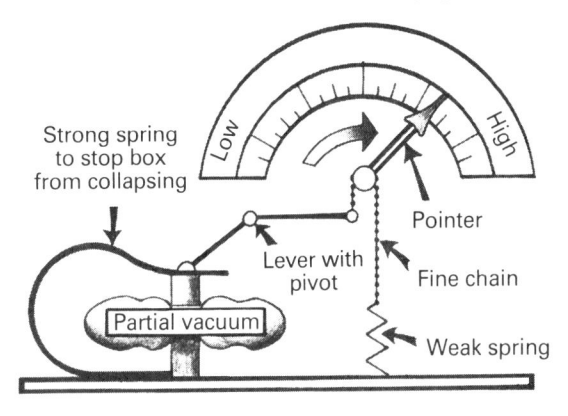

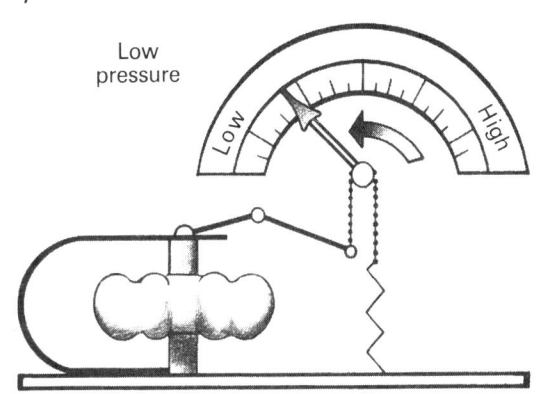

The word 'aneroid' means 'without liquid'.

People cannot see or feel atmospheric pressure. But it can often be very useful to them. A rubber 'sucker' is held onto a piece of glass by the pressure of the atmosphere.

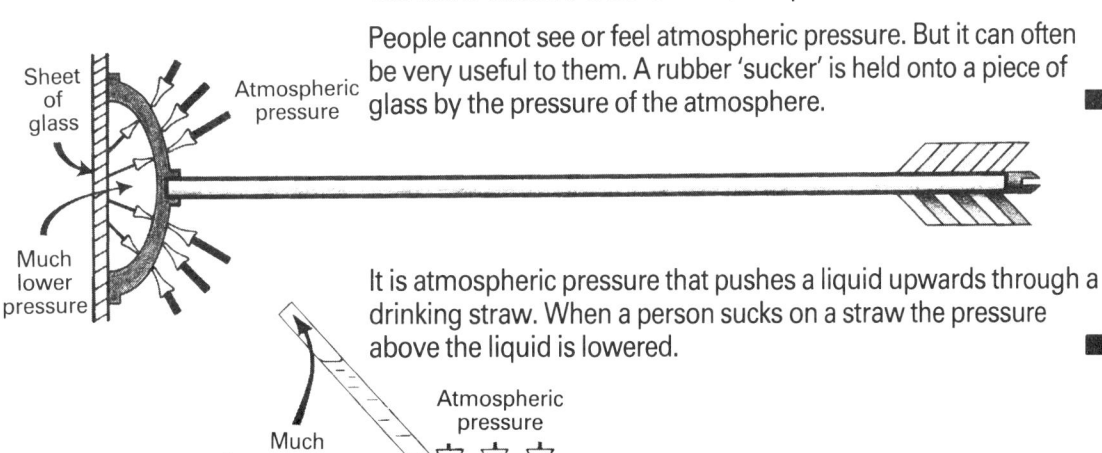

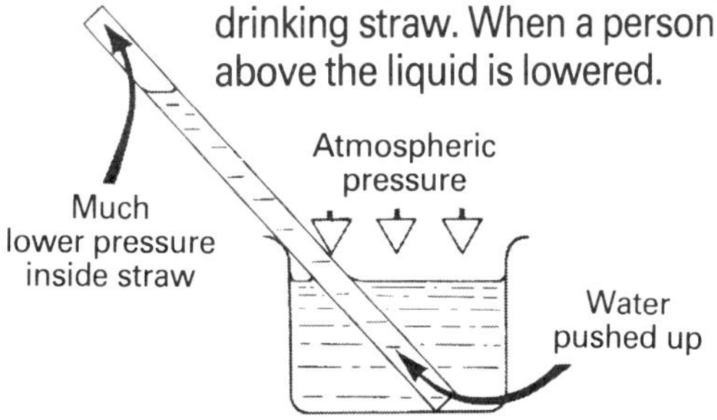

It is atmospheric pressure that pushes a liquid upwards through a drinking straw. When a person sucks on a straw the pressure above the liquid is lowered.

Questions 8

1. Why does a snowshoe have a large area, while an ice skate has a sharp blade?

2. This diagram shows a container full of water.
   (a) Draw three lines showing how the water would come out of the three holes.
   (b) At which hole is the pressure largest?
   (c) Explain why a dam is built thicker at the bottom than the top.

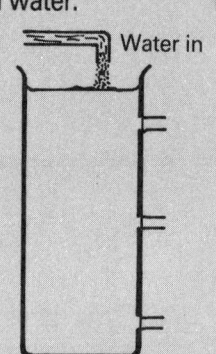

3. Use the formula:

   Pressure = $\frac{\text{Force}}{\text{Area}}$ to calculate the following:

   (a) Force = 50 N, area = 2 m², pressure = ?
   (b) Force = 500 N, area = 5 m², pressure = ?
   (c) Force = 720 N, area = 6 m², pressure = ?
   (d) Force = 3000 N, area = 4 m², pressure = ?
   (e) Pressure = 6 N/m², area = 3 m², force = ?

4. Suppose a man wearing snowshoes weighs 600 newtons. Each snowshoe has an area of 0·1 m². What pressure does he place on the snow?

5. This diagram shows part of an aneroid barometer.
   (a) What is it used for?
   (b) Label the parts A and B, and explain their use.
   (c) What is there inside B?
   (d) What does the word 'aneroid' mean?

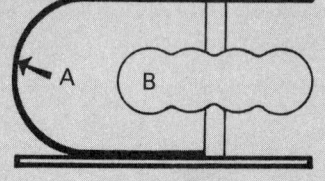

6. A tall column of liquid is used in one form of barometer to measure air pressure.
   (a) What is the liquid A normally used?
   (b) What is inside the tube at B?
   (c) Give an approximate height (h) of the liquid column when the barometer is at sea level in air.
   (d) Give one reason why water would be unsuitable for use as the liquid in a barometer. (LREB)

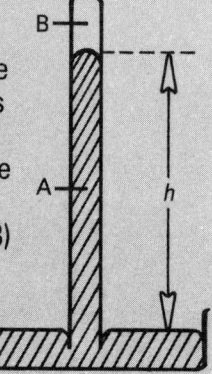

7. This diagram shows a pupil blowing into the tube A in order to measure the maximum pressure which his lungs can exert.

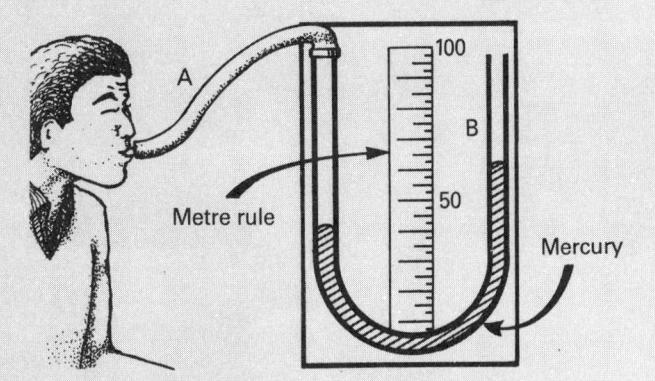

   (a) Name the piece of apparatus.
   (b) Write down the difference in liquid levels.
   (c) If the pupil now releases the pressure and repeats the experiment with a bung blocking the end of tube B:
      (i) how will the result differ from the result of the first experiment?
      (ii) Explain this difference. (YREB)

8. A 'U' tube is to be used as a manometer to measure lung pressure, by blowing down one side (C).

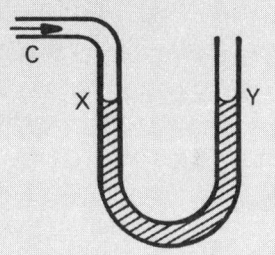

   (a) Give a reason why the levels X and Y are the same when no one is blowing down one side of the tube.
   (b) Which way would the levels move (up or down), when some one blows down the tube at C? Give a reason for your answer.
   (c) The following liquids could be used in a manometer: water of density 1 gram per cm^3; oil of density 0.8 gram per cm^3; salt solution of density 1.2 gram per cm^3. Which liquid would give the greatest difference in levels assuming that the same lung pressure is to be measured each time? (LREB)

CROSSWORD 2

Trace this grid on to a piece of paper before working out the answers.

Across

1. Gravity makes it difficult for you to walk—— (6)
4. An object with a high temperature is —— (3)
7. A force on the end of 13 down may make it —— (6)
8. Rubber —— will stretch easily (5)
11. When certain objects are rubbed together there is an —— force between them (13)
14. Force = —— × 18 across (12)
18. See 14 across (4)
19. They may attract each other or push each other apart (7)

Down

2. ——'s Law tells you that the more a 13 down is loaded, the more it extends (5)
3. A form of energy (5)
5. An astronaut is kept in —— by the force of gravity (5)
6. The —— of weight is the newton (4)
9. 16 down can be measured in —— (7)
10. If spilt, mercury does not —— the bench (3)
12. Another name for law (4)
13. See 2 down (6)
15. They need the force of their engines to make them accelerate (4)
16. Speed = distance travelled ÷ —— taken (4)
17. You can work out the —— of two vectors by drawing a parallelogram (3)

A parachutist: what forces are in action here? (see page 24 and 33)

Hot air balloons: how do they work? (see pages 49 and 73)

A special kind of photograph showing a model of a space shuttle in a wind tunnel. Notice the air patterns.

Concorde flying at very high speed. Can you see how streamlined the aircraft is? What force is it reducing by being this shape? (see page 33)

A crane using pulleys: many machines like this are still in use. (see page 38)

Saturn and its moons: a beautiful part of the Solar System. (see page 33)

A Formula One racing car. Where do you think its centre of gravity is? (see page 45)

The Stwlan Dam in Wales, holding the upper reservoir at Ffestiniog hydroelectric pumped storage power station. (see page 53)

Part 3

Heat Energy

Chapter 9

Temperature and thermometers

Heat energy and temperature scales

Heat is one form of energy and so it is measured in *joules*. But the temperature of something is a measure of how 'hot' or 'cold' it is, not how much heat energy it contains. Two pieces of steel can have the same temperature, but the heavier one contains more heat energy (in joules).

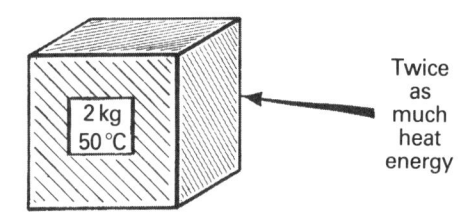

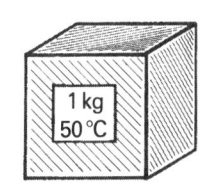

Temperature is always measured on a scale. The simplest scale is the Centigrade or *Celsius* scale, because it uses zero degrees (0 °C) as the freezing point of water and 100 degrees (100 °C) as the boiling point of water. These are called *fixed points*.

Another scale of temperature used in Physics is the *Kelvin* scale. This uses *Absolute Zero* as its lowest or zero point, which is the same as −273 °C. (Absolute zero is the point when all molecules are supposed to stop moving or vibrating.) The Kelvin scale starts at −273°C, so the melting point of ice is 273 kelvin, or 273 K, and the boiling point of water is 373 K.

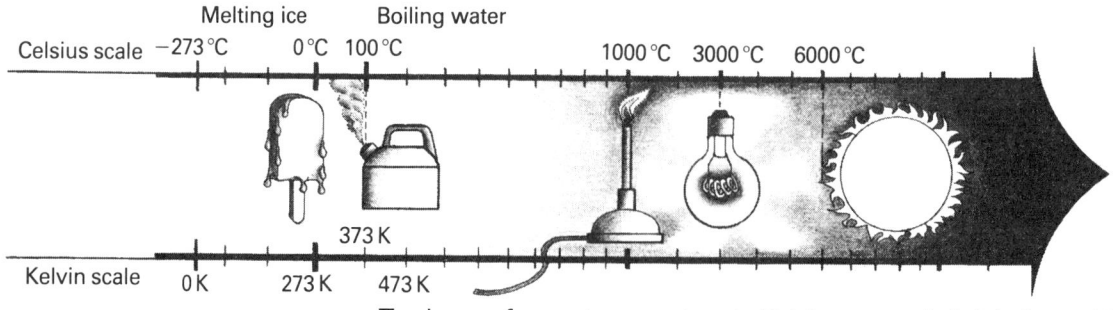

To change from a temperature in Celsius to one in kelvin just add 273. To change from a temperature in kelvin to one in Celsius subtract 273.

Mercury and alcohol thermometers

The temperature, or 'level of hotness', of something is measured with a thermometer. The main parts of a thermometer are the 'bulb' of liquid, a long, thin capillary tube, and a scale. As the liquid heats up it expands and moves along the tube.

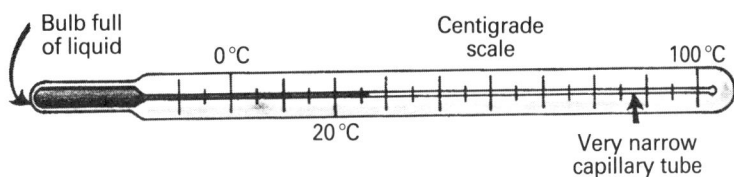

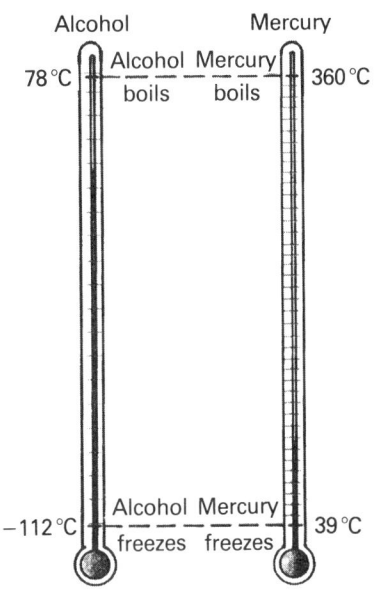

The two points, 0°C and 100°C, are called the lower and upper fixed points on a thermometer. The lower one can be found by putting the thermometer in pure melting ice, and the upper fixed point is found by placing the thermometer in steam from pure water, at normal pressure. Once these fixed points, 0°C and 100°C, have been marked on the thermometer scale, the distance between them is divided into 100 separate parts or 'divisions'. Then, each division on the scale stands for one degree Celsius of temperature.

Some thermometers use alcohol as their liquid while others use mercury. Alcohol is best for very low temperatures because it does not freeze until it reaches −112°C. Mercury freezes at −39°C, so it is useless in cold areas, like the North and South Poles. But mercury does not boil until it reaches 360°C, and so mercury thermometers can be used with very hot things. Alcohol boils at 78°C, so alcohol thermometers must not be used above this temperature.

The proper use of Alcohol and Mercury thermometers

Polar temp. −40°C

From 200°C oven

Clinical and 'thermoelectric' thermometers

A special kind of mercury thermometer is used in hospitals to measure a patient's temperature. It only needs a small scale, from 35 °C to 43 °C, so that it can give an accurate reading. It also has a small kink in its tube to stop the mercury from running back when the temperature is being read. This is why nurses are often seen shaking their thermometer, to get the mercury back in the bulb.

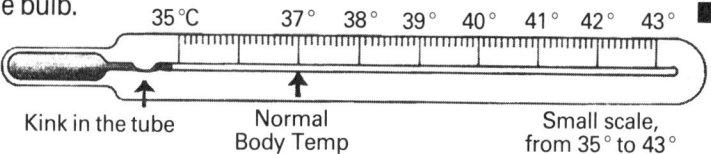

Kink in the tube — Normal Body Temp — Small scale, from 35° to 43°

Another useful thermometer for measuring very hot things like furnaces and molten metals over 360 °C, uses a *thermocouple*. This is the name of two metals, joined together in two places. When one of the joins is heated a small electric current is made, and can be seen on a meter. The size of the current indicates the temperature of the hot metals.

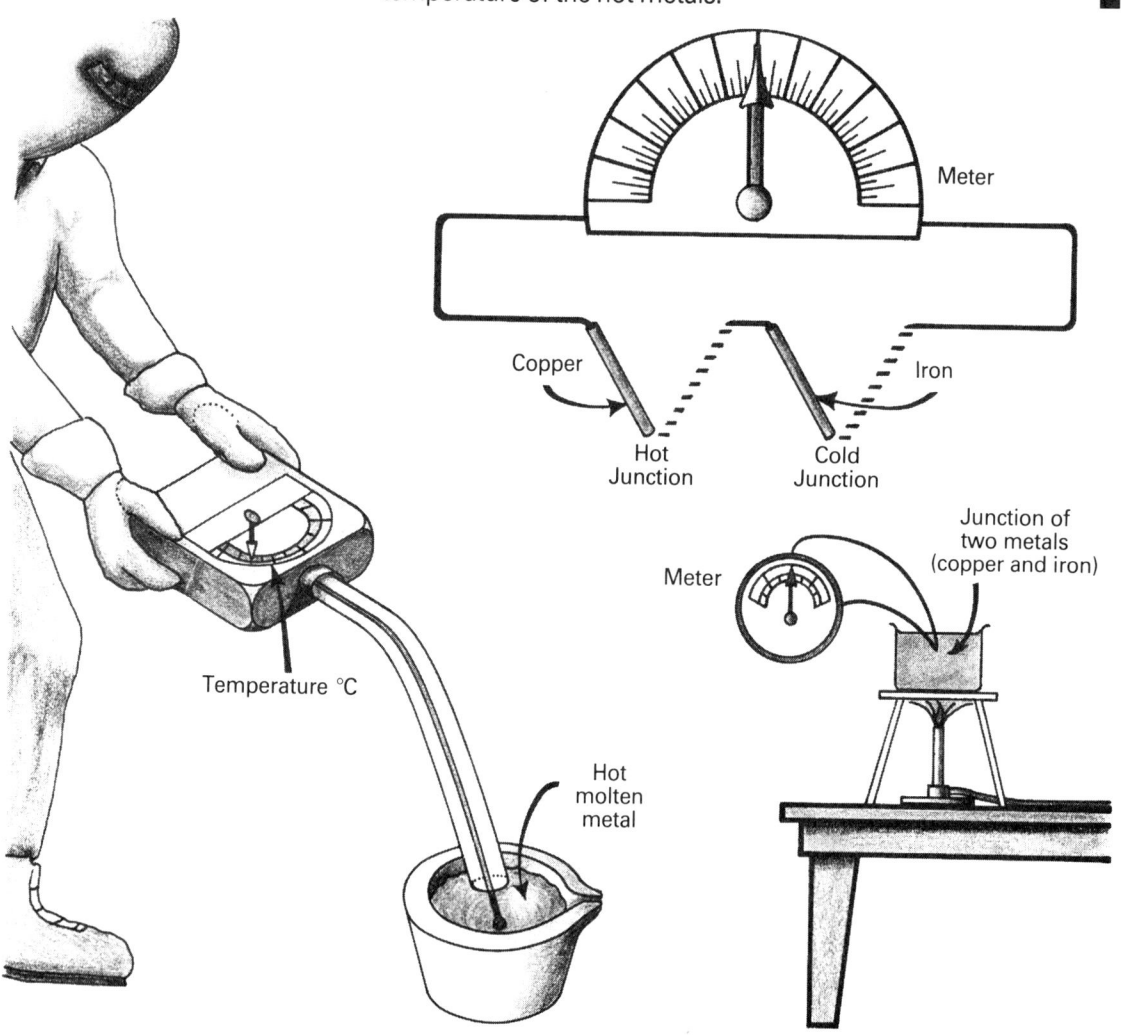

Questions 9

Copy the questions and fill in the missing words and numbers in Questions 1–4.

1. Water boils at __°C or __ kelvin. Water freezes at __°C or __ K. These are called the upper and lower __ points on the __ scale.

2. (a) A temperature of 50 °C is the same as __ K
   (b) 120 °C = __ K
   (c) 32 °C = __ K
   (d) 55 °C = __ K

3. (a) A temperature of 373 K is the same as __ °C
   (b) 584 K = __ °C
   (c) 1565 K = __ °C
   (d) 212 K = __ °C

4. A clinical thermometer is used in ____
   It has a small scale, from __ °C to __ °C
   Normal body temperature is __ °C

5. Which thermometer would you take with you on an expedition to the North Pole? Which thermometer would you use for measuring the temperature of boiling water? Explain your reasons.

6. This diagram shows a clinical thermometer. Draw this thermometer and label its important features, including a scale. Why do nurses shake these thermometers?

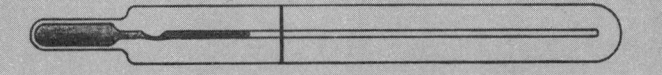

Chapter 10

Measuring heat energy

Joules and watts

Heat is a form of energy, and so it is measured in *joules*. A joule is a very small amount of heat energy and so heat supplies are often measured in *kilojoules*.

$$1 \text{ kilojoule} = 1000 \text{ joules} \quad (1 \text{ kJ} = 1000 \text{ J})$$

The *power* of a heating supply is measured in *watts*. If a supply has a power of 1 watt it supplies 1 joule of heat every second: 20 watts is the same as 20 joules per second; 500 W means 500 J/s; and so on. The power of a heat supply, say an electric kettle, an iron or a cooker, is usually measured in kilowatts:

$$1 \text{ kilowatt} = 1000 \text{ watts} \quad (1 \text{ kW} = 1000 \text{ W})$$

An electric kettle of 2 kW can supply 2000 J of heat energy every second.

Heat capacity and specific heat capacity

The heat capacity of an object depends on how much heat energy is needed to raise its temperature by 1 °C. If two objects are made of the same material, but one has twice the mass of the other, then its heat capacity is twice as large.

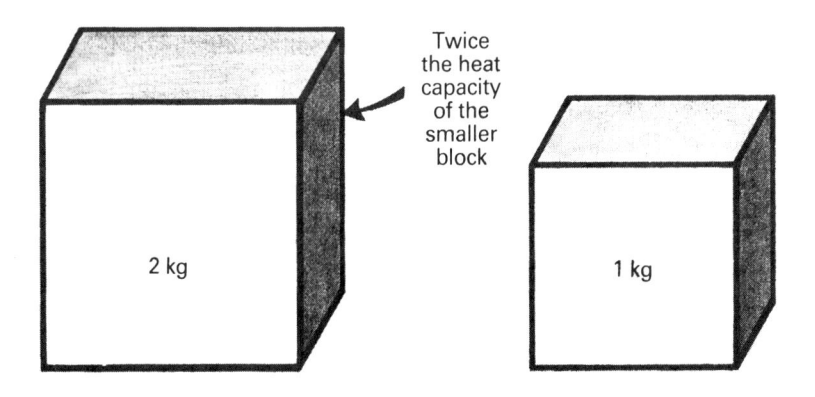

Twice the heat capacity of the smaller block

2 kg

1 kg

If the small one has a heat capacity of 400 joules for every degree Celsius, then the larger one has a capacity of 800 joules per °C, because it has twice the mass.

In physics we can compare the heat capacities of different materials by finding the heat capacity of one kilogram of the material. This is called the *specific heat capacity* of the material — it means the number of joules of heat energy needed to increase the temperature of one kg by 1 °C. Here are a few examples of specific heat capacities of some common materials.

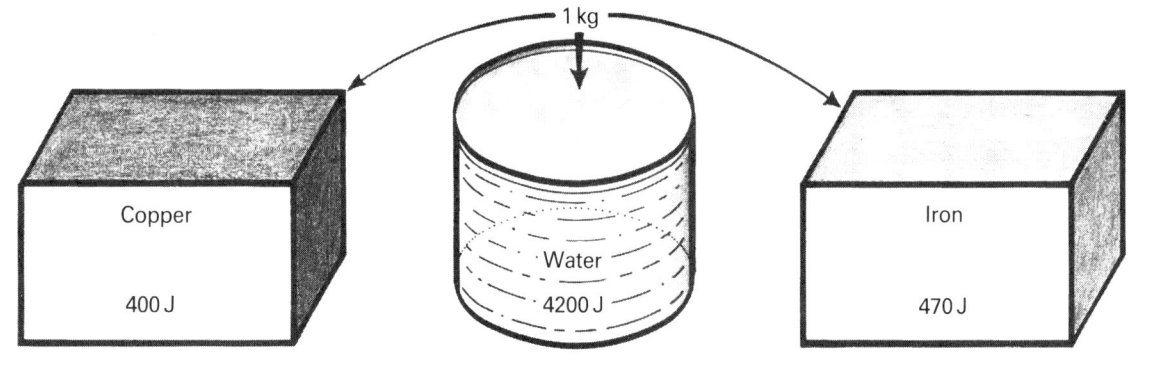

Copper 400 J

Water 4200 J

Iron 470 J

The specific heat capacity tells us the heat needed to warm 1 kg by 1 °C. For example, copper needs 400 J of heat to warm 1 kg by 1 °C. If 2 kg of copper are warmed by 1 °C, then double the heat is needed: 800 J. Also, if the copper is warmed by 2 °C, then the number of joules is doubled again:

> 400 J are needed to warm 1 kg of copper by 1 °C
> 800 J are need to warm 2 kg of copper by 1 °C
> 1600 J are needed to warm 2 kg of copper by 2 °C

A formula for the heat needed can be written as:

> Heat needed (in J) = Specific heat capacity (in J/kg/°C)
> × Mass (in kg)
> × Temperature change (in °C)

Heat 'exchanges'

When an object is warmed it takes heat in, or *absorbs* heat, which makes its temperature rise. If this hot object is placed into cold water then it immediately loses heat energy and cools down. Heat energy always travels from a hot object to a cooler one, until their temperatures are the same. This is called a *heat exchange*.

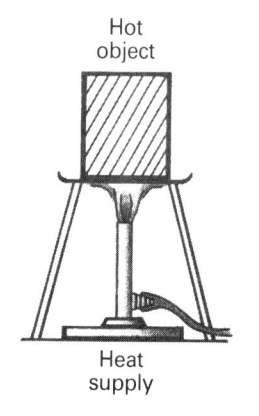

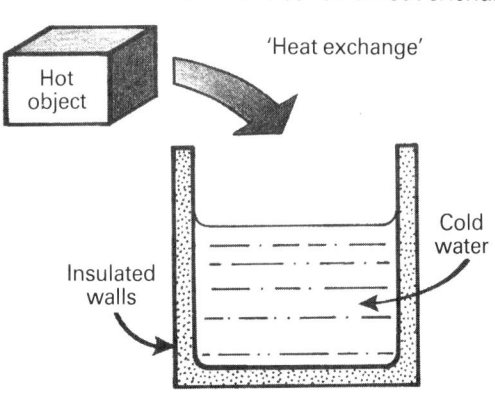

The hot object loses heat, while the cold water gains heat. Experiments with heat exchanges can be used to measure the specific heat capacity of different materials, e.g. copper, iron, and water. The heat lost by the hot object can be calculated by using the formula:

Heat lost = Specific heat capacity × Mass × Temperature lost

Most of this heat goes into the cold water — a small amount always escapes into the air around it. If we assume that all of this heat goes into the cold water then:

Heat lost by the hot object = Heat gained by the cold water

Once we know the specific heat capacity of water we can find the specific heat capacity of a metal, like copper, by placing a piece of hot copper in cold water.

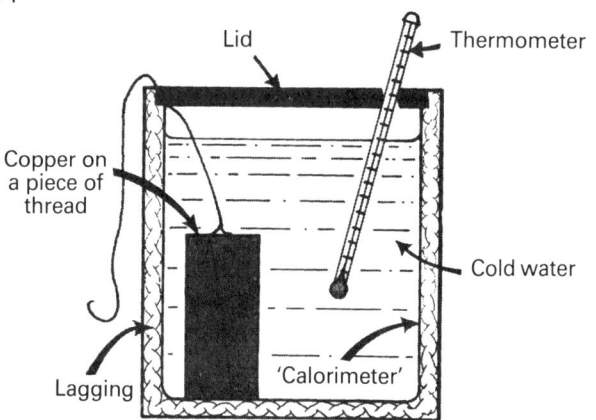

The masses of the hot object and the water have to be measured, as well as the changes in their temperatures as one cools down and the other warms up. The cold water is held in a specially insulated container called a *calorimeter*.

Questions 10

1. How many joules are there in:
   (a) 4 kilojoules (b) 6½ kJ (c) 3.5 kJ (d) 100 kJ?
2. How many kilowatts are:
   (a) 2000 watts (b) 5500 W (c) 9500 W (d) 500 W?
3. Copper has a specific heat capacity of 400 joules per kg per °C. Explain what this means.
4. How many joules of energy are needed to heat up:
   (a) 2 kg of copper by 2 °C
   (b) 10 kg of copper by 6 °C
   (c) 12 kg of copper by 10 °C?
   Put the answers in kilojoules as well.
5. Water has a specific heat capacity of 4200 J per kg per °C. Find the heat needed in each of these examples:
   (a) 1 kg of water being heated by 5 °C
   (b) 1 kg of water being heated from 20 °C to 60 °C
   (c) 2 kg of water being heated from 20 °C to 60 °C
   (d) 3 kg of water being heated from 40 °C to 80 °C
6. This diagram shows a saucepan full of soup being heated by burning gas. The gas supplies 1000 joules of heat every second.

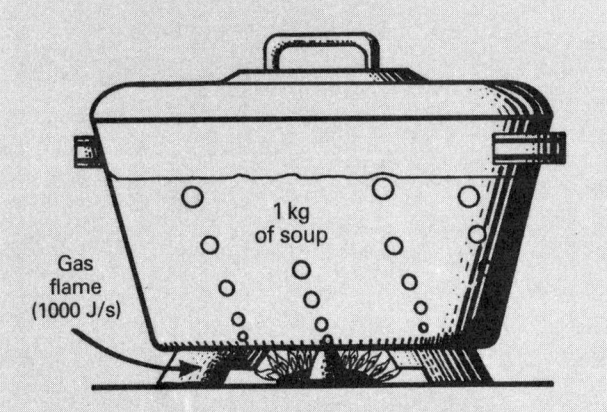

   [Diagram: saucepan containing 1 kg of soup being heated by a Gas flame (1000 J/s)]

   (a) How many joules does it supply in 10 seconds? How many joules in 20 seconds?
   (b) Suppose the specific heat capacity of the soup is 5000 joules per kg per °C. How long does it take to warm up by 1 °C?
   (c) How long will it take to warm up from 20 °C to 80 °C? (supposing that all the heat from the gas goes into the soup).
   (d) In a real kitchen, why would it take longer than this?

Chapter 11

Expansion of solids, liquids and gases

Solids expanding

All materials increase in size when they are heated — they *expand*. When they are cooled and their temperature drops they *contract*. Metals like brass, steel, copper, and iron expand as their temperature increases. This can be seen by heating a metal bar in a special clamp and then allowing it to contract. As the bar cools and contracts it suddenly snaps a pin which is placed in it.

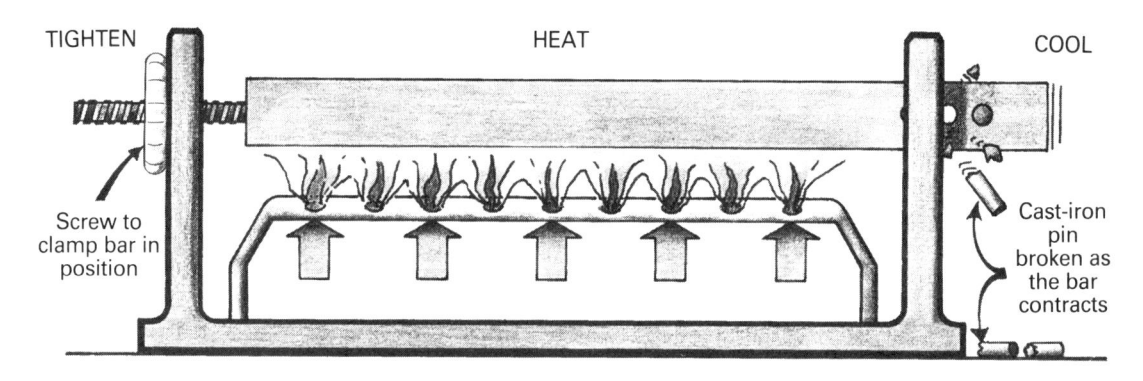

TIGHTEN — HEAT — COOL

Screw to clamp bar in position

Cast-iron pin broken as the bar contracts

Roads, buildings and bridges all get bigger on a hot day. They only expand by a few centimetres — but if they are not free to expand, a lot of damage can be caused. Roads made of concrete have small gaps left in them, for the concrete to expand into when it gets hot.

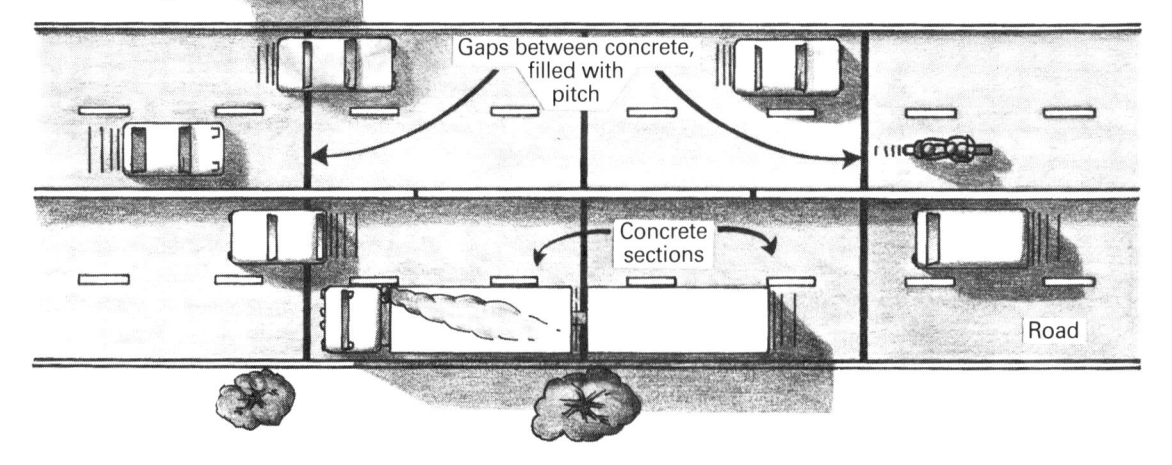

Gaps between concrete, filled with pitch

Concrete sections

Road

Gaps are left at the ends of bridges to allow the bridge to expand in hot weather. One end of the bridge rests on rollers.

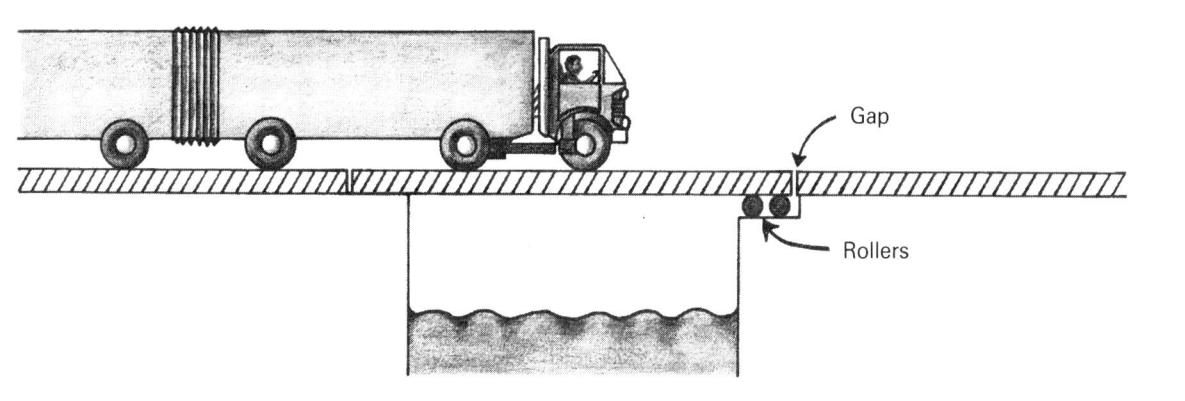

Using expansion

Some metals expand more than others when they are heated by the same amount. This can be very useful. A special 'strip' can be made by joining a piece of brass to a piece of steel. This is called a *bi-metallic strip.* When the strip is heated it gradually *bends* as the two metals expand.

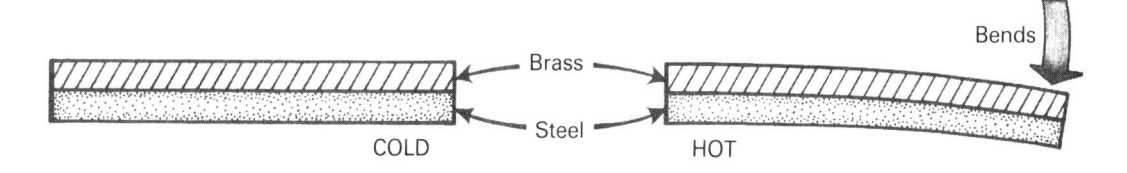

The brass expands more than steel, so the two metals make a curve with brass on the outside. A special metal called 'Invar' is often used instead of steel. This hardly expands at all when it is heated.

Bi-metallic strips are used in *thermostats* for switching things on and off automatically.

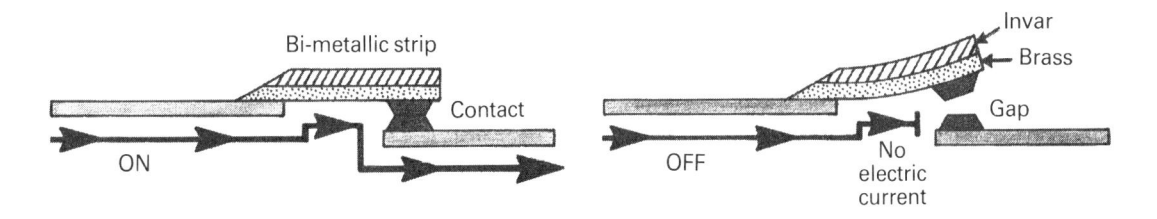

If the bi-metallic strip gets too hot it bends and breaks the electrical contact. This switches the electric current off. When the strip cools it straightens again. The current comes back on. So the bi-metallic strip is a kind of switch, controlled by heat. It is used in electric irons, kettles, fires, car indicators and central heating.

Liquids expanding

All liquids expand when they are heated. This can be shown by putting a liquid in a flask with a long tube inside it. As the liquid is heated it expands and rises up the tube.

Some liquids expand more than others when they are heated by the same amount.

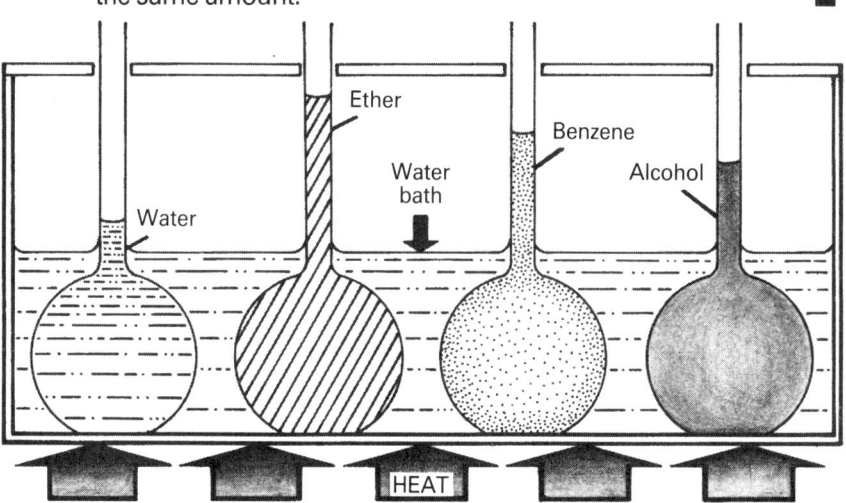

Alcohol expands quite a lot when it is heated. This is one of the reasons why it is used in thermometers.

The way that water behaves is very unusual. When it is *cooled* from 4 °C to 0 °C it actually *expands.* Water freezes at 0 °C and expands as it changes to ice. This is why water pipes sometimes burst in winter when the water inside them freezes.

For the same reason a pond hardly ever freezes completely in winter. The ice floats on top of the pond but the warmer water at 4 °C sinks to the bottom and does not freeze. Water reaches its maximum density at 4 °C, so the bottom of a pond is always the warmest part in winter. This means that fish can stay alive even in freezing cold weather.

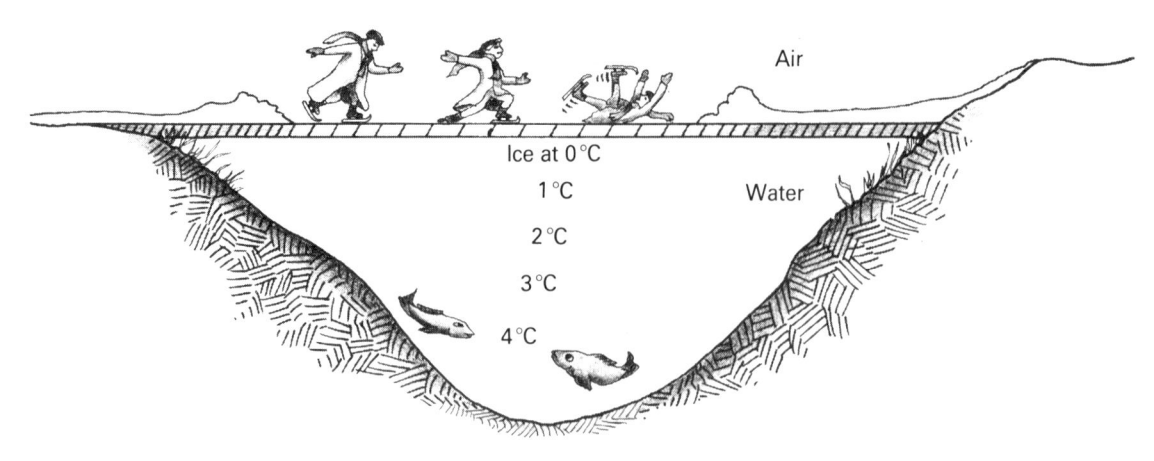

Gases expanding

The expansion of a gas, such as air, can be seen by trapping some air in a flask, then heating it gently by holding the flask. As the air is warmed it *expands* and pushes the water down the tube. When the air cools it *contracts* and the water comes back up the tube.

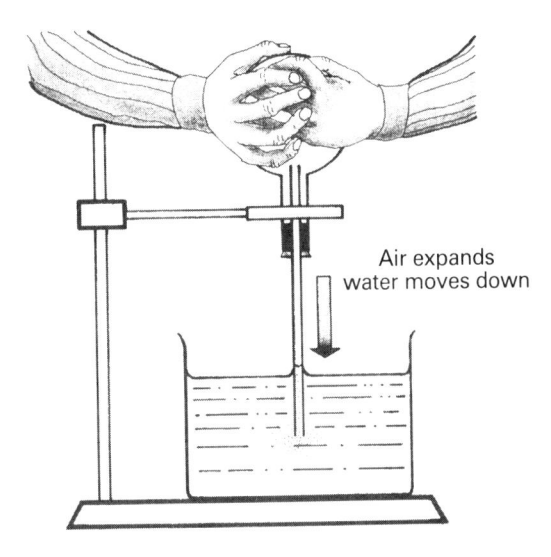

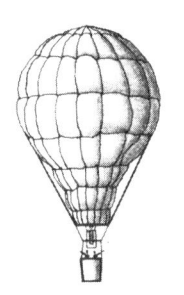

Air expands water moves down

Gases expand more than liquids, and a lot more than solids. Unlike solids and liquids all gases expand at about the same rate. But they only expand if they are allowed to. If you heat a gas and stop it from expanding its pressure builds up. Its molecules move faster and faster and press harder on the walls of the container. Eventually the pressure of a hot gas may cause an explosion.

When gases are allowed to expand they take up more space — they become less dense. Hot air is less dense than cold air and so it rises. This is why a hot-air balloon floats.

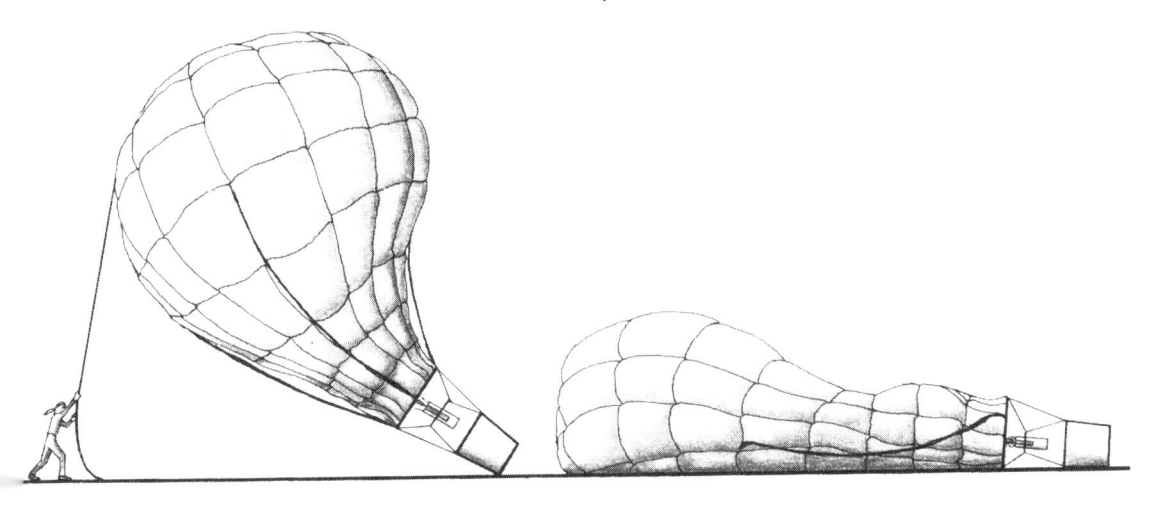

Rising hot air also carries heat from one place to another, as the next chapter explains.

Questions 11

1. Explain why:
   (a) bridges are often laid on rollers with a gap at one end,
   (b) concrete roads are put down in sections with a small gap between them.

2. This diagram shows a bi-metallic strip when it is cold.

   Brass
   Steel

   (a) How would this strip change if it was heated?
   (b) Why would it change in this way?
   (c) Write down three things that use bi-metallic strips.

3. Why do water pipes sometimes burst in winter?

4. Draw a diagram of a pond in winter, and explain why the fish are rarely frozen solid.

5. (a) (i) Describe what happens to the level of the water shown in the tube in diagram A, when the flask is heated.

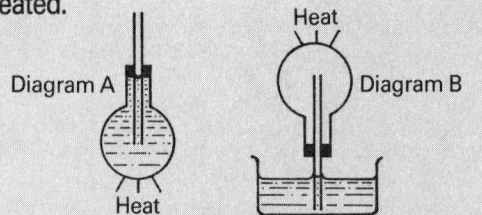

   Diagram A   Diagram B
   Heat   Heat

   (ii) Give reasons for your answer.
   (b) What would be observed when the flask in diagram B is warmed? Give a reason for your answer. (LREB)

6. (a) Describe what happens when a gas held in a container is heated, but not allowed to expand.
   (b) Explain why a hot air balloon rises.

7. The diagram shows a strip of iron and a strip of copper fastened together. The copper expands about twice as much as iron for the same temperature rise.

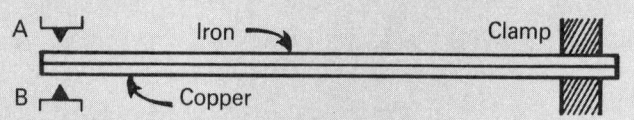

   A   Iron   Clamp
   B   Copper

   (a) If this compound strip were heated, which contact, A or B, would the strip touch? Give a reason for your answer.
   (b) Suggest a use for this device.
   (c) What would happen if the iron strip was replaced by copper and two copper strips heated together?
   (LREB)

8. Suppose that a metal screw-cap is fixed very tightly onto a glass jar. How could it be removed without using too much force?

74

Chapter 12

The way that heat travels

■■■■■■■■■■■■■■

Heat can travel in three different ways, called *conduction, convection* and *radiation.*

Conduction

The best materials for carrying heat by conduction are metals like copper, silver and brass — these are called good *conductors* of heat. Materials like wood, water and air conduct heat very slowly. These very bad conductors are called *insulators.*

Different materials can be compared to find the fastest conductor by coating rods of each material with wax and placing one end of each rod into a tank of hot water. The best conductor of heat melts the wax on the rod quickly, a long way along the rod. ■

Tank of hot water

Wax-covered rods

Lead rod— wax melts slowly

Wax melts quickly on copper rod

Scientists have a picture of the way that a conductor carries heat. The molecules inside a conductor move around very quickly when they are heated and bump into the molecules next to them. This in turn makes them move more quickly and collide with their neighbours. Eventually these collisions travel along the conductor until all the molecules move around more quickly and the whole rod becomes hot. ■

Molecules vibrate

Heat travels by conduction

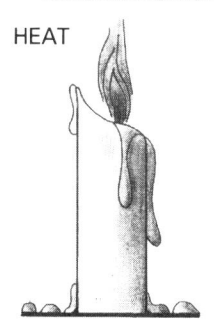

HEAT

Metals, such as copper and silver, are the best conductors of heat. They have tiny particles inside them, smaller than molecules, called *electrons.* These electrons are free to travel around inside the metal. When copper is heated these *free electrons* start to move faster. These moving electrons pass the heat from the hot end of the copper to the cool end. They are carriers of heat energy. (These free electrons also make copper and silver good conductors of *electricity.*)

Using conductors and insulators

Good conductors of heat are mostly metals, such as copper, iron or aluminium. They are used whenever heat needs to be carried quickly, for example in kettles, boilers or saucepans. The handle of a saucepan is always made from a bad conductor of heat, usually wood or plastic.

One of the best insulators of heat is *air*. Materials with a lot of air trapped in them, such as wool, feathers or fibre-glass are used as insulators in blankets, loft insulation or in the 'lagging' for pipes and hot-water tanks.

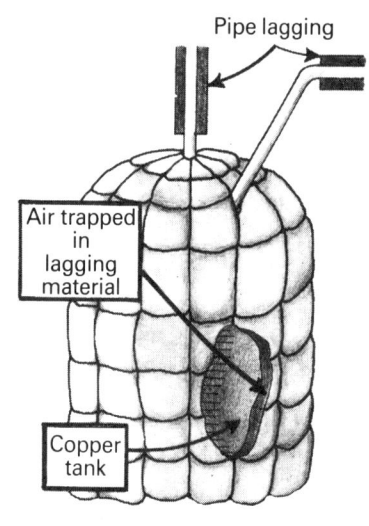

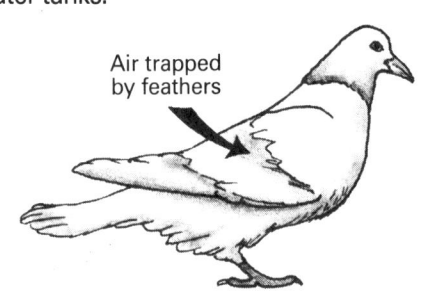

Air is used to insulate houses in *double-glazing*. A layer of air is trapped between two sheets of glass. Most houses built since 1930 have a 'cavity' of air between an inner and an outer wall. This is called a *cavity wall*. A cavity wall and double glazing both help to *insulate* a house.

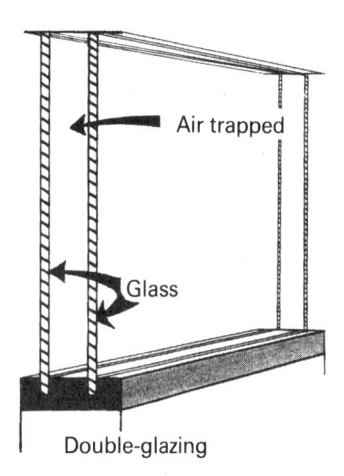

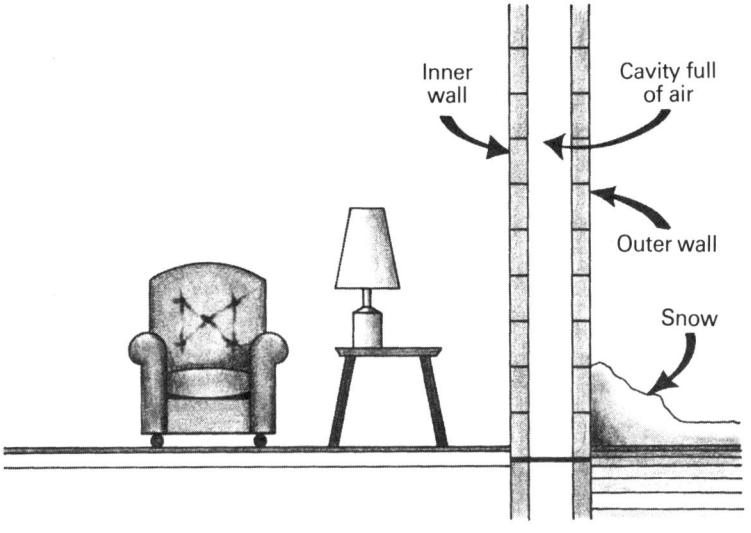

Convection

Another way that heat travels is by *convection*. This is the name given to currents in liquids and gases which carry heat upwards. When a gas or liquid is heated it expands, becomes less dense, and then rises — these upward currents are called *convection currents.* The hot air rising above a flame is one example of a convection current.

Convection currents are used in hot-water systems to make water circulate around the pipes in the system. Hot water from the boiler rises by convection to the hot-water tank. When the water cools it falls and goes back to the bottom of the boiler.

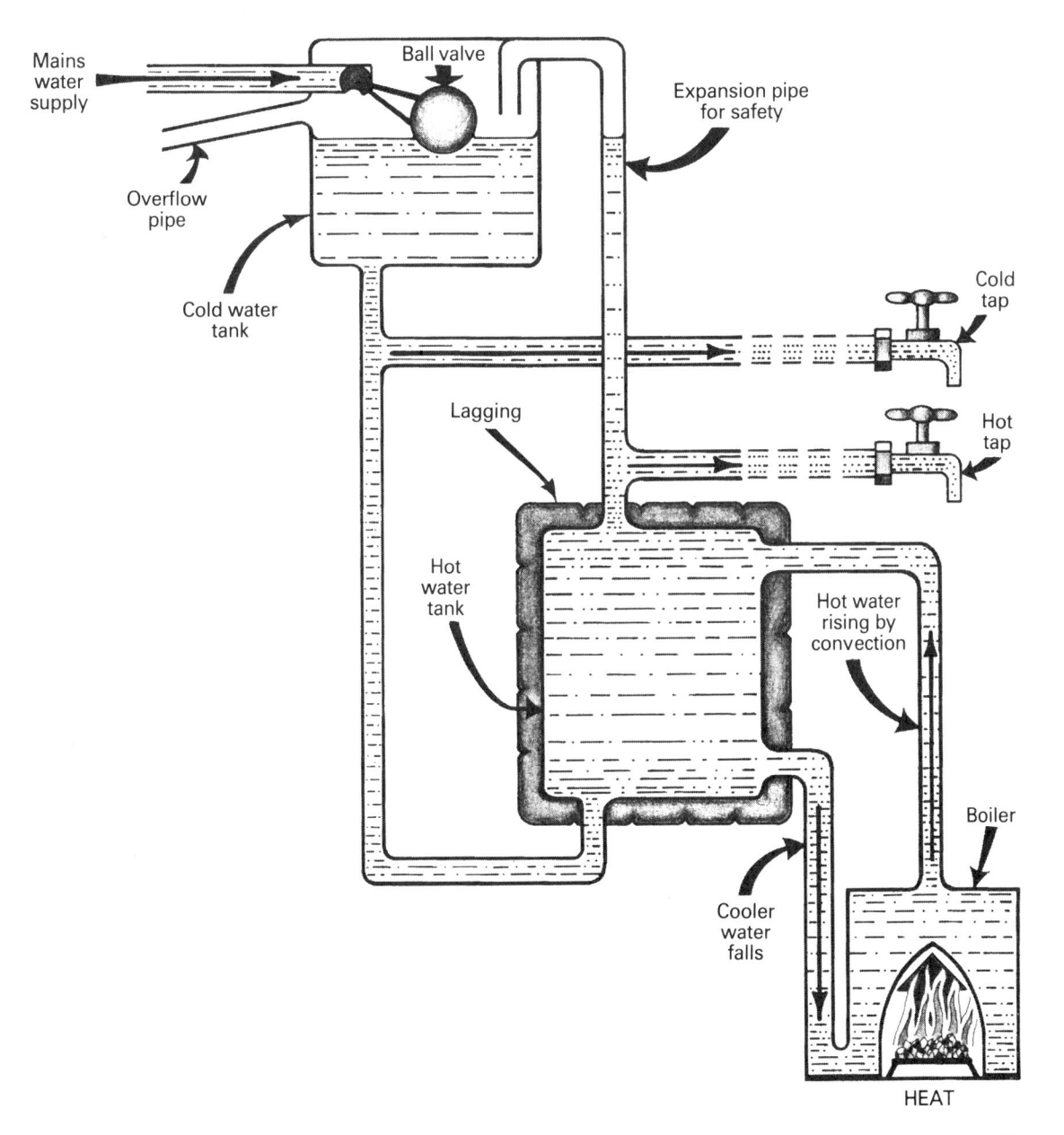

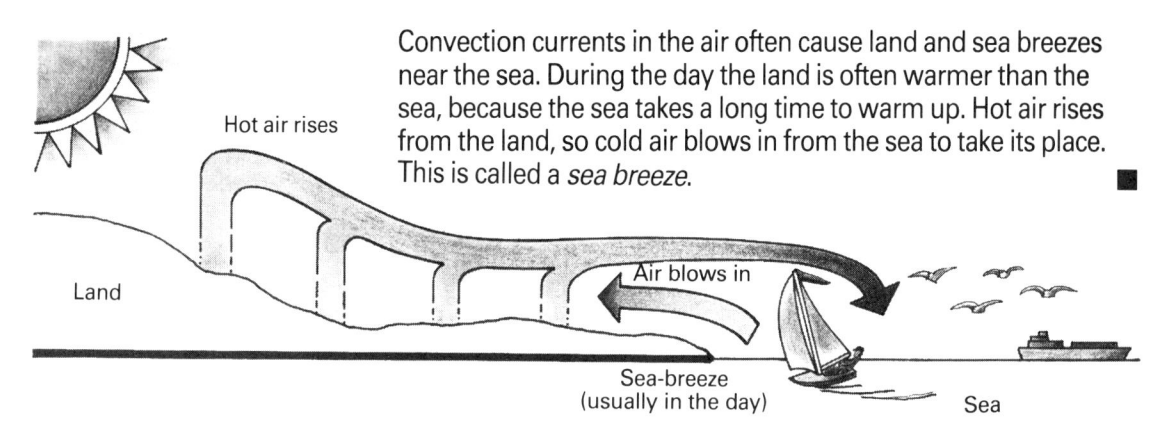

Convection currents in the air often cause land and sea breezes near the sea. During the day the land is often warmer than the sea, because the sea takes a long time to warm up. Hot air rises from the land, so cold air blows in from the sea to take its place. This is called a *sea breeze*.

At night, the sea is often warmer than the land and then warm air rises above the sea. The air above the land blows across to take its place, causing a *land breeze*.

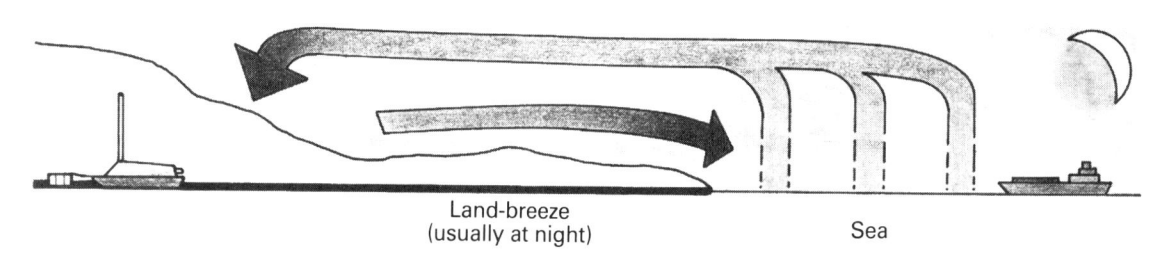

Warm air currents are also used to support a glider by carrying it upwards — these convection currents are called *thermals*.

Radiation

Heat travels well through metals by *conduction*. It travels through liquids and gases by *convection*. But heat can travel through empty space by *radiation*.

Heat travels most quickly by rays or radiation. These are heat rays or *infra-red rays,* which travel at a speed of 300 million metres per second, the same speed as light. The heat from the Sun reaches us by infra-red rays, which only take about 8 minutes to reach the Earth.

Heat rays can be detected by using a thermopile. This is made by joining two metals, like copper or iron, together in two places, or junctions. If heat rays fall on one of the junctions they warm it up and make a tiny electric current. This small current can be measured by a galvanometer.

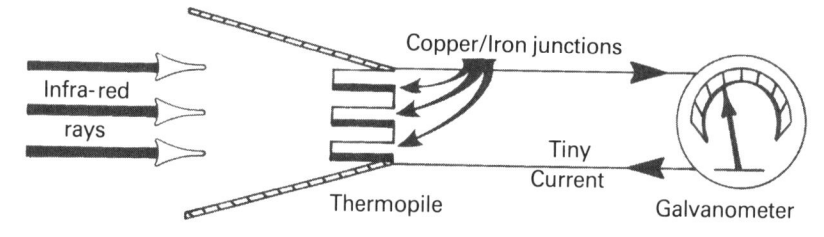

A thermopile can be used to find out which surfaces radiate heat best. Different surfaces like white, polished silver, and dull black are placed in front of the thermopile and heated by hot water. ■

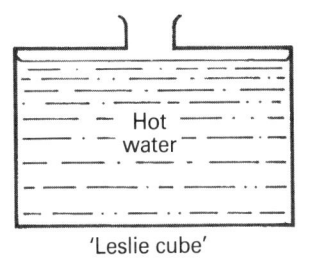

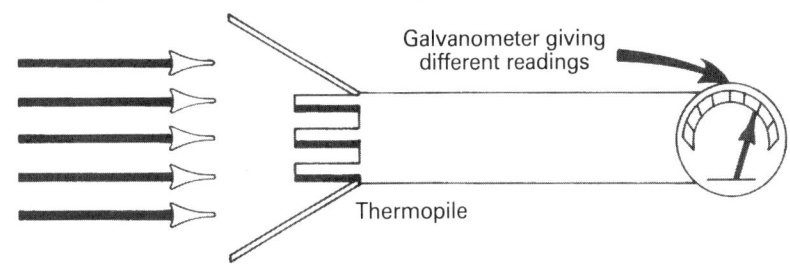

A special cube can be used with the different surfaces painted on each side of it. It is called a *Leslie cube*. We find that dull black surfaces are the best *radiators* of heat, while polished silver surfaces are the worst radiators.

However, silvered surfaces and white surfaces *reflect* heat much better than dull, black ones. This is why people wear white clothes in hot weather, and houses in hot countries, like Greece, are often painted white to keep them cool.

The vacuum flask

(a) Shiny silvered surfaces are used inside a vacuum flask to stop heat rays from escaping. The flask uses a glass bottle with two walls. Both these walls have a shiny silver coating. Silvered surfaces are poor radiators so they do not send out heat rays very quickly from one of the walls. The other wall is also shiny. This reflects back heat rays that try to escape.

(b) The space between the two walls has the air sucked out of it to leave a vacuum. The vacuum is very nearly empty space, containing very few molecules. So it conducts very little heat and only sets up very tiny convection currents.

(c) A stopper in the top of the flask prevents convection currents between the air inside and outside the flask. So very little heat is lost by convection. ■

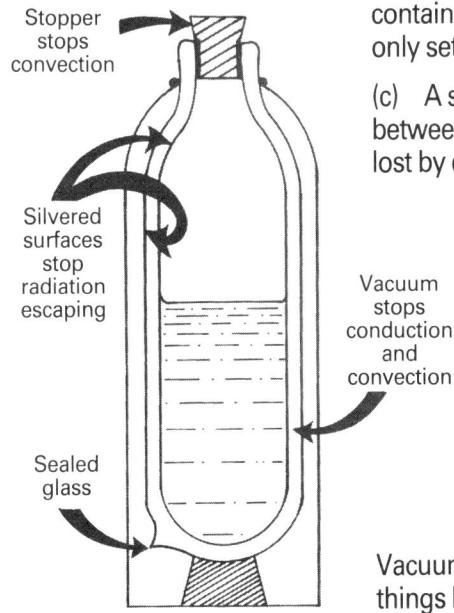

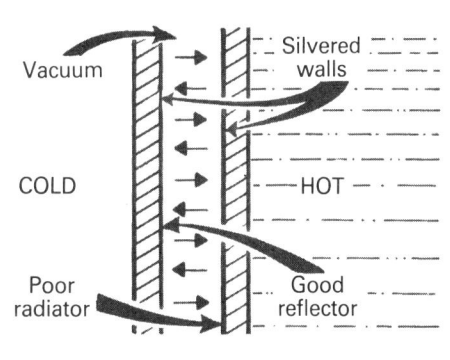

Vacuum flasks can either be used to keep cold things cold or hot things hot because the heat travels very slowly in either direction.

Questions 12

1. Write down four good conductors and four bad conductors of heat.
2. Try to explain why metals are good heat conductors.
3. Describe three ways of insulating a house which involve using *air* as an insulator.
4. Complete the following sentences by choosing one of the words in the list below. Each word may be used more than once. The first one is done for you as an example.

   insulation, conduction, radiation, convection, condensation

   e.g. Fibre glass is placed in roof spaces for the purpose of *insulation*.

   (a) Saucepans may have a copper base because heat travels well through copper by means of ___.
   (b) Houses may have cavity walls because heat does not travel well through air by means of ___.
   (c) Cavity walls may be filled with plastic foam to stop heat travelling through air by means of ___.
   (d) Petrol storage tanks may be painted white because white surfaces do not easily absorb heat by ___.
   (e) Heat travels across a vacuum by means of ___.
   (SWEB)

5. Explain why:
   (a) Houses in hot countries are often painted white.
   (b) Birds 'fluff up' their feathers in winter.
   (c) A string vest can keep a person warm.
   (d) The boiler of a hot water system is always at the bottom.
   (e) People wear white clothes in summer.

6. The diagram shows the inside of a vacuum flask with the outer case removed. Give details asked for about parts A, B and C.

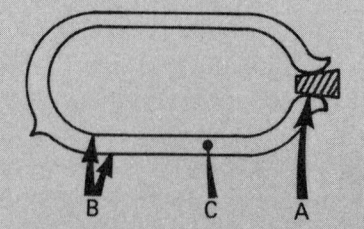

   (a) Name part A. What might it be made from? How does it help to prevent heat loss from the liquid in the flask?
   (b) What is the coating on the parts labelled B? How does this help to prevent heat loss?
   (c) What is at C? How does this help to prevent heat loss?
   (LREB)

7. This diagram shows a typical domestic hot-water system. Five interconnecting pipes are labelled A to E.

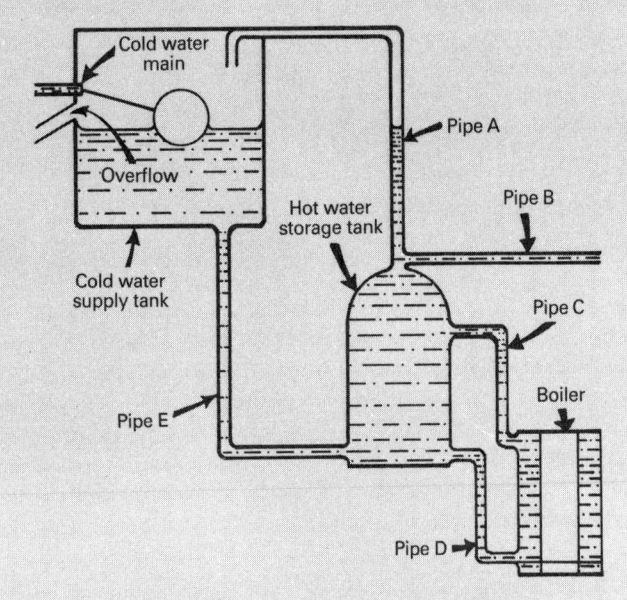

(a) Through which pipe does hot water leave the boiler?
(b) To what is the right-hand end of B connected?
(c) Why is the left-hand end of pipe B attached near the top of the hot water storage tank?
(d) What is the name of pipe A?
(e) What is the purpose of pipe A? (EMREB)

8. A lighted electric lamp is placed midway between two glass bulbs, A and B, both containing air. One bulb, A, is silvered and the other, B, is blackened. There is coloured water in the U-tube which connects the two glass bulbs. At first P and Q are on the same level. After the lamp has been left switched on for a short time the coloured water levels change.

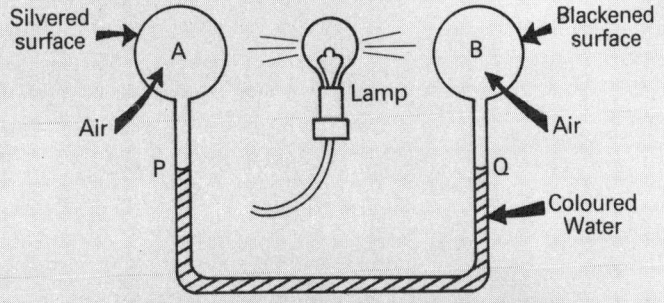

(a) What happens to the air pressure in bulb A?
(b) What happens to the air pressure in bulb B?
(c) Is the pressure in A greater than, equal to or less than that in B?
(d) Give a reason for your answer to (c).
(e) Which level, P or Q, rises? (EMREB)

Chapter 13
Melting, boiling and evaporation

Change of state

When a piece of ice, at 0 °C, is heated it melts and becomes liquid. If the water formed is heated up to about 100 °C, it boils and eventually changes to a gas, called *steam*.

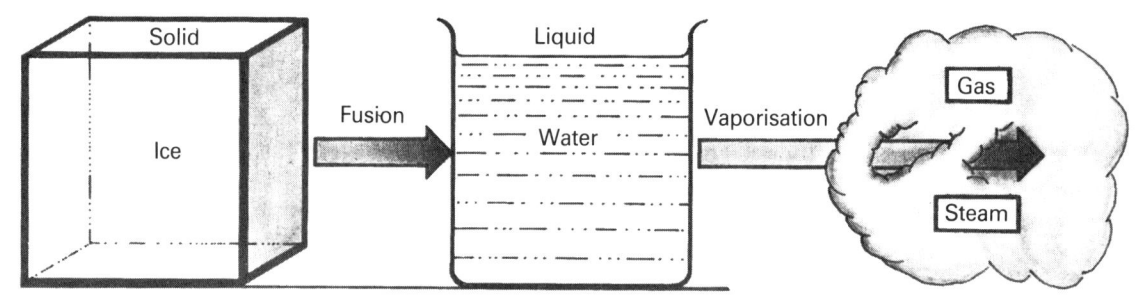

When a solid melts to form a liquid or a liquid boils to become a gas we say the substance changes its *state*. Heat is needed to melt or boil a substance and this heat is called *latent heat*. This latent heat is needed to make the molecules of a solid vibrate faster and faster until it melts and the molecules are in a more free liquid state. The heat needed is called *latent heat of fusion* ('fusion' means 'melting'). When a liquid boils heat energy is needed to help the molecules break away from the liquid and form a gas or vapour. This is called *latent heat of vaporisation*.

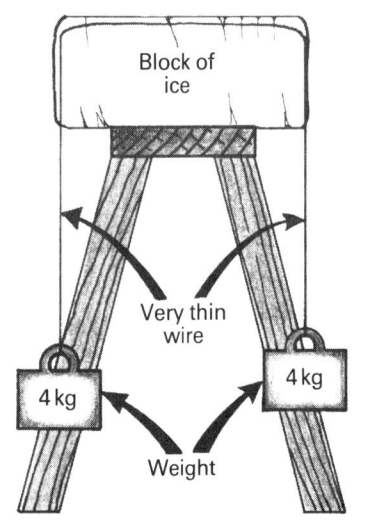

Melting and boiling

The temperature when ice melts, or when water freezes, is called its melting or freezing point. This is usually 0 °C for pure water. But if salt is added to water the freezing point is lower, sometimes −10°C. This is why the sea around England hardly ever freezes. The roads in winter are often covered in salt so that water on the roads will not freeze so easily.

Melting can also be affected by pressure. A very thin piece of wire can be used to 'cut through' a block of ice.

The thin wire creates a large pressure on the ice. This pressure helps to melt it. As the wire cuts through the ice below it, the water above freezes again.

The *boiling point* of water can also change. Salted water has a higher boiling point than pure water. It may boil at 101 °C or even 102 °C, instead of at 100 °C.

The boiling point of water also depends on the pressure of the air above it. In a pressure cooker water can be made to boil at 120 °C because of the high pressure above it. ■

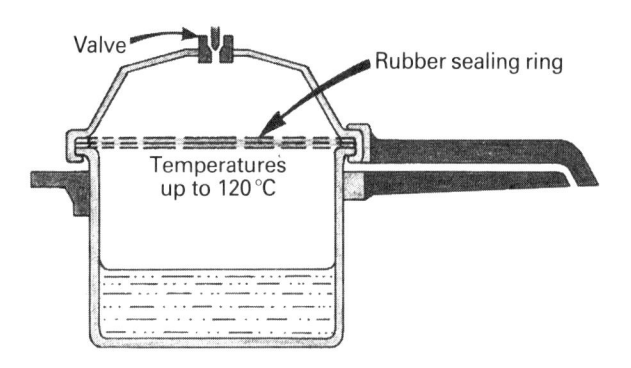

If the pressure above water becomes less than normal, it boils at below 100 °C. At the top of a high mountain water can be boiled at 90 °C, or even less, because atmospheric pressure there is much less than normal. At the top of Mount Everest, nearly 9000 metres above the sea, water would boil at about 71 °C.

Specific latent heat

Latent heat is the name given to the heat energy needed to melt a solid or to boil a liquid at its boiling point. *Specific latent heat* is the heat needed to melt or boil one kilogram (or sometimes one gram) of a substance. The specific *latent heat of fusion* of ice is the heat needed to change one kilogram of ice into water at 0 °C. 340 000 J of heat are needed to melt 1 kg of ice (or 340 J for 1 g). The specific heat of *vaporisation* of water is the heat energy needed to change 1 kg (or 1g) of water into steam at 100 °C. In fact it is about six times bigger than the latent heat of fusion: 2 000 000 joules per kilogram or 2000 joules per gram. ■

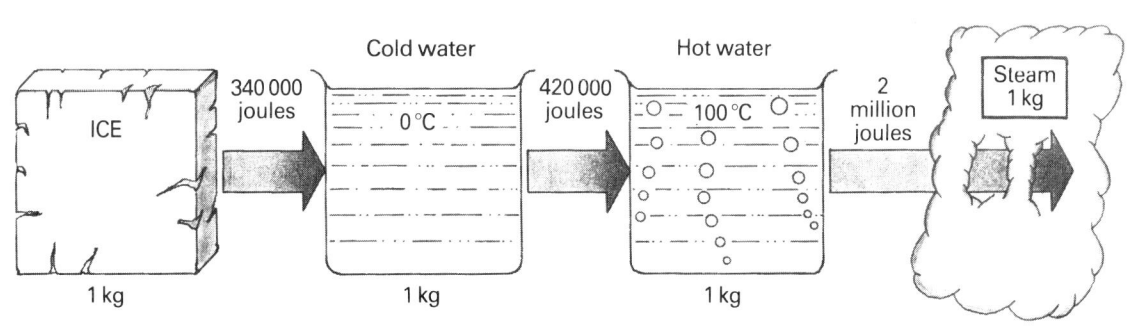

Suppose one kilogram of pure ice is heated at a steady rate until it all melts. Then the water from it is heated at the same rate until boiling point (100 °C). Finally the water is boiled away to make steam. A graph can be drawn showing the three different stages. The graph is flat where the ice is melting and where the water is boiling. The temperature stays the same. All the heat supplied is used as *latent heat,* for melting and then later for boiling.

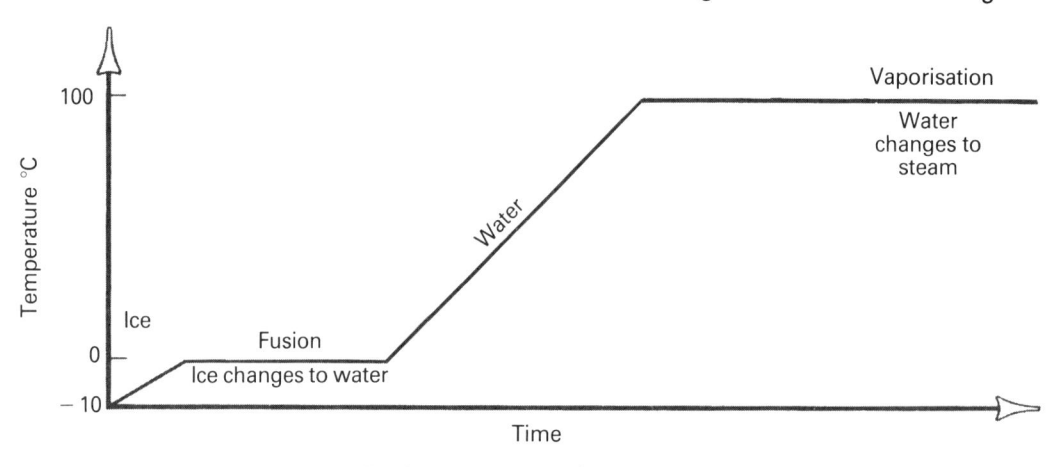

It takes 340 000 J of heat to melt 1 kg of ice. If 2 kg are melted, then 680 000 J are needed — 3 kg need 1 020 000 J. The larger the mass of ice, the more the latent heat needed to melt it.

Evaporation and condensation

When any liquid is left standing for some time it gradually disappears or *evaporates* into the air. The molecules in the liquid are slowly escaping into the atmosphere. The ones with the highest energy (moving fastest) escape first and this means that the rest of the liquid loses energy and cools down. This is called *cooling by evaporation.*

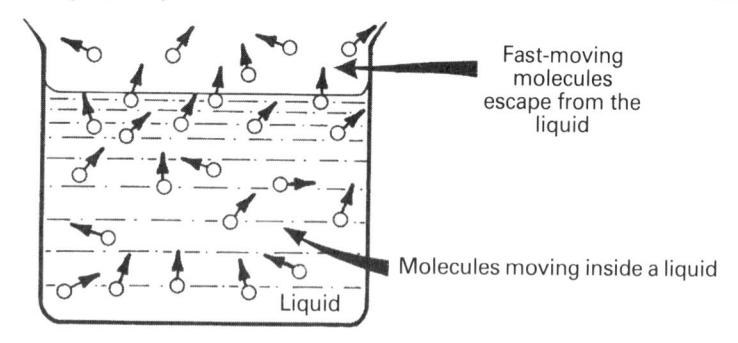

When a person sweats, or perspires, the sweat on his body evaporates and absorbs heat energy from him. This heat is used as latent heat, to change the liquid sweat into vapour. This heat comes from his body and so the person cools down.

Some liquids, such as petrol and *ether,* evaporate very easily. When air is blown through liquid ether it quickly becomes a vapour. If the ether is in a container standing on some water, the water soon turns to ice. As the ether evaporates it takes heat from the water.

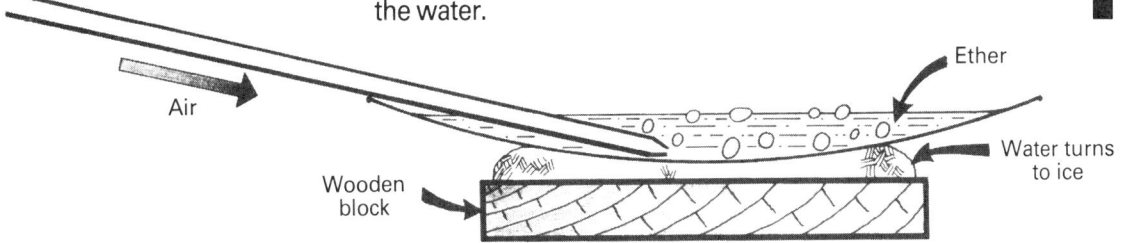

The latent heat needed to evaporate the ether is taken from the water, so the water freezes.

This shows that evaporation produces cooling, a fact which is used in *refrigerators.* A liquid called *freon* is used in a fridge. Like ether it evaporates easily.

Inside the fridge the freon *evaporates* and takes heat away from the fridge and its contents. This cools the inside of the fridge down.

A pump carries the freon vapour out of the fridge. Outside the fridge the freon is compressed by the pump and changes back to a liquid again. It condenses. As it condenses it gives out the heat that it took away from the inside of the fridge. This is why the pipes at the back of a fridge are warm.

The same liquid is pumped back inside the fridge, evaporates again, cools the inside, and so on.

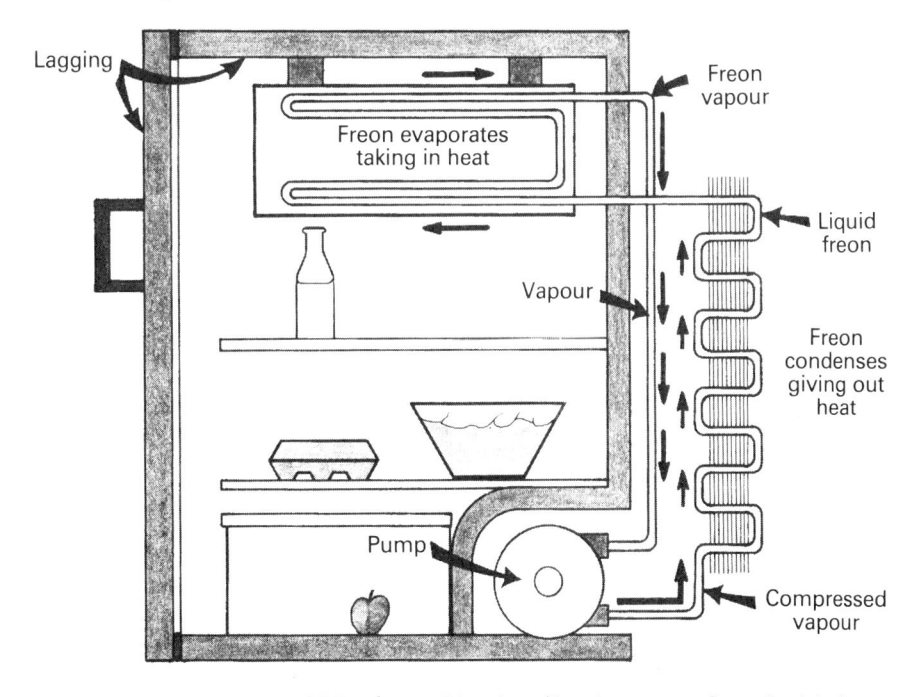

All the time a fridge is working heat is taken away from inside it and given to the air outside it.

Water vapour in the air

The air around us always contains some water vapour. Warm air can hold more water vapour than cold air. When warm air is suddenly cooled down some of this water vapour changes back to a liquid. The vapour *condenses.* On cold nights the air sometimes cools enough to make a *dew*— the water vapour inside the air condenses on the ground or the roofs of cars. Condensation of water vapour in the air can also be seen on the cold tap in a steamy bathroom, or the insides of windows on a cold day.

Washing will dry quickly on a warm, windy dry day when most of its surface is exposed to the air. Liquids can be made to evaporate quickly by:

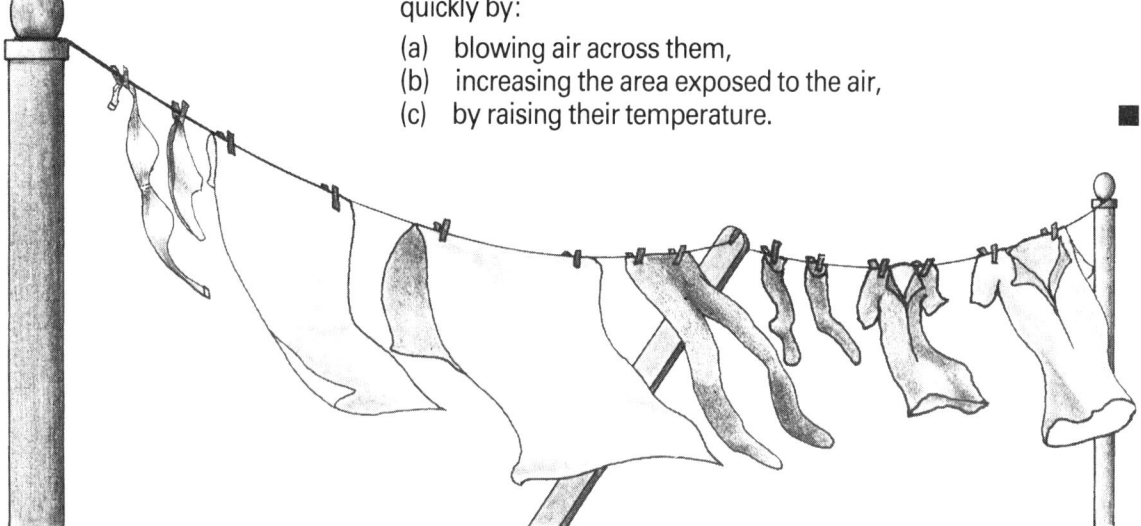

(a) blowing air across them,
(b) increasing the area exposed to the air,
(c) by raising their temperature.

If the air above them is warm and dry this helps to speed up evaporation.

When the air is damp, or humid, and already contains a lot of water vapour washing dries slowly. Also the sweat on your body evaporates more slowly if the air is humid. The dampness or humidity of the air can be measured by a special instrument consisting of two thermometers, one wet and one dry. When the air is very dry the water around the wet bulb evaporates quickly and the reading drops. On a very damp humid day, or in a steamy bathroom, both thermometers show the same reading because the water cannot evaporate. The instrument is called a *wet-and-dry bulb hygrometer.*

Questions 13

1. What is meant by *latent heat?* What do the words *fusion* and *vaporisation* mean?
2. If salt is added to water what happens to its boiling point? What happens to its freezing point?
3. When does water boil in a pressure cooker? Why is it useful for cooking? When would water boil at the top of Mount Everest?
4. If 340 joules of heat are needed to melt 1 g of ice how much heat is needed to melt:
   (a) 10 g   (b) 15 g   (c) 20 g   (d) 50 g
   of ice?
5. 2000 J is needed to change 1 g of water into steam at 100 °C. How much heat is needed for:
   (a) 10 g   (b) 15 g   (c) 20 g   (d) 50 g
   of water.
6. This diagram shows air being blown through ether:
   (a) What happens to the film of water under the beaker? Why?
   (b) Why is ether used for this experiment?
   (c) What other liquid could be used?
   (d) Could the wooden block be replaced by a copper block? Give a reason.

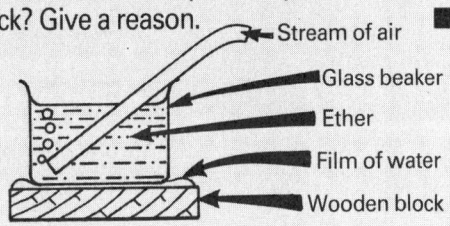

   Stream of air
   Glass beaker
   Ether
   Film of water
   Wooden block

7. What is this instrument called?

   Dry bulb
   Wet bulb
   Water

   Why is one reading usually less than the other?
   What could you notice about the two readings on a warm, dry day; or in a very steamy bathroom?
8. Explain why:
   (a) the cold tap in a bathroom is often covered in condensation, but not the hot tap,
   (b) a dew is formed on a cold night,
   (c) a person feels cool when he sweats,
   (d) washing dries quickly on a warm, dry, windy day.

Chapter 14

Using heat energy

Heat engines

Any engine which changes heat energy from a burning fuel into kinetic energy, or movement, is called a *heat engine*. The best examples are: the *steam engine*, the *petrol engine*, the *diesel engine*, the *jet engine* and the *rocket engine*.

The first heat engine was the steam engine which was used mainly for pulling trains. Its heat energy is made by burning coal or wood. This heat is used to change water into steam at high pressure. The steam pressure is then used to drive a piston backwards and forwards. In car and diesel engines the fuel is burnt inside a cylinder where the piston moves up and down. These are called *internal combustion engines*.

Petrol engines

In a petrol engine energy is obtained by exploding a mixture of air and petrol with a spark. This explosion is used to drive a piston. As the piston moves up and down inside a cylinder the engine goes through a four-stroke cycle.

(a) the *intake stroke*. The piston moves down and a mixture of petrol and air is drawn into the cylinder through the inlet valve.
(b) the *compression stroke*. The piston moves up and compresses the petrol–air mixture into a small space. Both valves are tightly shut.
(c) the *power stroke*. Just as the piston reaches the top of its compression stroke the spark plug makes a tiny electric spark. This explodes the petrol, forcing the piston down.
(d) the *exhaust stroke*. The piston moves up again, the exhaust valve opens and the burnt gases are pushed out.

Another type of petrol engine is called the *two-stroke engine*. These are used in mopeds, lawnmowers and small boats. Instead of valves the cylinder has holes, or *ports,* on the side which are opened and shut by the piston as it moves past them. There are three ports: the *exhaust port,* the *inlet port* and the *transfer port.*

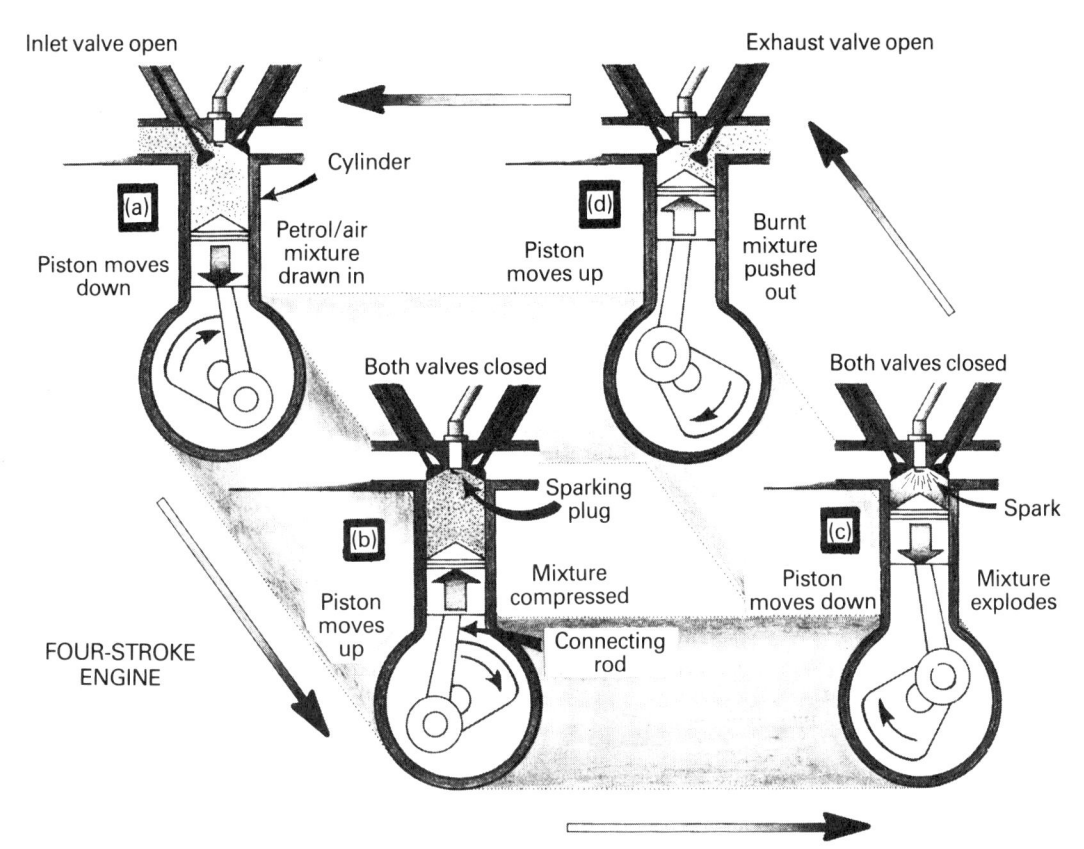

FOUR-STROKE ENGINE

(a) Inlet valve open. Piston moves down. Cylinder. Petrol/air mixture drawn in.

(b) Both valves closed. Piston moves up. Sparking plug. Mixture compressed. Connecting rod.

(c) Both valves closed. Piston moves down. Spark. Mixture explodes.

(d) Exhaust valve open. Piston moves up. Burnt mixture pushed out.

As the piston moves up and compresses the mixture, the inlet port is left open. This lets fresh petrol and air into the cylinder. In other words, the *compression and intake* strokes happen at the same time. Then the mixture explodes and forces the piston down. The exhaust port is left open and out go the burnt gases. In other words, the *power and exhaust strokes* happen at the same time.

As the piston moves down the transfer port is left open. This lets fresh mixture into the top of the cylinder. (The piston is specially shaped to stop fresh and burnt gases mixing.) The piston moves up again, compresses this fresh mixture, the mixture explodes, and so on.

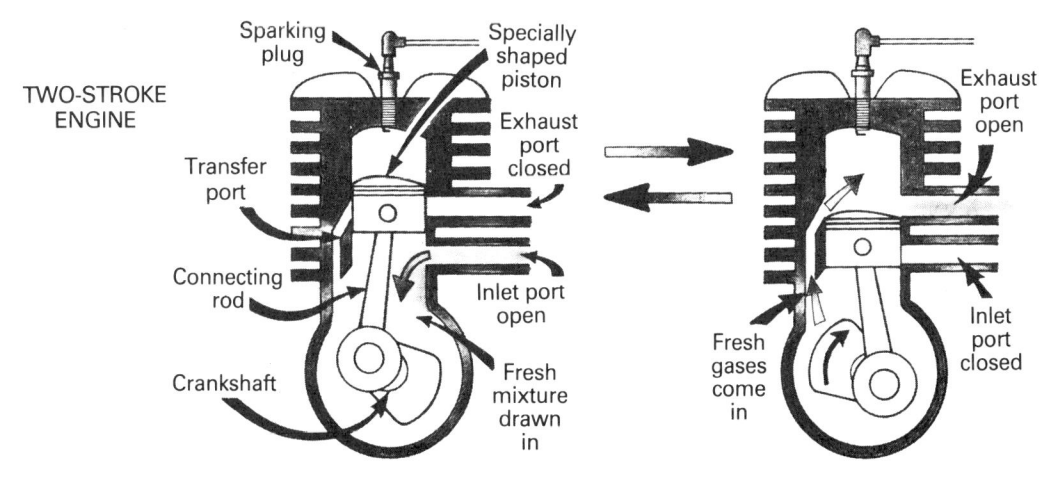

TWO-STROKE ENGINE

Sparking plug. Specially shaped piston. Exhaust port closed. Transfer port. Connecting rod. Inlet port open. Crankshaft. Fresh mixture drawn in.

Exhaust port open. Fresh gases come in. Inlet port closed.

The *diesel engine* is another internal combustion engine. It uses diesel fuel (instead of petrol) to produce heat energy. A diesel engine does not use a spark plug, because enough heat is made by compressing the fuel to make it explode. Diesel engines are used for heavy loads such as a train, a lorry, buses or taxis.

Jet and rocket engines

A more modern heat engine, invented in 1940, is the *jet engine*. Heat energy, made by burning jet fuel, is changed to kinetic energy as the hot gases from the engine are forced out of the back of the engine. This forces the engine forwards with a terrific thrust.

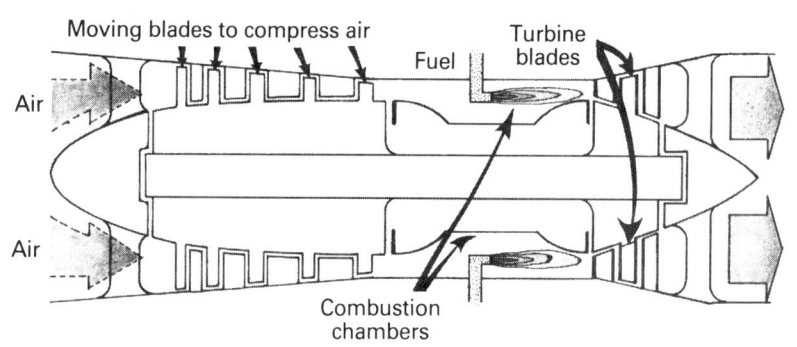

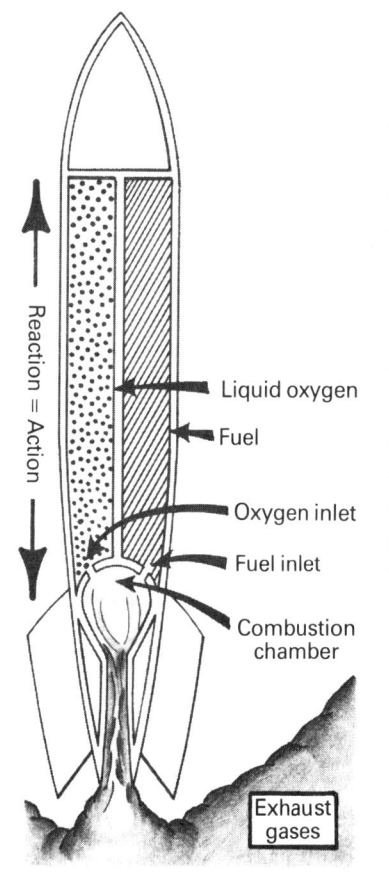

Rocket engines work in the same way as jet engines except that rockets carry their own supply of *liquid oxygen.* This means that they can fly in space where there is no air. The liquid oxygen mixes with the rocket fuel and burns in a special combustion chamber. Very hot, fast moving gases are forced out of the back of the rocket through a *nozzle.* As the gases move backwards the rocket is pushed forwards.

This is an example of *Newton's Third Law,* sometimes written as: 'Every action has an equal and opposite reaction.' The action, the hot gases rushing backwards, gives a reaction, the rocket being pushed forwards. When a person fires a bullet forwards from a gun, he is pushed backwards. If a balloon is blown up and then let go, it moves forwards, as the air inside it moves backwards. Jets and rockets are pushed forward in a similar way.

Questions 14

1. Describe what is meant by a *heat engine,* including the energy changes involved.
2. Draw a labelled diagram of the four-stroke cycle of a petrol engine. Explain what happens on each stroke.
3. This is a diagram of part of a four-stroke petrol engine. ■

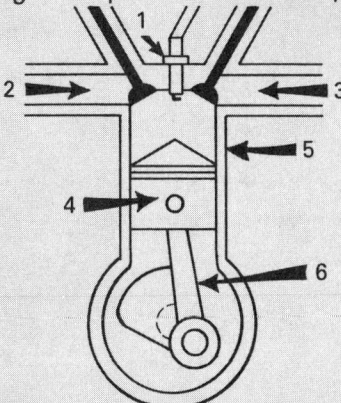

    (a) Label the parts numbered 1–6.
    (b) How is a diesel engine different from this?
4. What are four-stroke engines used in? Which vehicles use two-stroke engines? Which ones use diesel?
5. Label this diagram of a two-stroke engine, by showing:
    (a) the exhaust port, the inlet port and the transfer port,
    (b) the piston and the connecting rod.
    Describe how this is different from a four-stroke engine. ■

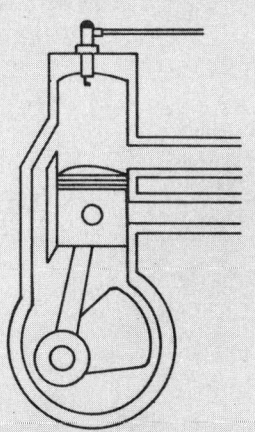

6. Fill in the missing words:
    'A rocket engine carries its own liquid ____ so that it can fly in ____. Jet and rocket engines both use the principle of action and ____. The action is the rush of hot ____ from the back of the jet, while the reaction is the forward ____ on the engine. Both engines are examples of ____ engines'.

CROSSWORD 3

Trace this grid on to a piece of paper before working out the answers.

Across
1 They measure temperature (12)
5 It expands when cooled from 4 °C to 0 °C (5)
7 It is easy for swimmers to —— in the 18 down 21 across (5)
8 Another name for a pivot (7)
12 A temperature of 313 K is the same as ——°C (5)
13 Latent heat is needed to turn —— into water (3)
14 Steam is a —— (3)
15 If a solid sinks in a liquid the liquid is the —— dense of the two (4)
19 The three ways in which heat may be transferred are conduction, ——, and radiation (10)
21 See 7 across (3)
22 The —— the gas pressure, the more liquid moves up a manometer (8)

Down
2 Fibre glass is not a good conductor of —— (4)
3 It is used in 1 across (7)
4 When water boils it changes its —— (5)
6 They travel forward as their gases move backwards (7)
7 The number of strokes in the engine of most cars (4)
9 Mechanical advantage = —— ÷ effort (4)
10 Parts of a car's engine (7)
11 A type of engine invented in 1940 (3)
15 A —— is a sort of 'force multiplier' (5)
16 A vacuum flask is used to make the heat —— as small as possible (4)
17 If a force of 36 N is applied over an area of 4 m^2 the pressure is equal to —— N/m^2 (4)
18 See 7 across (4)
20 The density of a material that sinks can be found using an Archimedes' —— (3)

An electric locomotive. These are much more fuel efficient than the old diesel locomotives. (see page 88)

The shuttle about to be launched. (see page 90)

A glider using convection currents or thermals. (see page 78)

Houses in London with solar panels used for domestic water heating: even in Britain these panels can help to conserve fuel.

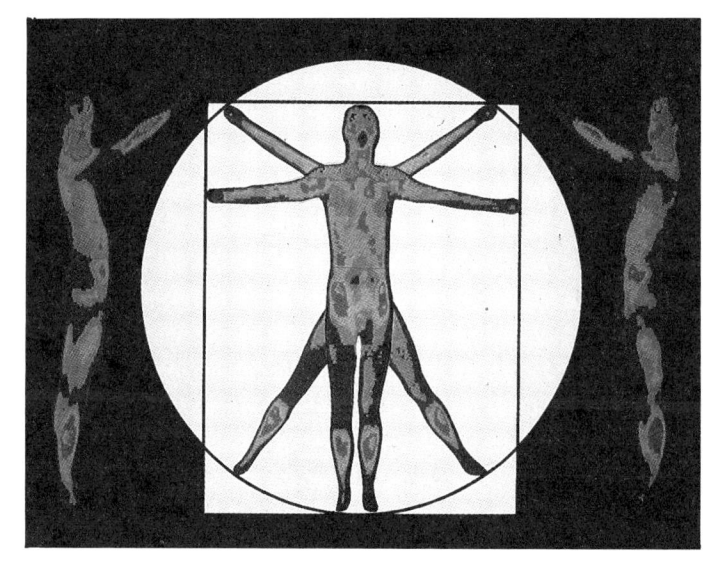

A body "Thermograph". The colours show different skin temperatures ranging from the darkest (coolest) to white (hottest).

A house "Thermograph". The lighter colours show areas of greatest heat loss. (see page 76)

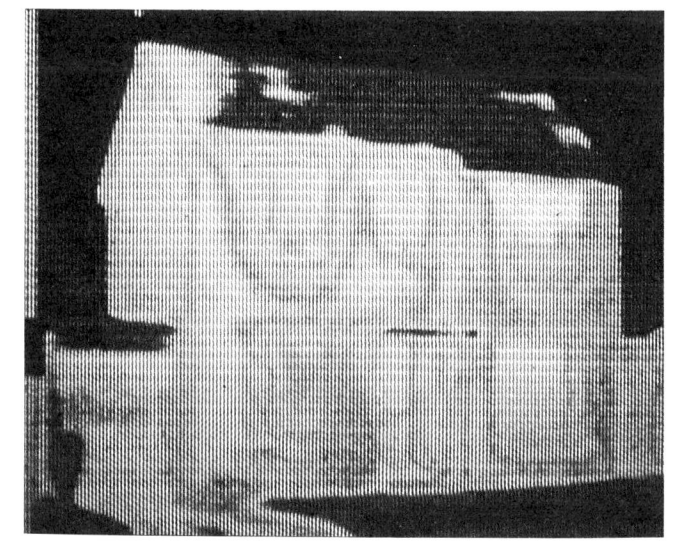

Two girls using a digital thermometer to measure water temperature. These thermometers are also used in industry to measure and regulate temperatures in furnaces.

Part 4

Light & Sound Energy: Waves

Chapter 15

How does light travel?

Rays and beams

Light is one type of radiation. It travels at a speed of 186 000 miles per second or 300 000 000 metres per second. This means that a ray of light takes about 8 minutes to reach us from the Sun. Light energy usually travels in straight lines that we call rays, but whenever we see light we see these rays collected together as a beam of light. So we talk of *sun-rays* and *sun-beams.* Beams of light can have three different shapes.

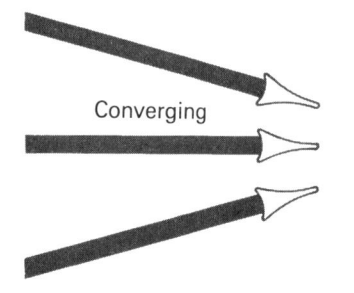

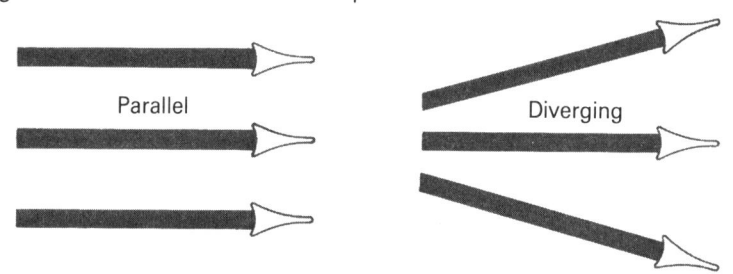

Converging Parallel Diverging

Searchlights and car headlamps usually make a parallel beam of light.

Some materials do not allow light to travel through them — they are *opaque.*

Shadows and eclipses

When light rays are stopped by something opaque, a shadow is made because light normally travels in straight lines and cannot bend around corners.

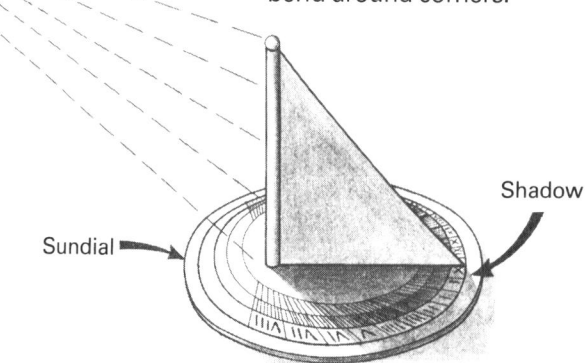

Sun

Sundial

Shadow

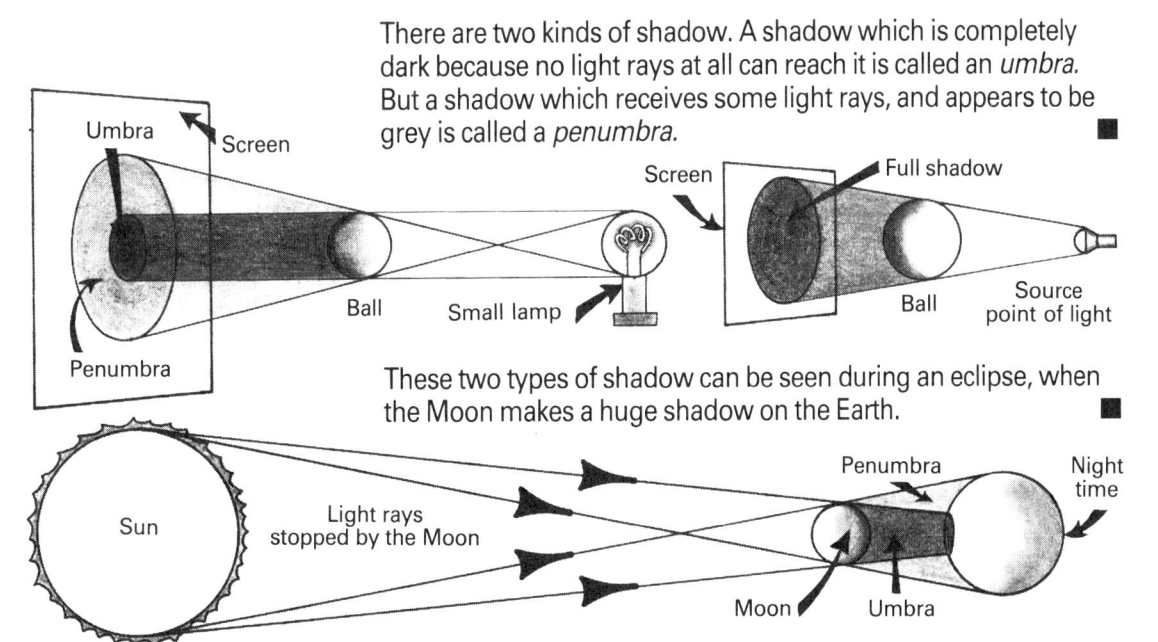

There are two kinds of shadow. A shadow which is completely dark because no light rays at all can reach it is called an *umbra*. But a shadow which receives some light rays, and appears to be grey is called a *penumbra*.

These two types of shadow can be seen during an eclipse, when the Moon makes a huge shadow on the Earth.

If a person sees the eclipse from the umbra part of the Moon's shadow, he sees a total eclipse because none of the Sun's light rays (or heat rays) can reach him. If he is standing in the penumbra, he can still see some of the Sun, and so he only sees a partial eclipse.

Total eclipse (in the umbra)

Partial eclipses (from different parts of the Earth)

Pinhole cameras

A very simple type of camera can be made from a closed box with a screen at one end and a tiny pinhole at the other. Light rays from an object travel in straight lines and cross over at the pinhole. This makes an upside down, or *inverted,* image at the back of the camera.

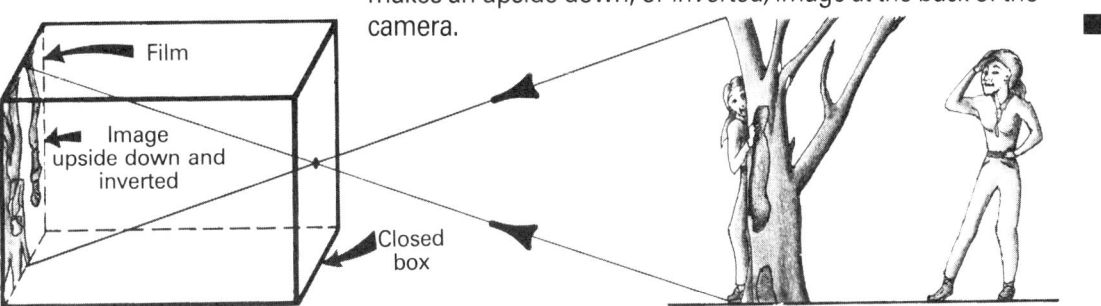

With a tiny pinhole the image is sharply focused but very faint. A larger pinhole makes the image brighter but not so clear — the image is blurred. Modern cameras have a larger hole at the front with a lens to focus the image on to the film at the back of the camera (see Chapter 18).

Questions 15

1. How far can a ray of light travel in one second?
2. On a sunny day, why does a man's shadow get longer later in the day? (Draw two diagrams.)
3. The two types of shadow are called ___ and ___. What is the difference between them?
4. This diagram shows an eclipse of the Sun. Describe with a drawing what you would see if you were standing on Earth.
   (a) in region A,
   (b) in region B,
   (c) in region C.
   (d) Draw a labelled diagram to show an eclipse of the Moon.
5. A lamp is used to illuminate an object (a ball) in order to cast a shadow on a screen as shown in this diagram.

   (a) What are the names of the two shadow areas shown in the diagram?
   (b) Draw in two rays from point A and two rays from point B which just touch the ball and pass on to the screen, showing how the two shadow areas are formed.
   (c) If the arrangement in the diagram were regarded as an eclipse of the Sun, which object would represent the Sun, the Earth, the Moon?
6. A pinhole camera is shown, being used to form an image of the filament of a lamp on the screen at the back of the camera.

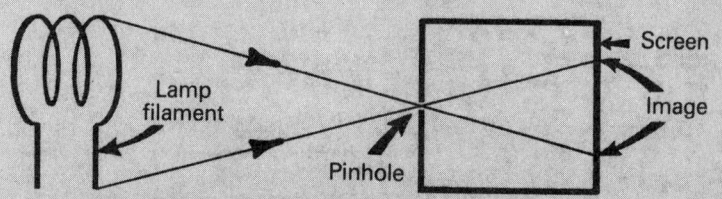

   (a) Describe the image formed on the screen.
   (b) State one way in which the image would change if you enlarged the hole of the camera.
   (c) In what way is the image improved by placing a suitable lens over the large hole?
   (d) What type of lens could this be?

Chapter 16
Reflecting light

Plane mirrors and the laws of reflection

When light rays or beams hit a shiny surface they bounce off it. This is called *reflection.* Smooth and shiny surfaces are the best reflectors, and so these are used to make mirrors. Ordinary flat mirrors are called *plane mirrors.*

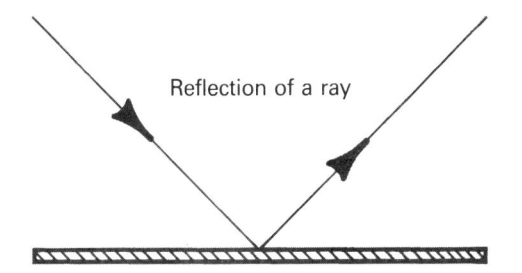

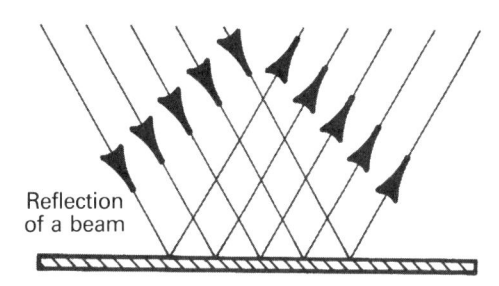

Reflection of a ray

Reflection of a beam

There are two laws of reflection.

The first law says that the incident ray, the reflected ray and a line drawn at right angles to the mirror, *the normal,* are all in the same surface or plane. They can all be drawn on the same flat sheet of paper.

The second law says that when a light ray is reflected from a mirror it always leaves the mirror at the same angle as it hit it.

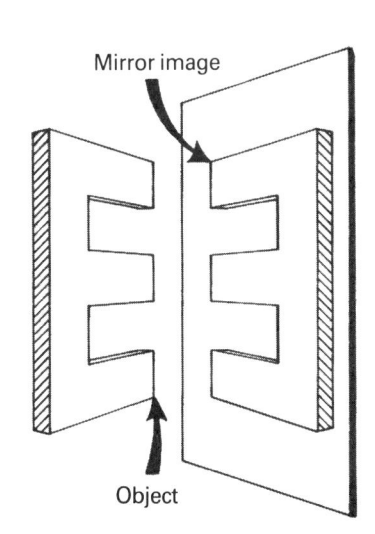

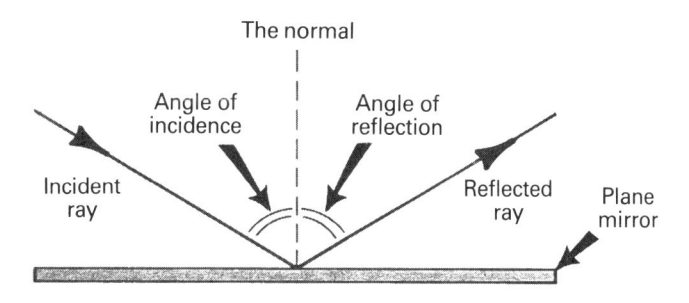

The two angles are called *the angle of incidence* and *the angle of reflection.* These angles are always the same.

Whenever you see something in a plane mirror it always looks the wrong way round, or right-to-left. A right-handed tennis player or cricketer looks left-handed in a mirror. His image is left-handed.

What you actually see in a mirror is called the *image*. The image in a plane mirror is always:

the same size as the object in front of it;

as far behind the mirror as the object is in front.

If you stand 50 cm in front of a plane mirror, your image will be 50 cm behind it.

Using plane mirrors

Plane mirrors are used in cars. A car driver can look into his driving mirror and see the mirror image of the traffic behind him.

The word AMBULANCE can be painted on an ambulance the wrong way round: ƎƆNAJUᙠMA . When a car driver sees the word in the mirror it looks the right way round.

Two plane mirrors can be used to make a *periscope*. The two mirrors are fixed at an angle of 45°. A periscope like this can be used to look over the top of an obstacle.

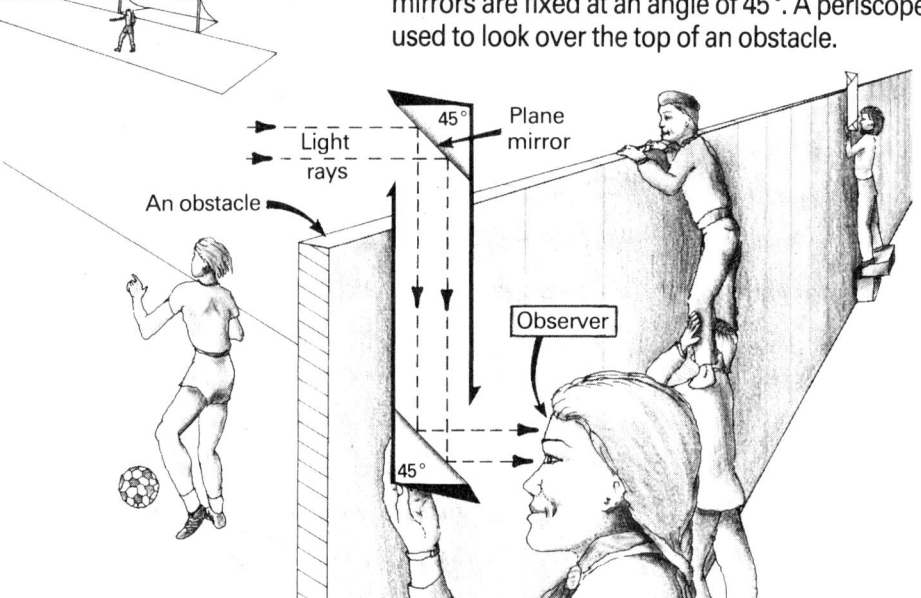

Curved mirrors

Some mirrors are curved instead of being flat or 'plane'. These can be used to give different images. There are two main types: *concave*, which curve inwards, and *convex*, which bulge outwards.

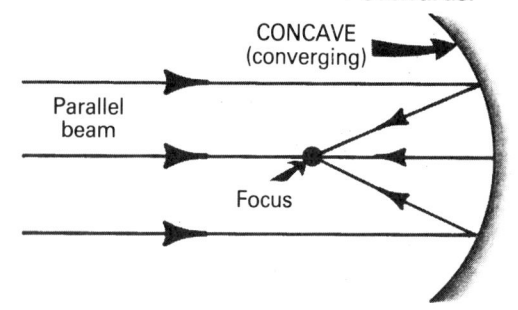

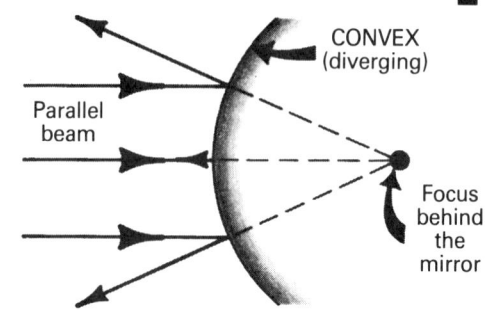

If a parallel beam of light shines onto a concave mirror the mirror focuses all the rays to one point. This is called the *focus* of the mirror. A concave mirror is a converging mirror because it makes a parallel beam into a *converging* beam.

But with a convex mirror a beam of light is reflected outwards, to make a *diverging* beam. The rays do not come to a focus — we say that the focus is behind the mirror.

Using curved mirrors

Both types of mirror are useful because of the different ways they reflect light. Convex mirrors are used in supermarkets and large shops to look out for shoplifters.

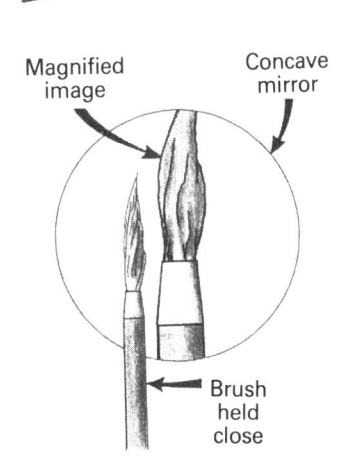

Rays coming in from a wide angle

Store detective

Convex mirror

Magnified image

Concave mirror

← Brush held close

A person looking into a convex mirror can see through a very wide angle, so he is able to keep his eye on a lot of people at the same time. The mirror makes people look smaller. Convex mirrors are often used on the side of a car as car wing mirrors. The driver can see through a much wider angle than he can with a plane mirror.

Convex mirrors make things look smaller. But *concave* mirrors are used as shaving mirrors because they can make an object look a lot bigger.

When an object is held close to a concave mirror the image seen is much larger than the object. It is *magnified*.

A special type of concave mirror is used in torches, car headlamps and searchlights to make a strong, parallel beam of light. These mirrors are shaped like the end of a rugby ball — they are called *parabolic mirrors*.

Strong parallel beam of light

Bulb

Parabolic mirror

Finding images

A special type of diagram can be drawn to find the image formed by an object in front of a mirror. It is called a *ray diagram*. An arrow is used to stand for the object. Then two rays of light are drawn, coming from the top of the object. These rays strike the mirror and are reflected off it. Here is an example of a concave mirror.

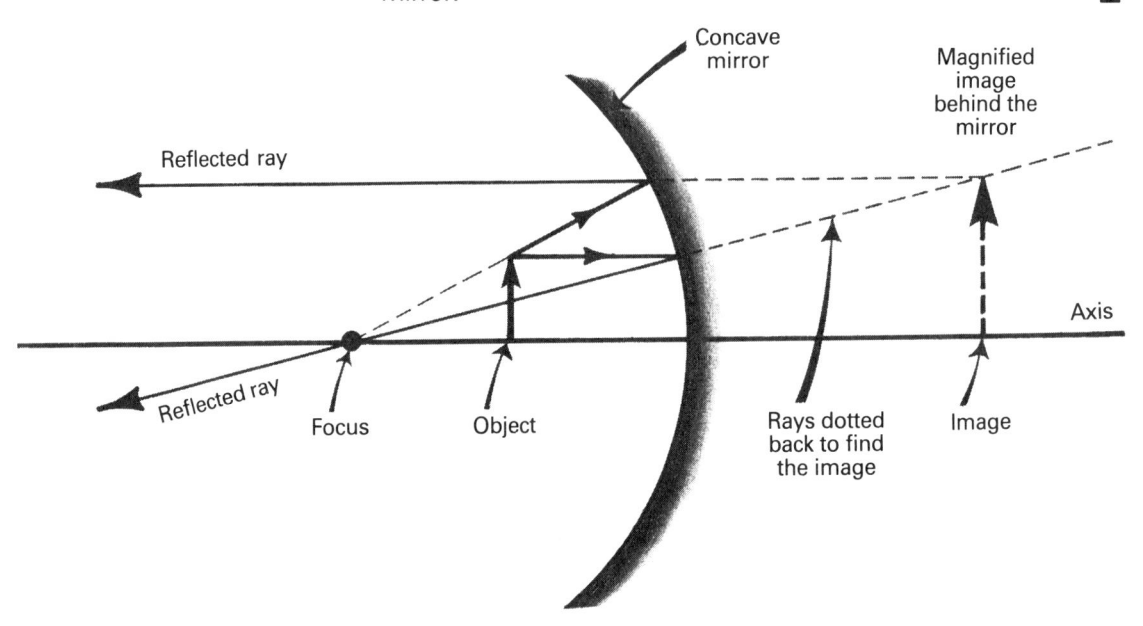

A line is drawn through the centre of the mirror called the *axis*. One ray of light from the object travels straight to the mirror, parallel to the axis. This ray is reflected off the mirror and comes back through the focus. A second ray of light coming from the focus through the top of the object is drawn. This ray is reflected by the mirror and goes back parallel to the axis. The two reflected rays are now 'dotted back' behind the mirror. The point where they meet is the exact position of the image.

Ray diagrams like these are useful for finding where an image is and how large it is. Ray diagrams will be used again in later chapters.

Questions 16

1. Sketch the diagram below and draw the image that would be formed in the mirror. Do the same for these letters: N, R and L.

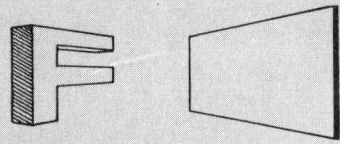

2. Draw a diagram which shows a ray of light meeting a plane mirror at an angle of incidence of 30°. Put in: the reflected ray, the normal and the angle of reflection.

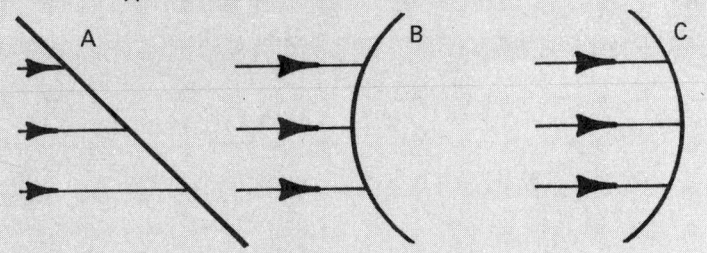

3. What types of mirror are A, B and C?

   Draw the paths of the rays of light after they have been reflected by each mirror.

4. Draw this table and complete it to show the uses of each mirror:

Mirror	Diagram	Use
Plane		
Diverging		
Converging		

5. This diagram shows a 'magnifying' mirror. Draw the diagram and show where the *image* is formed using two rays.

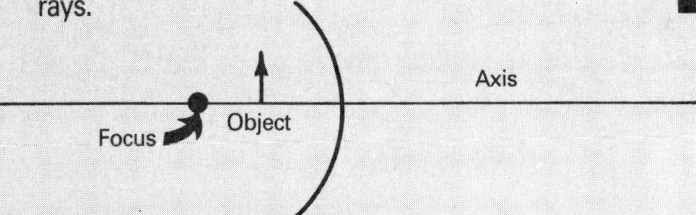

   What kind of image is seen in:
   (a) a plane mirror,
   (b) a convex mirror?

6. Draw a diagram to show how a periscope can be used to see over the top of a high wall.

7. A person stands four metres in front of a plane mirror. How far away from him will his mirror image be? If he moves one metre nearer the mirror, how far away will the image be now?

103

Chapter 17: Refraction of light

What is refraction?

When a ray or beam of light passes from one substance or material into another it bends, so changing its course. This bending of light rays as they pass from one material to another is called *refraction*.

A pencil, or a stick, placed in water appears to be bent because the light rays from it are *refracted* as they travel from water into air.

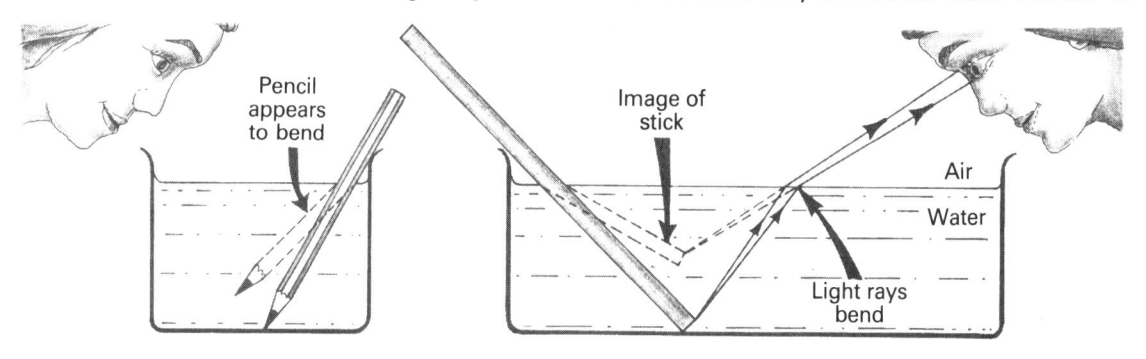

Light rays are also refracted by a *glass block* when they pass through it at an angle.

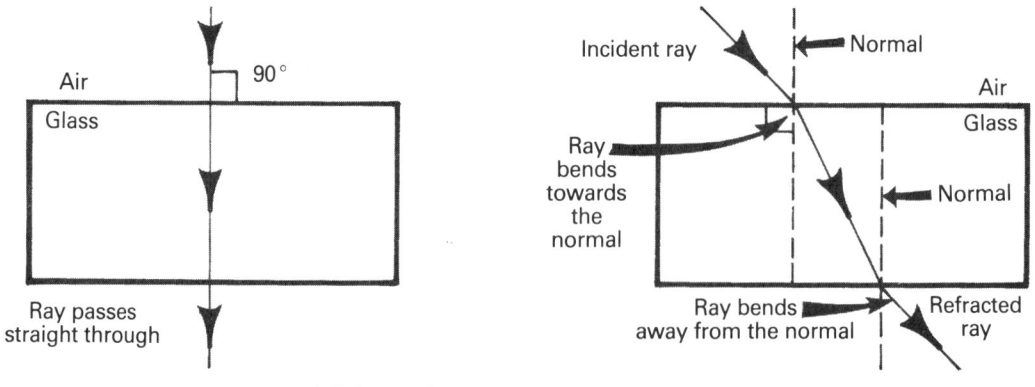

A light ray bends towards the normal as it goes into the glass. It bends away from the normal as it leaves the glass.

Refraction of light occurs because light rays are slowed down as they leave air and enter a different material. Light travels faster in air than it does in water and glass.

Real and apparent depth

The bottom of a swimming pool appears closer than it really is when you look at it from above. This is caused by the refraction of light rays coming from the bottom of the pool.

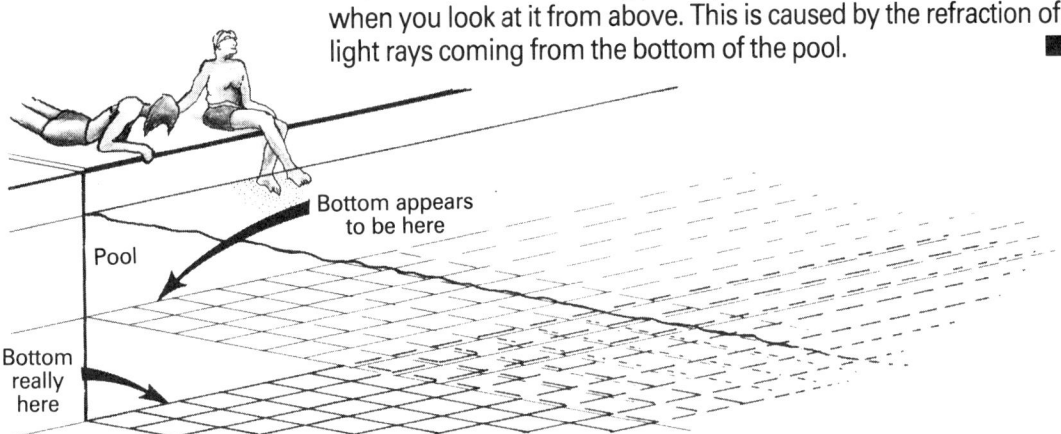

Bottom appears to be here

Pool

Bottom really here

An object in water looks closer than it really is. As the light rays leave the water they are refracted and appear to come from just above the object.

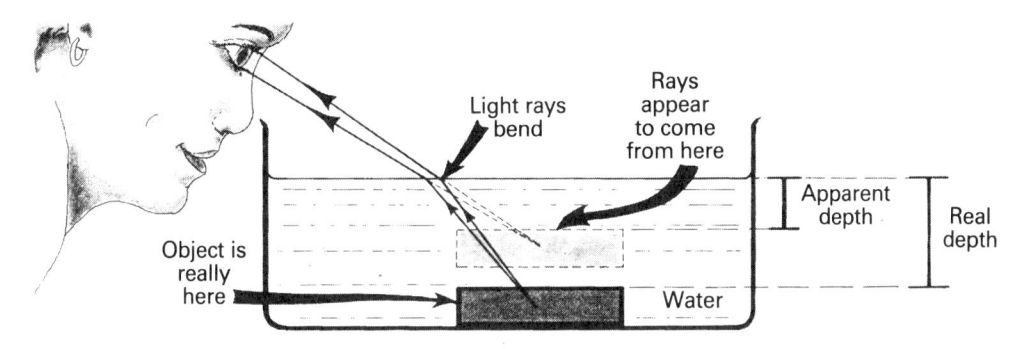

Light rays bend

Rays appear to come from here

Apparent depth

Real depth

Object is really here

Water

The actual depth of the *object* is called the *real depth*. The depth of the *image*, where the object appears to be, is called its *apparent depth*.

Total internal reflection

Sometimes a ray of light inside a glass block does not pass out through the edge of the block into the air. Instead, it is reflected back into the block.

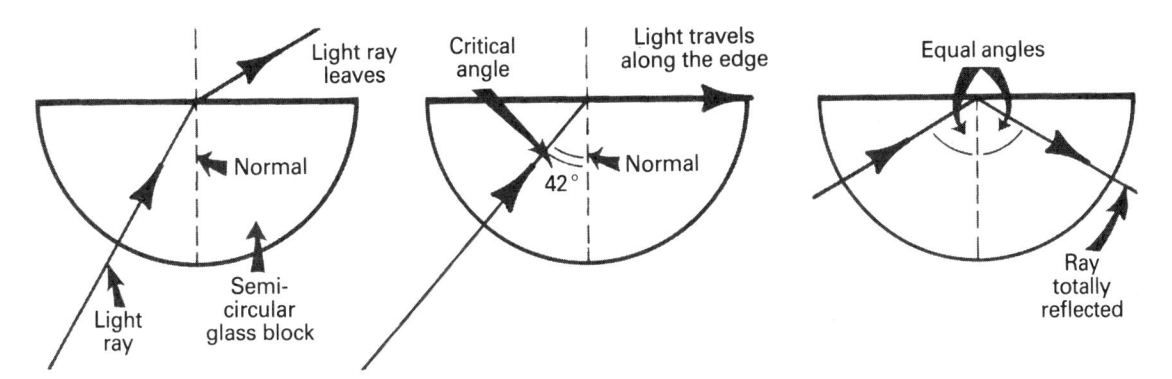

Light ray leaves

Normal

Semi-circular glass block

Light ray

Critical angle

Light travels along the edge

Normal

42°

Equal angles

Ray totally reflected

This is called *total internal reflection*. Total internal reflection only happens when the light ray meets the edge of the block above a certain angle. This angle is called the *critical angle*.

Total internal reflection also happens in water. Most light rays from an object under water travel out into the air. But if a ray meets the water surface above a certain angle it is reflected back into the water.

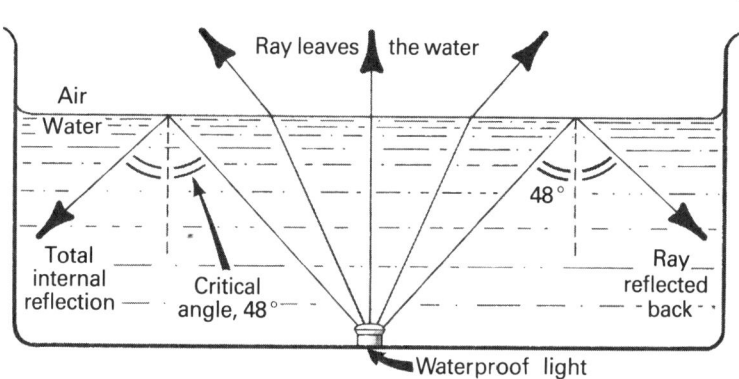

Total internal reflection is used in specially designed prisms, called *45° prisms*. They can be used like mirrors to reflect light off one of their faces.

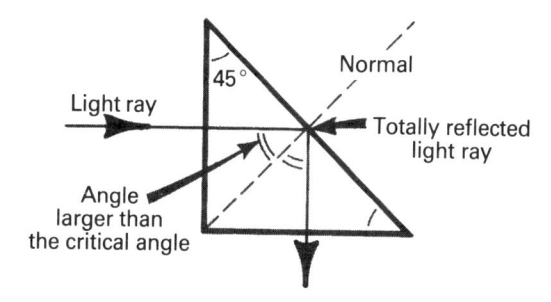

In fact these prisms are better reflectors than mirrors. They are used in good periscopes, and in special prism binoculars.

Refraction in lenses

Lenses are shaped so that they refract light in certain ways. A lens which curves outwards is called a *convex* lens. One which curves inwards is a *concave* lens.

When a parallel beam of light meets a convex lens it is refracted so that all the rays meet at one point. This is called the *focus*.

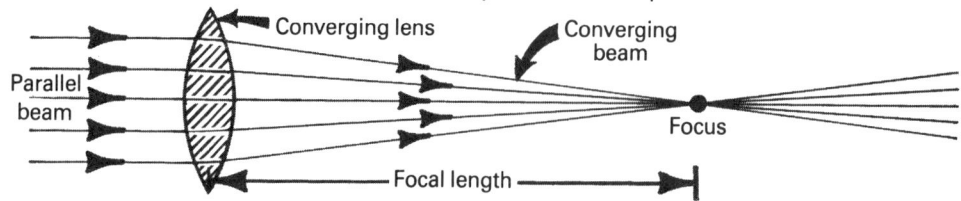

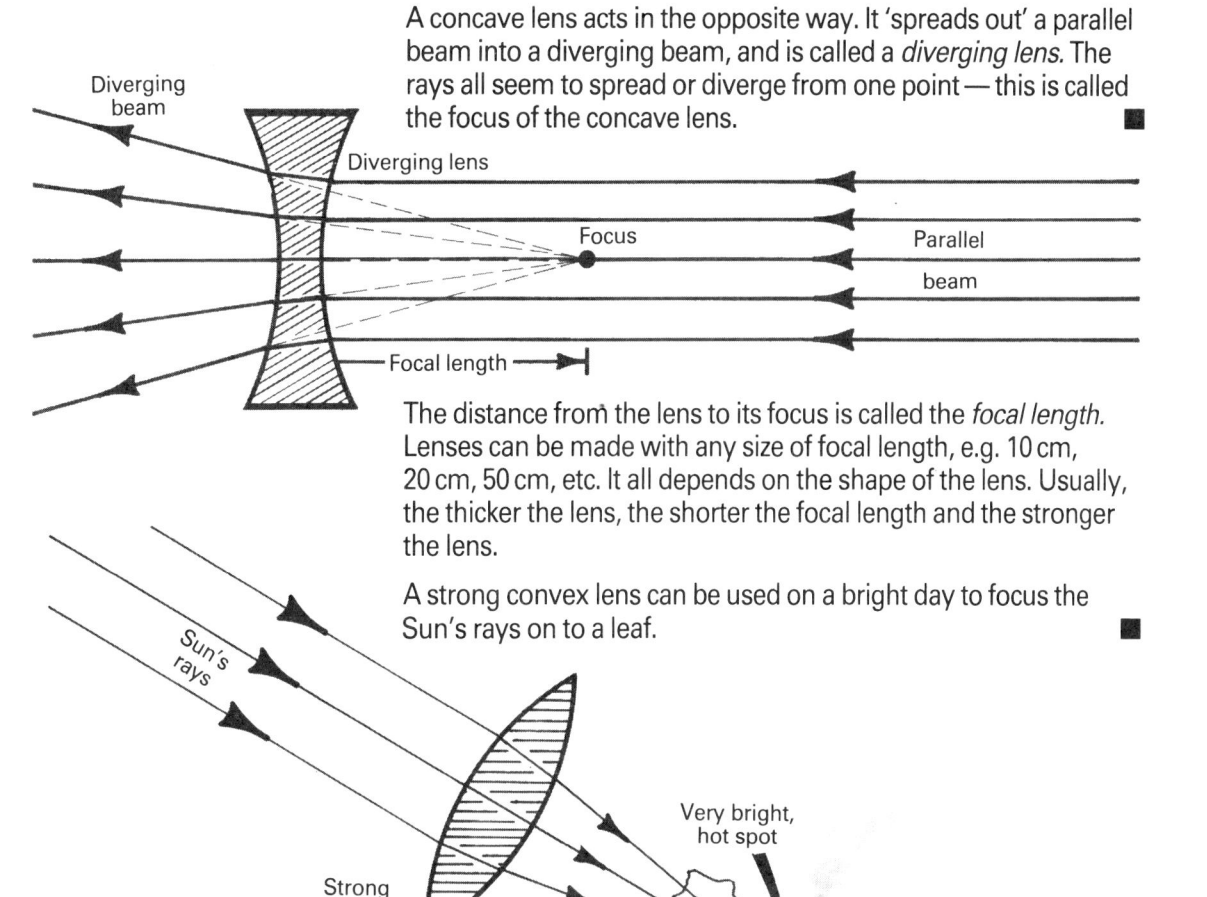

A convex lens changes a parallel beam into a converging beam, so it is called a *converging lens*.

A concave lens acts in the opposite way. It 'spreads out' a parallel beam into a diverging beam, and is called a *diverging lens*. The rays all seem to spread or diverge from one point — this is called the focus of the concave lens.

The distance from the lens to its focus is called the *focal length*. Lenses can be made with any size of focal length, e.g. 10 cm, 20 cm, 50 cm, etc. It all depends on the shape of the lens. Usually, the thicker the lens, the shorter the focal length and the stronger the lens.

A strong convex lens can be used on a bright day to focus the Sun's rays on to a leaf.

The distance from the lens to the paper is roughly equal to the focal length.

Using lenses

Lenses have very many uses, in things like: cameras, telescopes, microscopes, binoculars, spectacles and so on. Instruments that use lenses are called *optical instruments* (see Chapter 19).

The simplest use for a convex lens is the *magnifying glass*. If a small object is viewed through a strong convex lens it appears much larger.

A *ray diagram* can be used to work out the exact position and size of an image. Two rays from the top of the object need to be drawn: the first ray travels parallel to the axis. It is then refracted through the focus of the lens. The second ray goes through the top of the object, straight through the centre of the lens. It is not refracted at all.

Rays dotted back

Magnified image

Ray parallel to axis, refracted through focus

Object

Focus

Axis through centre of lens

Rays never meet

Ray passes through centre of lens

The two rays do not meet on the right-hand side of the lens. They have to be dotted backwards. The point where they meet gives the exact position where the image appears to be. An image like this can be seen but it cannot be focused on a screen. It is called a *virtual* image.

Questions 17

1. Draw a simple diagram of a beam of light rays being refracted by a glass block. Which way does the beam bend:
   (a) on entering the block,
   (b) as it leaves the block?
2. Name three materials that will refract light. What causes refraction?
3. Explain the meaning of *real depth* and *apparent depth*. Why does an object on the bottom of a swimming pool look closer than it really is?
4. Draw and complete these diagrams to show the path of each light ray.

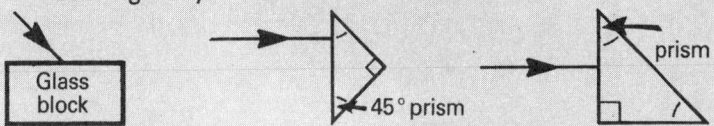

   Glass block   45° prism   prism

5. Explain, with a diagram, how two 45° prisms can be used to make a periscope.
6. (a) What types of lenses are A and B?

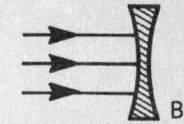

   A   B

   (b) Draw in the shape of each beam after it travels through the lens.
   (c) Name three instruments that use lenses.
7. Complete the following ray diagrams to show the formation of the image. In each case draw two rays of light.

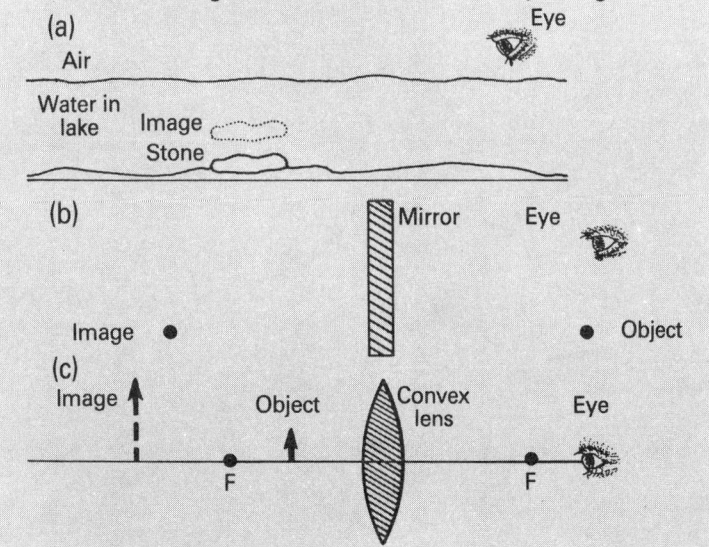

   (a) Eye / Air / Water in lake / Image / Stone

   (b) Mirror / Eye / Image / Object

   (c) Image / Object / F / Convex lens / F / Eye

8. What is a *virtual image*?

Chapter 18
Optical instruments

The human eye

The eye is probably the best optical instrument we have, although it only has one convex lens. The power or focal length of this lens can be controlled by special muscles, called *ciliary muscles*. The lens is used to focus light rays on to the back of the eye, or *retina*. This sends a message through the *optic nerve* to the brain.

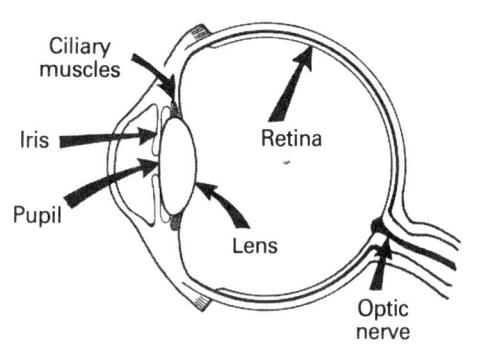

When you look at a distant object your eye muscles make the lens thinner. The light rays from the distant object are then focused on the retina. When you look at an object close to you the eye muscles make the lens fatter, or more convex, so that the object is again focused.

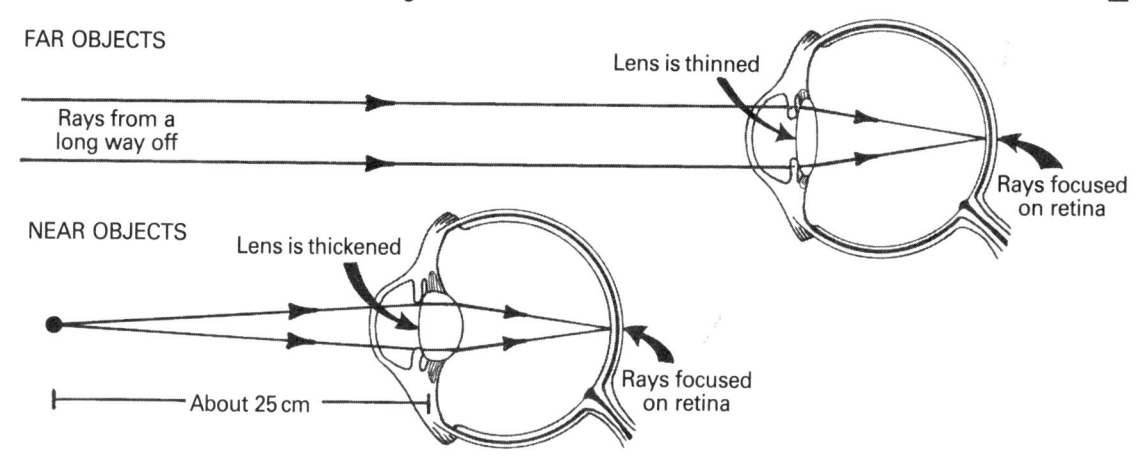

FAR OBJECTS
Rays from a long way off
Lens is thinned
Rays focused on retina

NEAR OBJECTS
Lens is thickened
About 25 cm
Rays focused on retina

This ability of the eye lens to become fatter and thinner when you view objects at different distances is called *accommodation*.

The amount of light entering our eyes is controlled by the *pupil*. This is an opening in front of the eye lens which can get larger or smaller depending on the brightness of the objects we are looking at. At night the pupil becomes wide open, to let as much light in as possible. But on a bright day the pupil shrinks to avoid straining our eyes.

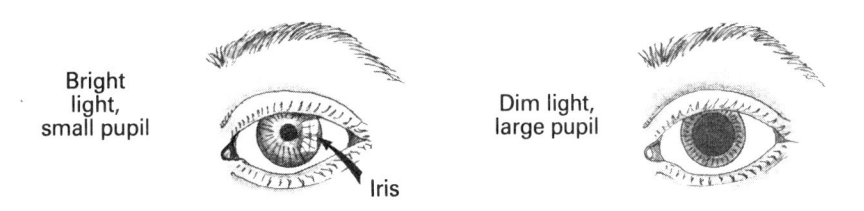

Bright light, small pupil

Dim light, large pupil

Iris

The lens camera

One instrument made by man which is like the human eye is the lens camera. Like the eye it has a lens at the front. This focuses light rays on to the film at the back of the camera (like the retina).

Roll of film

Film

Upside down image

Shutter

Aperture

Light rays

Movable lens

Object

The position of the lens at the front can be altered in more expensive cameras. This means that light rays from objects at different distances can be focused on to the film. This is just like the accommodation of the eye.

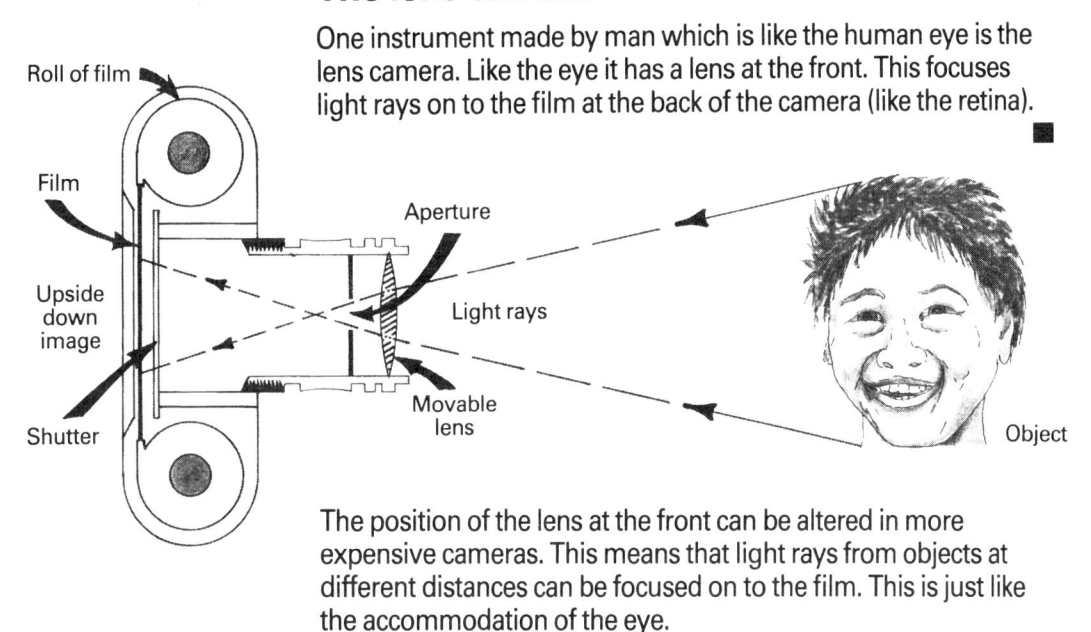

The amount of light entering the camera is controlled by altering the size of its *aperture*. This is the opening at the front of the camera, like the pupil of the eye. In bright light a camera needs a small aperture. In dim light it needs a large aperture.

In both the camera and the eye an image is formed on the film or retina which is upside down. This is called an *inverted* image.

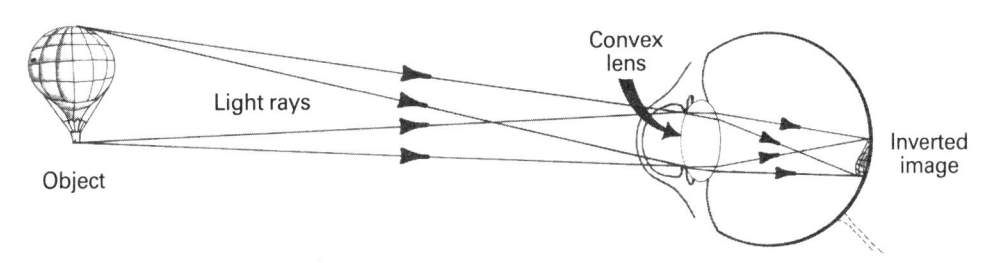

Object

Light rays

Convex lens

Inverted image

Defects of vision and spectacles

The two main defects of vision are *long sight* and *short sight*. If a person is short-sighted he cannot see objects in the distance clearly, such as a football or cricket match. His eye lens does not focus the light rays from far away objects exactly on to the retina. The rays are focused just in front of the retina.

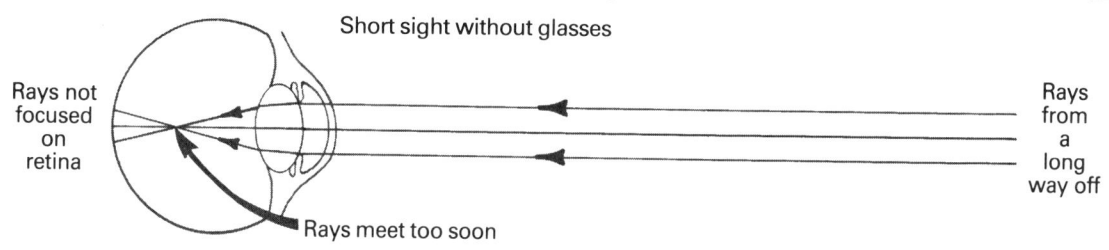

Short sight without glasses

Rays not focused on retina

Rays from a long way off

Rays meet too soon

If the short-sighted person wears spectacles with a concave or diverging lens the light rays spread or diverge just before they reach the eye, and then are focused exactly on the retina.

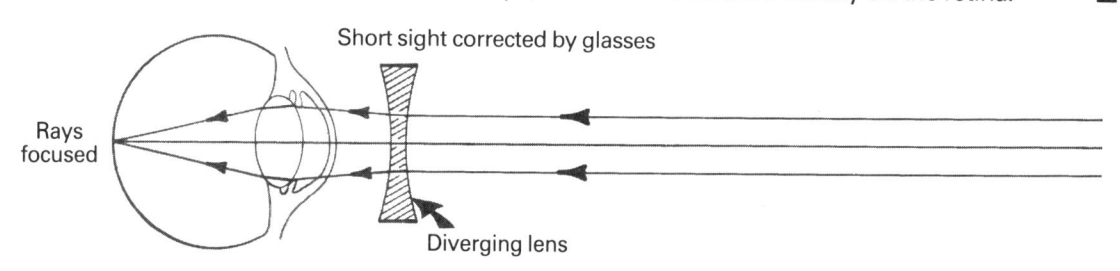

Short sight corrected by glasses

Rays focused

Diverging lens

Long sight is exactly the opposite. A long-sighted person can see distant objects very clearly. But he cannot see things near to him or read at the normal distance. This is about 25 cm from the eye, for adults. The rays from a near object are focused behind the retina.

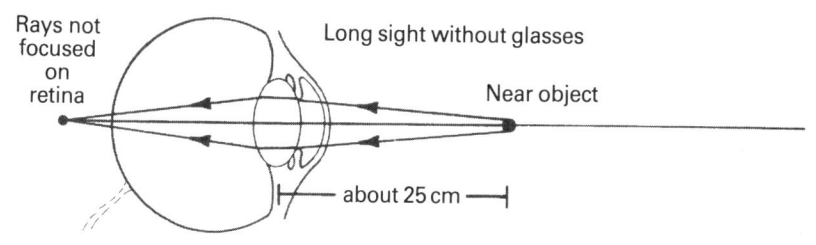

Long sight without glasses

Rays not focused on retina

Near object

about 25 cm

A long-sighted person must wear spectacles which have a convex or converging lens. This brings in, or converges, the rays before they reach the eye so that they focus exactly on the retina.

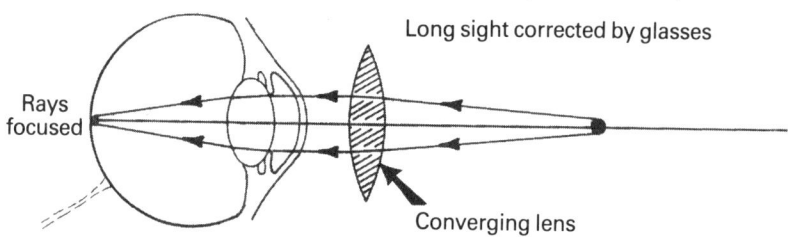

Long sight corrected by glasses

Rays focused

Converging lens

Other optical instruments

Many optical instruments can be made from lenses and mirrors. The simplest optical instrument is a magnifying glass, which is just a simple convex lens. Two convex lenses of the right focal lengths can be used to give much more magnification in the *microscope*.

Another useful optical instrument is the *projector*. This uses a lamp, a concave mirror and convex lenses to project an image on to a screen. In a slide projector an image is made of a slide — in a cine projector different images are made on the screen as a film is pulled past the lamp.

A *telescope* can be made by using two convex lenses of the right focal length. The lens at the front of the telescope is called the *objective*. The lens at the back is called the *eyepiece*. The objective lens has a long focal length, say 50 cm. The eyepiece lens needs a short focal length, say 10 cm. ∎

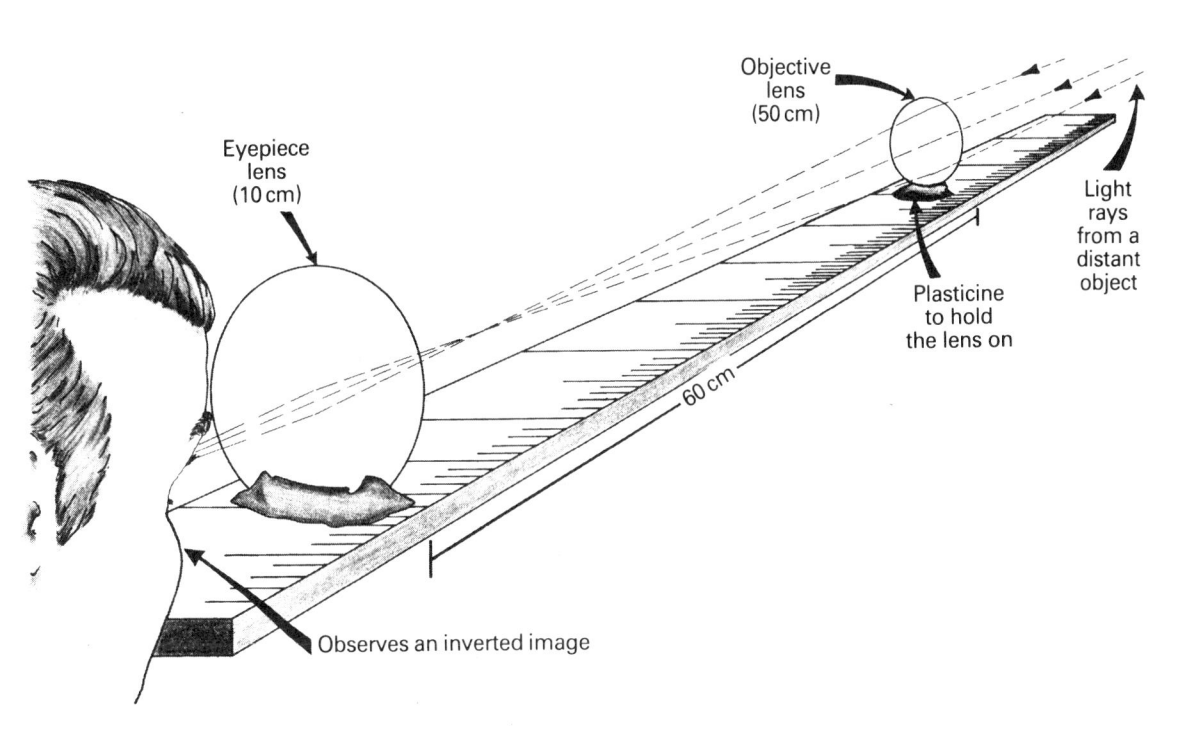

The two lenses can be held by plasticine on a metre rule. They need to be 60 cm apart if their focal lengths are 50 cm and 10 cm. The image seen is upside down.

This is called an *astronomical telescope*. Bigger telescopes use a huge concave mirror instead of an objective lens — they are called *reflecting telescopes*. Nowadays scientists learn about the universe by collecting *radio waves* from outer space as well as light rays. Giant *radio telescopes* are used. The study of waves of all kinds is the subject of the next chapter.

Questions 18

1. Fill in the missing words: 'In the normal human eye light rays are focused by the ____ on to the back of the eye or ____. The amount of light entering the eye is controlled by the ____. The lens makes an ____ image on the back of the eye.'
2. Describe in your own words how the human eye is like a lens camera.
3. Fill in the missing words: 'The amount of light entering a camera depends on the size of the ____. The light rays are focused on to the film by a ____.'
4. These diagrams show one eye with short sight and one with long sight.

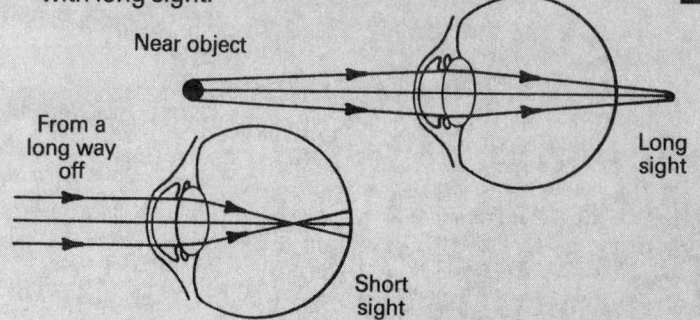

   Near object

   Long sight

   From a long way off

   Short sight

   (a) Describe what is wrong with each eye.
   (b) Draw the spectacles that will correct the person's eyesight.
   (c) How do the spectacles do this?
5. Name three optical instruments and explain what each one is used for.
6. This diagram shows the outline of a camera.

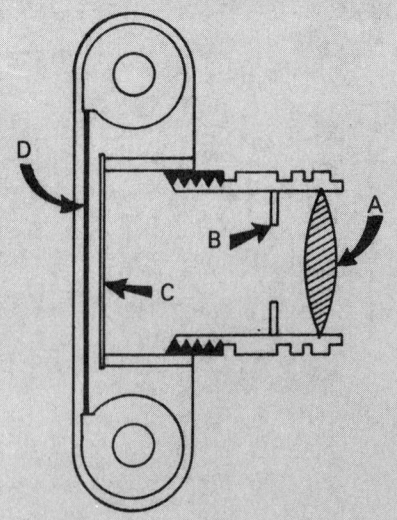

   (a) Name the four parts A, B, C and D and describe their action.

(b) A camera is often compared with the human eye. Complete this diagram of an eye, marking on it the names of the four parts which act like the parts A, B, C and D in the camera diagram. (WY and LREB) ■

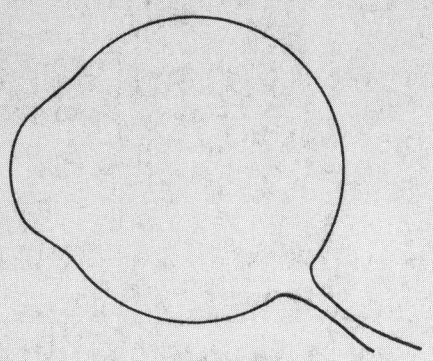

7. The diagram shows an eye which is receiving rays from a distant object. ■

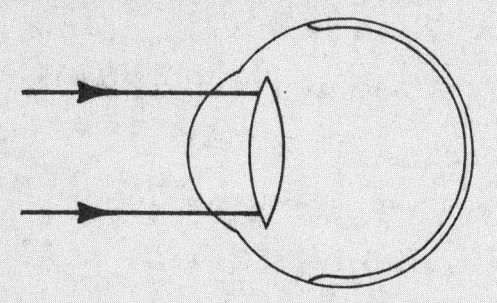

   (a) Complete the diagram to show the eye lens correctly focusing the rays from the distant object.
   (b) What happens to the lens when it focuses rays from a near object?
   (c) Label the retina of the eye in the diagram.
   (d) Explain how the eye adjusts itself to varying conditions of brightness. (YREB)

8. Here is a short passage from *Lord of the Flies* by William Golding:

   'Ralph moved the lenses back and forth, this way and that, till a glossy white image of the declining sun lay on a piece of rotten wood. Almost at once a thin trickle of smoke rose up and made him cough. Jack knelt too and blew gently, so that the smoke drifted away, thickening, and a tiny flame appeared. The flame, nearly invisible at first in that bright sunlight, enveloped a small twig, grew, was enriched with colour, and reached up to a branch which exploded with a sharp crack. The flame flapped higher and the boys broke into a cheer.
   "My specs!" howled Piggy. "Give me my specs!" '

   Piggy was short-sighted. What is wrong with the physics here?

Chapter 19
Colours of light and the spectrum

The spectrum

In 1666 Sir Isaac Newton discovered that white light was actually made up of seven different colours. Newton shone sunlight through a prism and found that the light was split into the colours of the *spectrum:* Red, Orange, Yellow, Green, Blue, Indigo and Violet (these can be remembered by the sentence: 'Richard of York gave battle in vain'). The splitting of white light into the seven separate colours of the spectrum is called *dispersion*. (See the cover.)

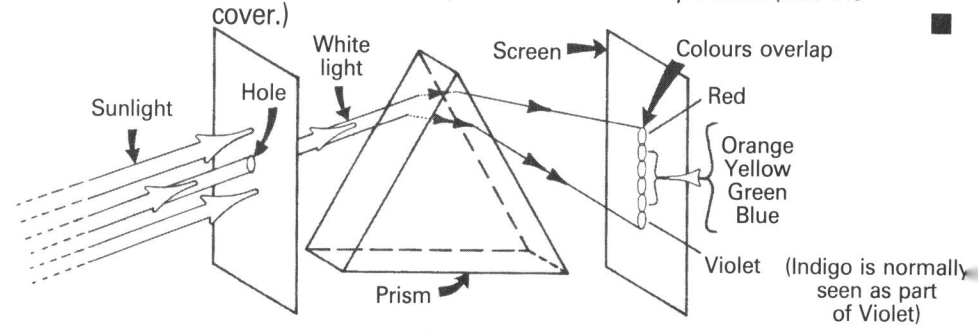

There are two types of spectrum: *pure* and *impure*. Newton's spectrum was impure because the seven colours overlapped and were not completely separate. When the colours are separated so that each can be seen clearly a pure spectrum is made. This can be done by placing a lens on one side of the *prism.*

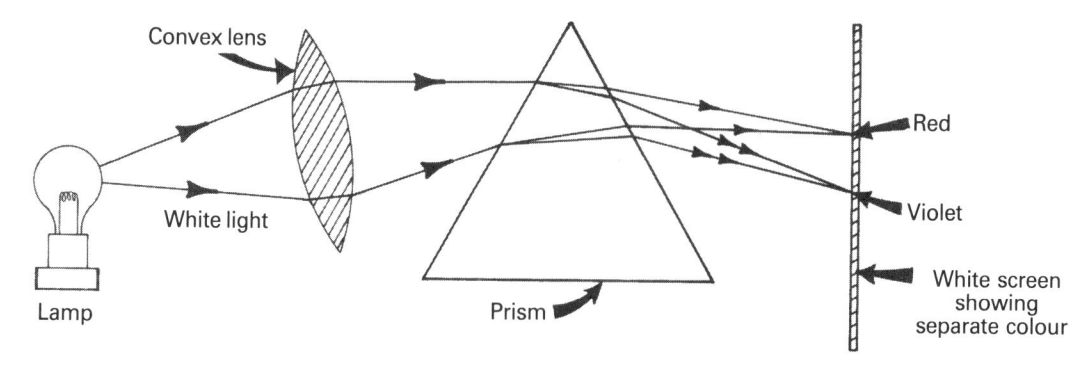

A rainbow is the best example of a spectrum in everyday life. Drops of rain act like tiny prisms and split, or disperse, white sunlight into the seven colours of the rainbow.

Reasons for the spectrum

Dispersion is caused by the different colours of light travelling at slightly different speeds in glass or water. Red light travels more slowly than violet light in glass. This means that violet light is refracted more by a prism than red. The seven colours leave the prism at slightly different angles. Red light is refracted the least, violet the most.

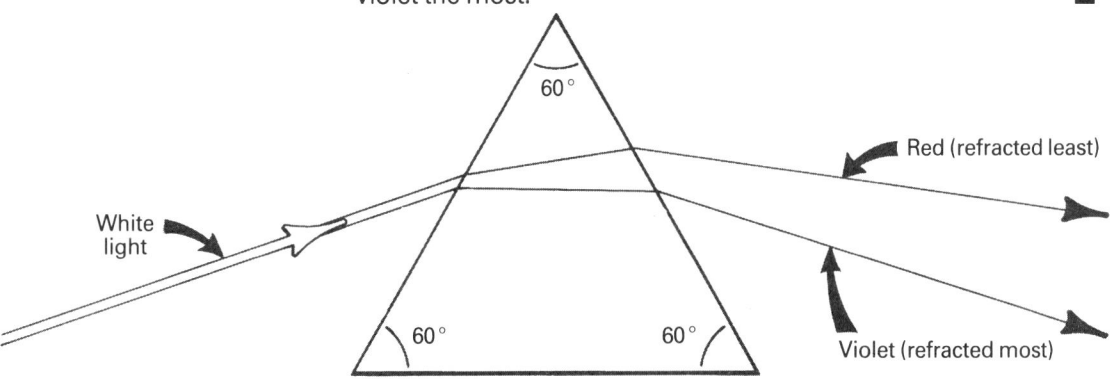

Recombining the spectrum

Isaac Newton also found that the colours of the spectrum can be changed back into white light, or *recombined,* by using another prism. The second prism is placed next to the first, but faces the opposite way.

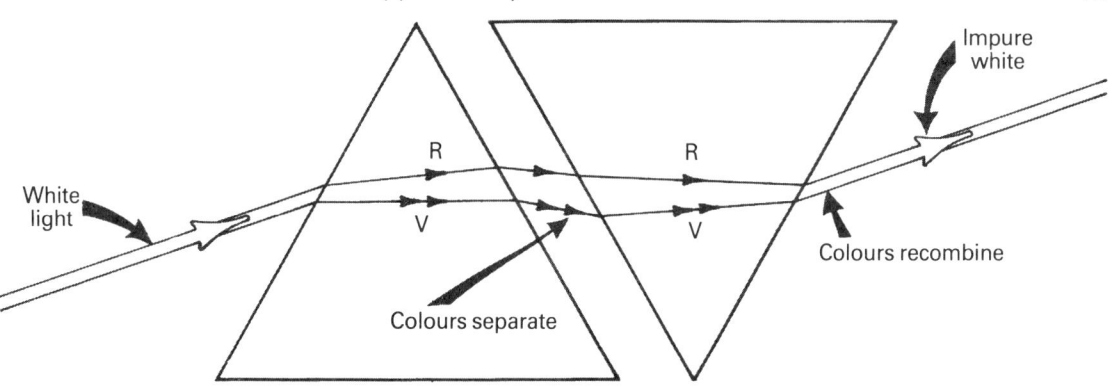

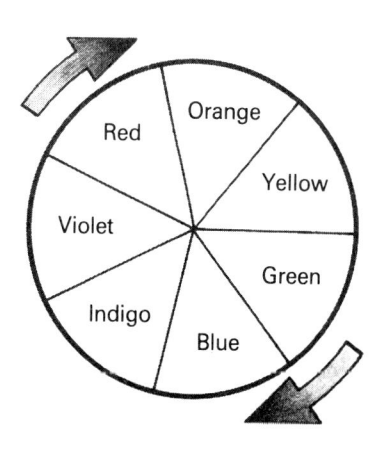

Another way of producing impure white light is by dividing a disc into seven equal parts. One of the colours of the spectrum is painted on to each part. When the disc is spun very quickly the colours merge together. The disc appears to be roughly white.

Colour mixing

There are two types of colour mixing: mixing by adding different coloured *lights* and mixing by adding *paints* or *pigments*.

The three main coloured lights are red, green and blue. These are the three *primary colours* in science. If red, green and blue lights are added they form white light. Red and blue light make *magenta*. Red and green light make *yellow*. Green and blue light make *cyan* (a blue-green or turquoise colour).

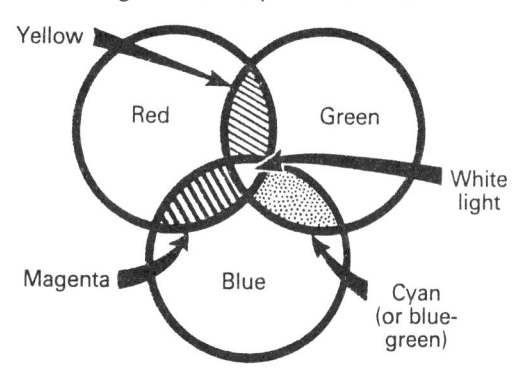

Colour television pictures are made up from the three primary colours. The picture consists of millions and millions of tiny glowing dots: some red, some blue and some green. The light from the glowing dots mixes to form all the different colours you see on the screen.

Questions 19

1. What are the seven colours of the spectrum? Describe, with a diagram, how Isaac Newton produced these colours with a glass prism.
2. Why does white light separate into different colours? Which colour is refracted most and which is refracted least? Explain why.
3. Give some examples where the spectrum can be seen in everyday life.
4. Describe how the colours of the spectrum can be re-combined to make roughly white light.
5. If each of these circles stands for a coloured light on a screen, what are the colours at A, B, C and D?

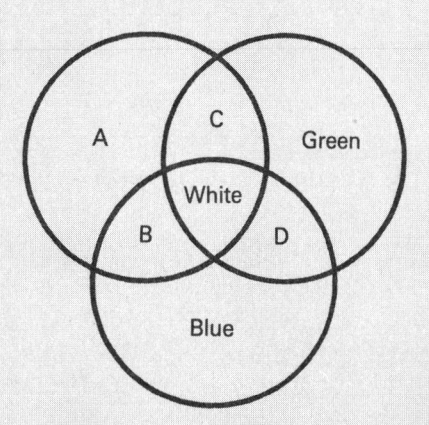

6. These diagrams show thin parallel beams of white light falling on to a glass prism and a glass block.

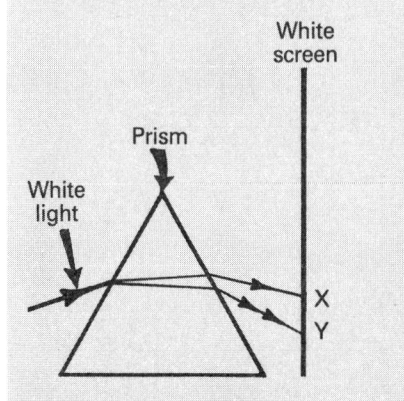

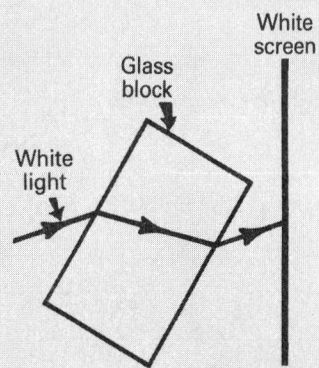

   The ends of the observed spectrum are labelled X and Y
   (a) What colour is observed at X?
   (b) What colour is observed at Y?
   (c) With the glass block no spectrum is seen on the screen. Suggest a reason for this.

   (LREB)

Chapter 20: Waves

Types of wave

A wave is one way of carrying energy from one place to another. There are many types of wave: water waves, ripples on a pond, sound waves, radio waves, light waves and so on. The study of waves is an important part of physics.

Some types of wave can be arranged into one family or group called *the electro-magnetic spectrum*. The important waves in this group are: radio waves, infra-red rays, light waves, ultra-violet rays, X-rays and gamma rays.

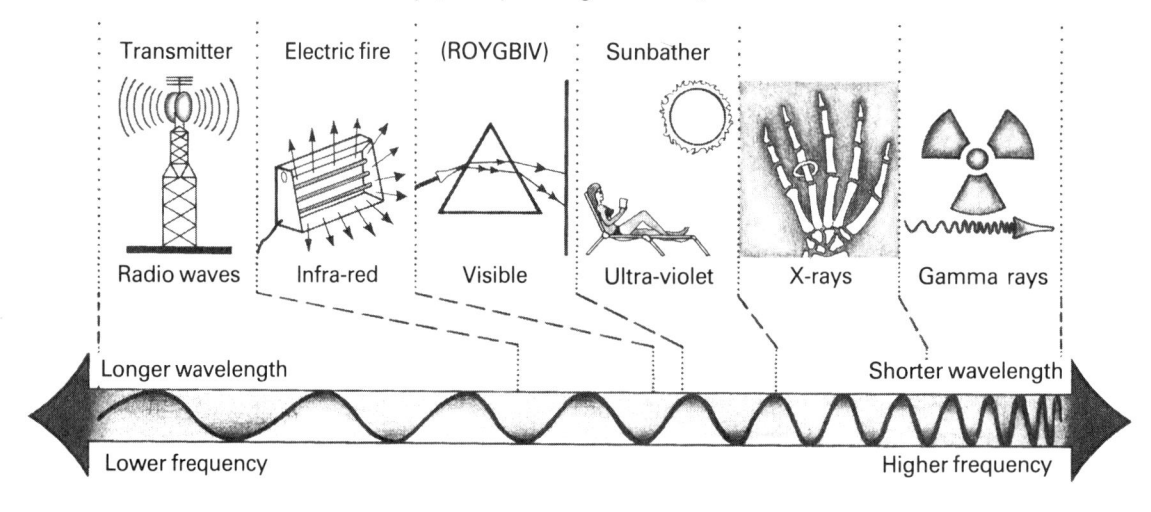

Transmitter	Electric fire	(ROYGBIV)	Sunbather		
Radio waves	Infra-red	Visible	Ultra-violet	X-rays	Gamma rays

Longer wavelength ←——————————————→ Shorter wavelength
Lower frequency ←——————————————→ Higher frequency

Infra-red rays are the same as heat rays. Radio waves carry radio and TV messages. Light rays are the only rays that we can see with our eyes. Ultra-violet rays come from the Sun, or from a 'sun-lamp'. They are invisible but they cause sun-burn. X-rays can be used to take photographs of the inside of our bodies, bones for example. Finally, gamma rays are very dangerous waves which can penetrate metal.

All these waves:
(a) travel at the same speed of 300 million metres per second,
(b) travel in straight lines (this is why they are often called 'rays'),
(c) can travel in a vacuum,
(d) have their own *wavelength* and *frequency*.

Radio waves have quite a long wavelength. Some radio stations use waves several hundred metres long. The waves with the shortest wavelength are gamma and X-rays. They are also the most dangerous and penetrating.

Longitudinal and transverse waves

All waves are either *longitudinal* or *transverse* depending on the vibrations that cause the wave.

Ripples on a pond, or waves on the sea, are transverse waves — as the wave travels along, the water particles vibrate up and down. A piece of cork on a pond moves up and down as a ripple moves past it.

In a transverse wave the vibrations are at *right angles* to the direction of the wave. All the waves in the electromagnetic spectrum are transverse waves.

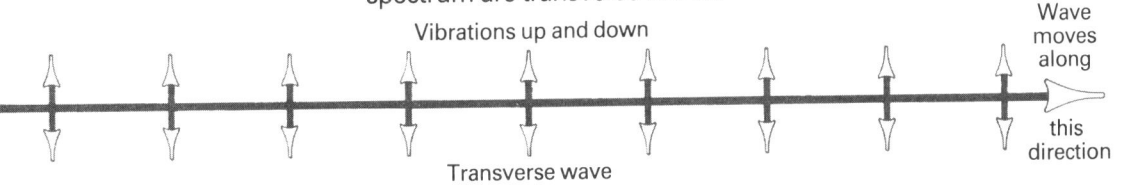

Vibrations up and down

Wave moves along this direction

Transverse wave

In a longitudinal wave the vibrations causing the wave are in the same direction as the wave itself.

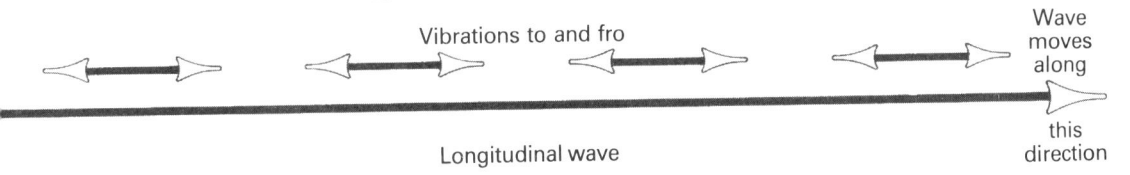

Vibrations to and fro

Wave moves along this direction

Longitudinal wave

A sound wave is one example. The sound wave from a tuning fork is longitudinal. The prongs of the fork and the air next to it vibrate backwards and forwards in the same direction as the wave itself.

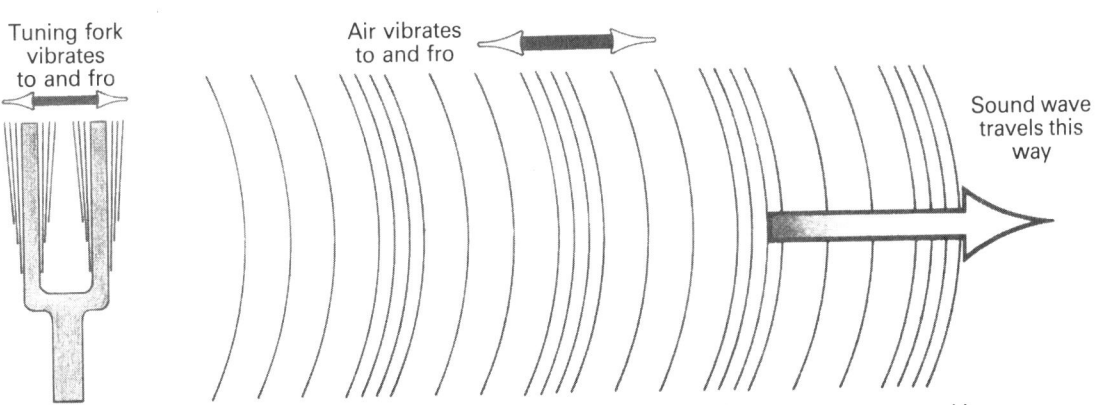

Tuning fork vibrates to and fro

Air vibrates to and fro

Sound wave travels this way

Unlike light and heat rays, sound waves cannot travel in a vacuum. They always need a substance or a *medium* to travel in. Air, water, steel and many other substances will carry sound waves.

Features of waves

Every wave in physics has three important features which make it different from others. They are *frequency*, *wavelength* and *wave speed*.

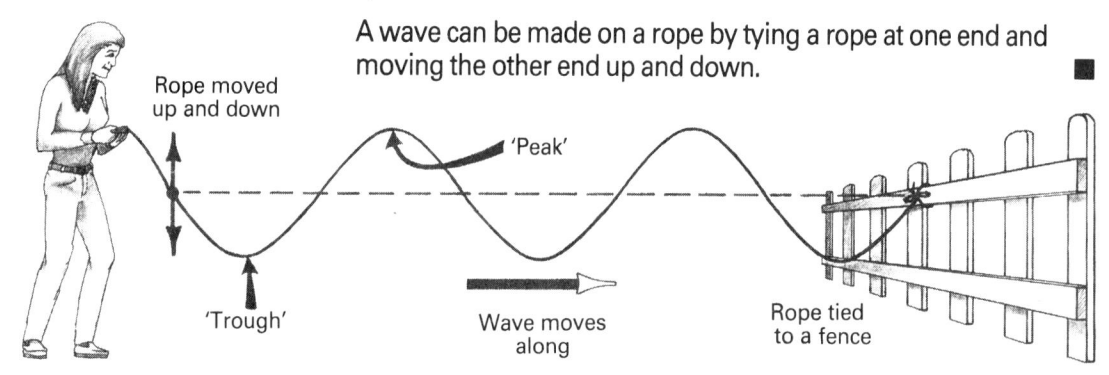

A wave can be made on a rope by tying a rope at one end and moving the other end up and down.

A ripple on a pond seen from the side would look the same: a 'peak', followed by a 'trough', another peak and another trough all along the wave. In other words a wave is a series of peaks and troughs.

The up-and-down or backwards-and-forwards movement of a wave can be shown on a graph.

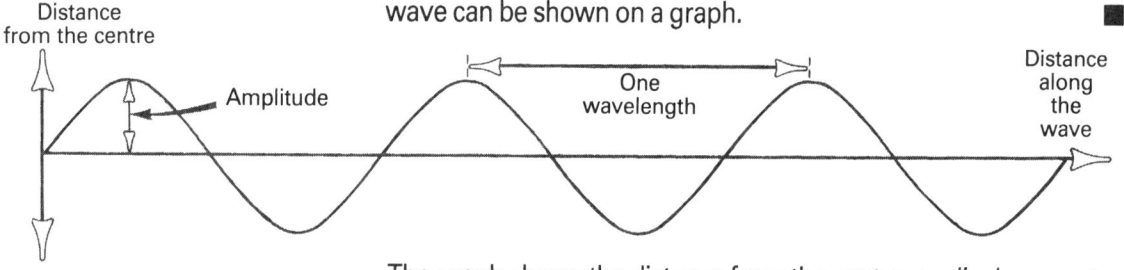

The graph shows the distance from the centre, or *displacement*, of the particles at different places along the wave.

The *wavelength* is the distance between two peaks next to each other on the wave.

The height of the wave is called its *amplitude*.

The *frequency* of a wave is the number of complete waves made in one second.

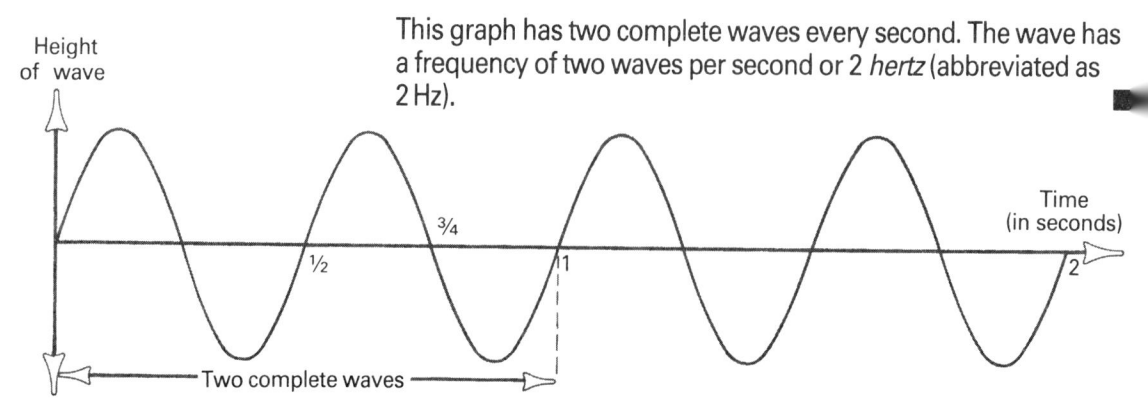

This graph has two complete waves every second. The wave has a frequency of two waves per second or 2 *hertz* (abbreviated as 2 Hz).

The higher the frequency of a wave the shorter its wavelength becomes. Radio waves have a lower frequency and a longer wavelength than X-rays.

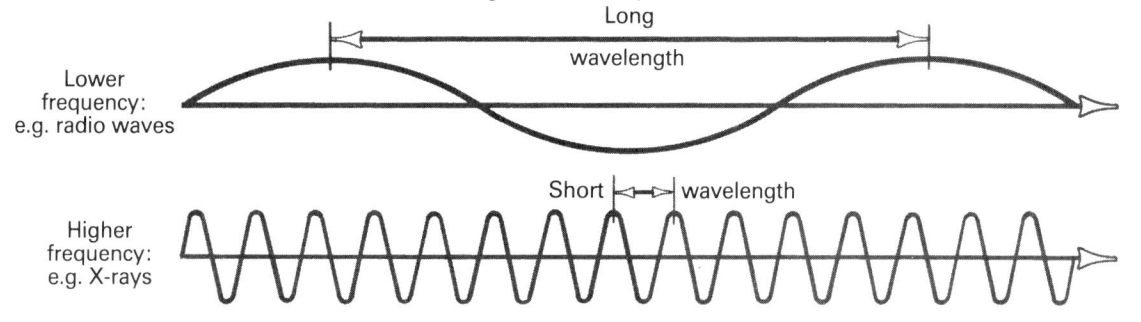

Lower frequency: e.g. radio waves — Long wavelength

Higher frequency: e.g. X-rays — Short wavelength

The *speed* of a wave can be worked out if you know its wavelength and frequency. Suppose a wave has a wavelength of 3 metres and a frequency of 2 waves every second. Its wave speed is then 3 metres × 2 = 6 m/s. In other words:

Wave speed = Frequency × Wavelength
(in m/s)   (in Hz)   (in m)

If v stands for wave speed, f for frequency and the Greek letter λ (lambda) stands for wavelength:

$$v = f \times \lambda$$

This formula can be put into a triangle.

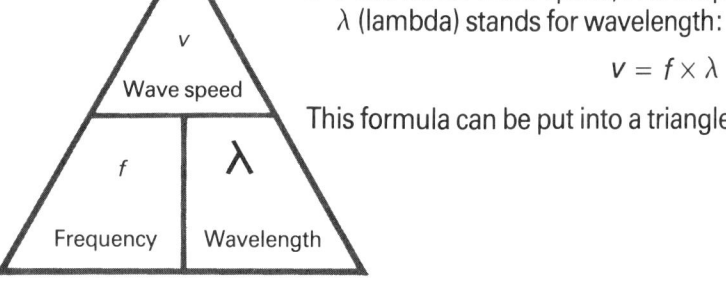

For example, if f = 50 Hz, λ = 2 m,
then the wave speed, v = 50 × 2 = 100 m/s.

Properties of waves

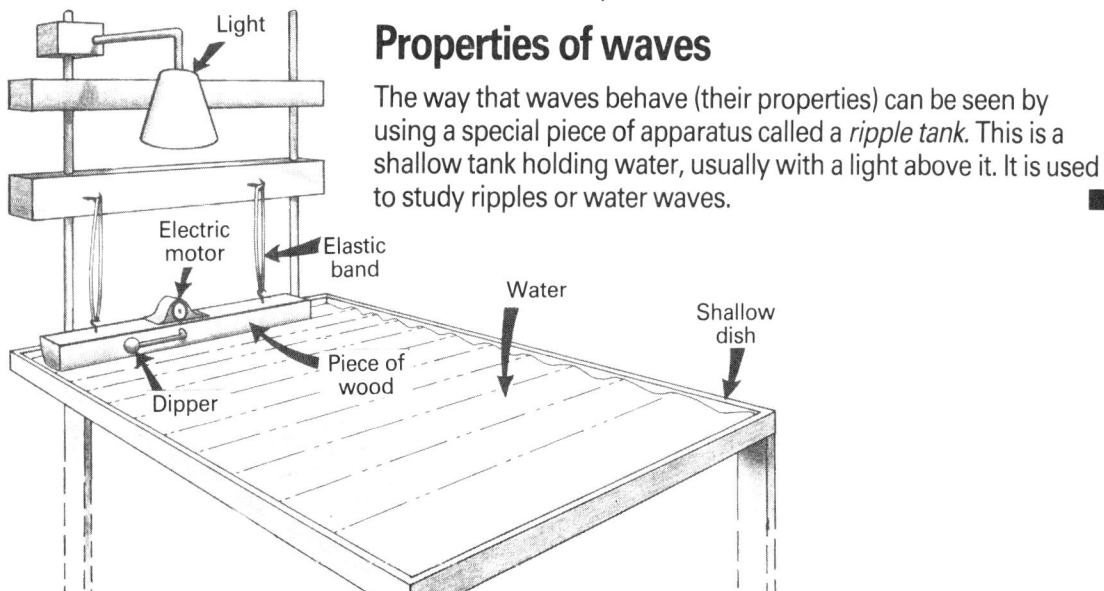

The way that waves behave (their properties) can be seen by using a special piece of apparatus called a *ripple tank*. This is a shallow tank holding water, usually with a light above it. It is used to study ripples or water waves.

Two kinds of water wave can be made in a ripple tank: *circular* waves and *plane* waves.

Plane waves can be made by a flat piece of wood vibrating up and down in the tank. A circular wave is made by a 'dipper' vibrating on the surface of the water.

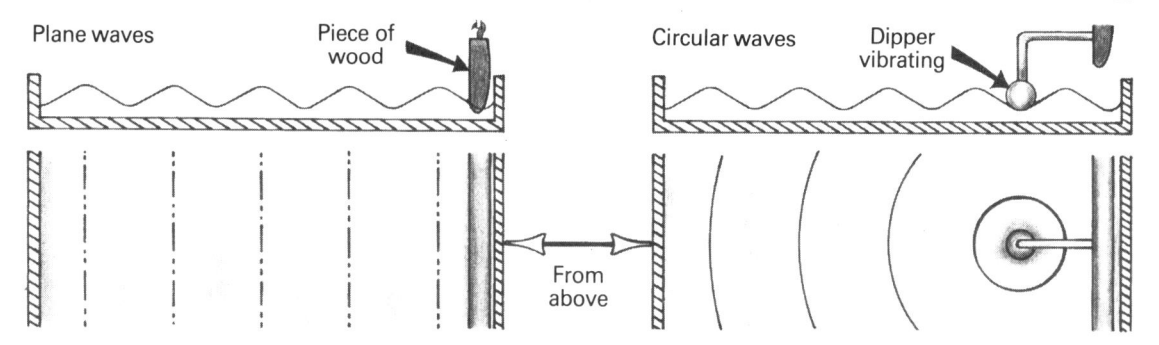

The tank can be used to show that waves can be *reflected, refracted* and *diffracted*.

(a) *Reflection.* Waves in the tank are reflected when they meet an obstacle of any shape. A concave obstacle in the tank reflects plane water waves towards one point or focus. A convex reflector spreads or diverges the waves. All waves can be reflected in a similar way: light waves, sound waves, radio waves, heat rays and so on.

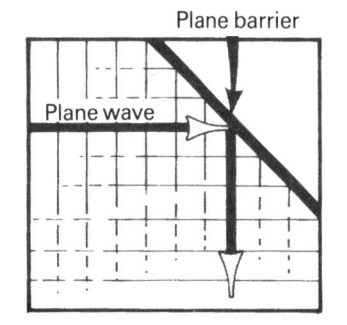

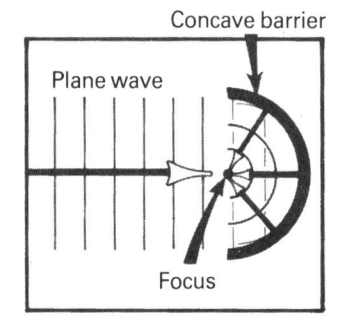

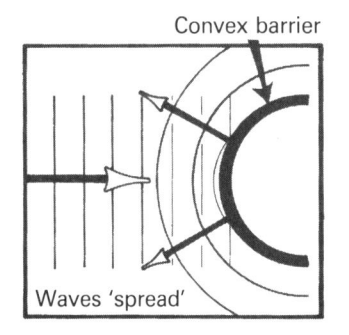

(b) *Refraction.* Water waves can also be refracted, or bent, in a ripple tank when they pass from deep water to shallow water. This is just like the refraction of light rays when they travel from one material into another. Radio waves are refracted high up in the atmosphere. When they reach a special layer called the *Appleton layer* they change direction.

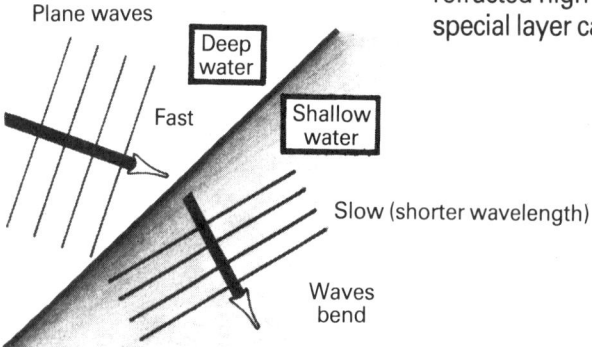

(c) *Diffraction.* A more unusual property of waves is called diffraction. This means that a wave can bend round an obstacle, or spread out after passing through a slit. Waves are diffracted most when the slit is about the same size as their wavelength. Sound waves can be diffracted by a slit as wide as a door. But light waves are only diffracted by a tiny slit, less than a millimetre wide. ■

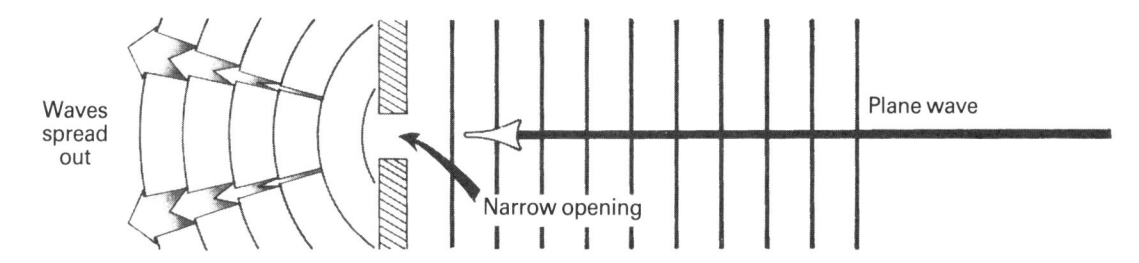

Interference

The final property which is shown by all waves is called *interference.* This occurs when two waves meet and interfere with each other. It can be shown in a ripple tank by placing two vibrating dippers close to each other. The circular waves from the dippers meet and create an *interference pattern.* ■

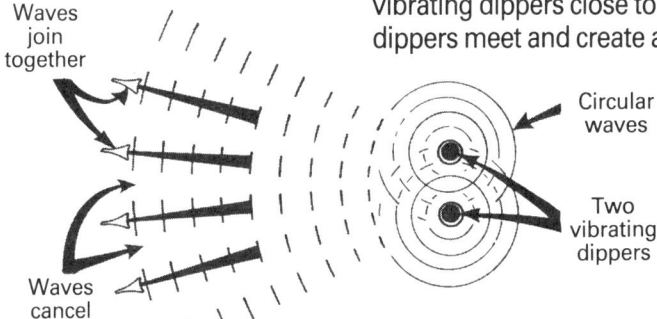

Where a *peak* of one wave meets a trough from the other the two waves cancel each other out. This is called *destructive interference.* ■

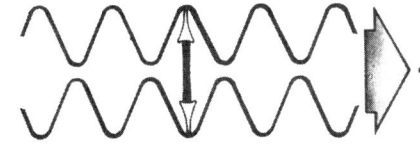

Peak meets trough . . . and . . . they cancel each other out

But if a *peak* of one wave meets a *peak* from the other the two waves join together. They *reinforce* each other. The waves join to make a much stronger wave, with twice the amplitude. This is called *constructive interference.* ■

Peak meets peak . . . and . . . there is twice the height

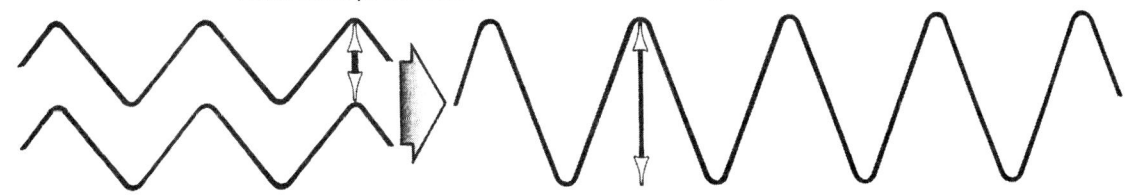

125

Questions 20

1. If this diagram shows the electromagnetic spectrum, what waves do the letters A to F stand for?

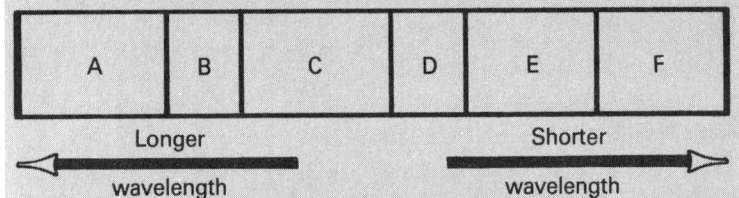

| A | B | C | D | E | F |

   ⟵ Longer wavelength   Shorter wavelength ⟶

   What do these waves have in common?

2. What is the difference between longitudinal and transverse waves? Give some examples of each type.

3. Draw a graph of a wave to show what is meant by: wavelength and amplitude.

4. Use the triangle to work out the missing quantity:

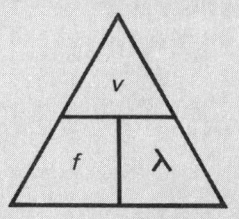

   (triangle with v on top, f and λ below)

   (a) frequency = 10 Hz, wavelength = 2 m, wave speed = ?
   (b) f = 200 Hz, λ = 0.1 m, v = ?
   (c) for a radio wave, f = 200 000 Hz, λ = 1500 m. What is the speed of the radio wave?
   (d) v = 320 m/s, λ = 2 m, f = ?
   (e) v = 340 m/s, f = 170 Hz, λ = ?
   (f) v = 1500 m/s, f = 250 Hz, λ = ?

5. Describe how a ripple tank can be used to demonstrate that waves can be:
   (a) reflected from a barrier,
   (b) refracted,
   (c) diffracted by a slit.

6. These two diagrams show waves meeting a plane surface. In diagram (a) the waves are reflected. In diagram (b) the waves are refracted. Draw each diagram neatly and accurately to show what happens to the waves.

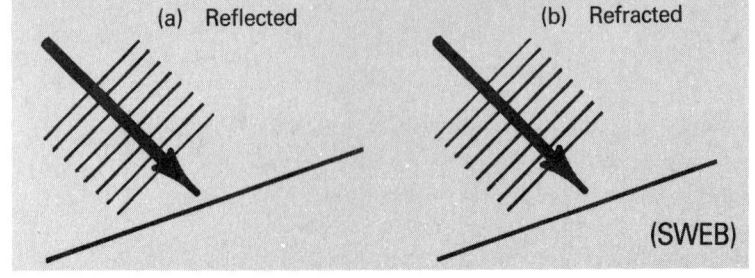

   (a) Reflected   (b) Refracted

(SWEB)

7. This diagram represents a transverse wave:

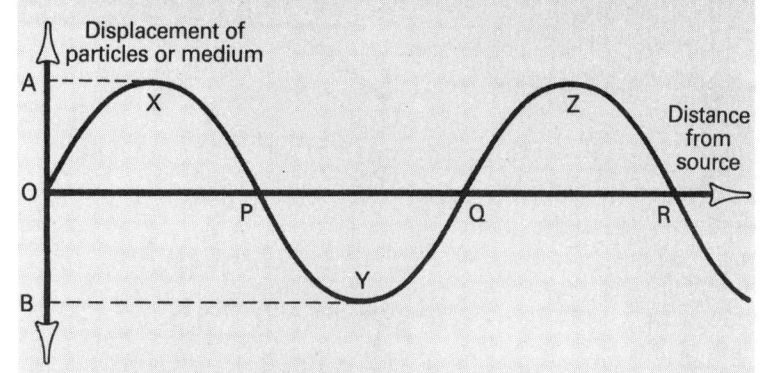

(a) Which one of the following distances is equal to the amplitude of the wave?
AB, AO, AX, BY.
(b) Which one of the following distances is equal to one wavelength of the wave?
XP, PQ, OQ, XY.
(c) State one example of a transverse wave.
(d) State one example of a longitudinal wave.
(e) What do you understand by the term frequency of a wave? (EMREB)

8. Use a diagram to explain how:
(a) two waves interfere with each other to cancel each other out,
(b) two waves join together and reinforce each other.

Chapter 21
Sound waves and sound energy

Movement of sound waves

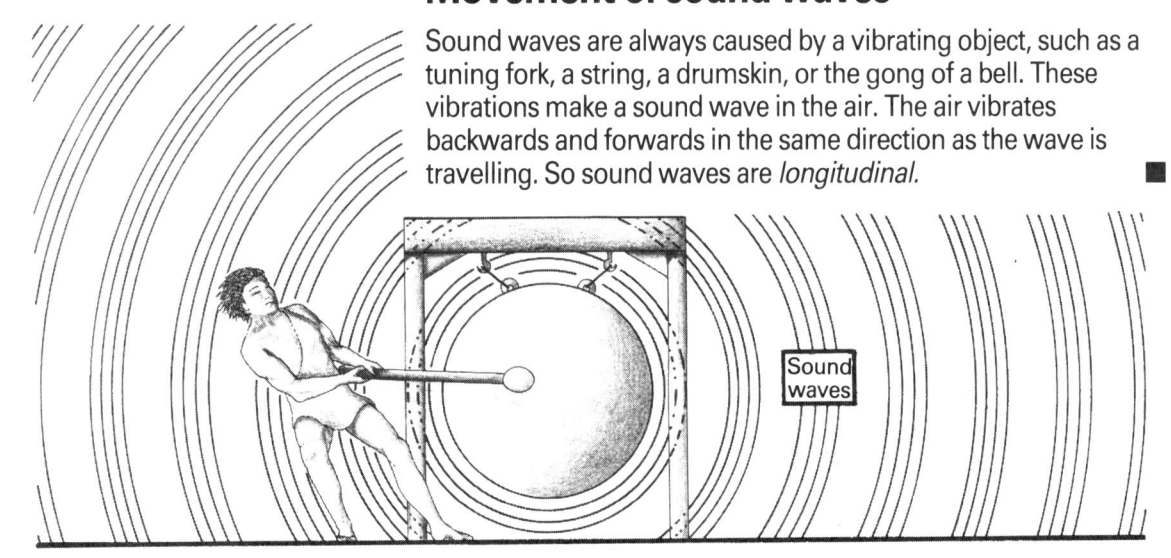

Sound waves are always caused by a vibrating object, such as a tuning fork, a string, a drumskin, or the gong of a bell. These vibrations make a sound wave in the air. The air vibrates backwards and forwards in the same direction as the wave is travelling. So sound waves are *longitudinal*.

As the sound wave travels in air the vibrations *compress* the air at some parts of the wave, and stretch or *rarefy* the air at other points. All along the sound wave there are places of *compression* and *rarefaction*.

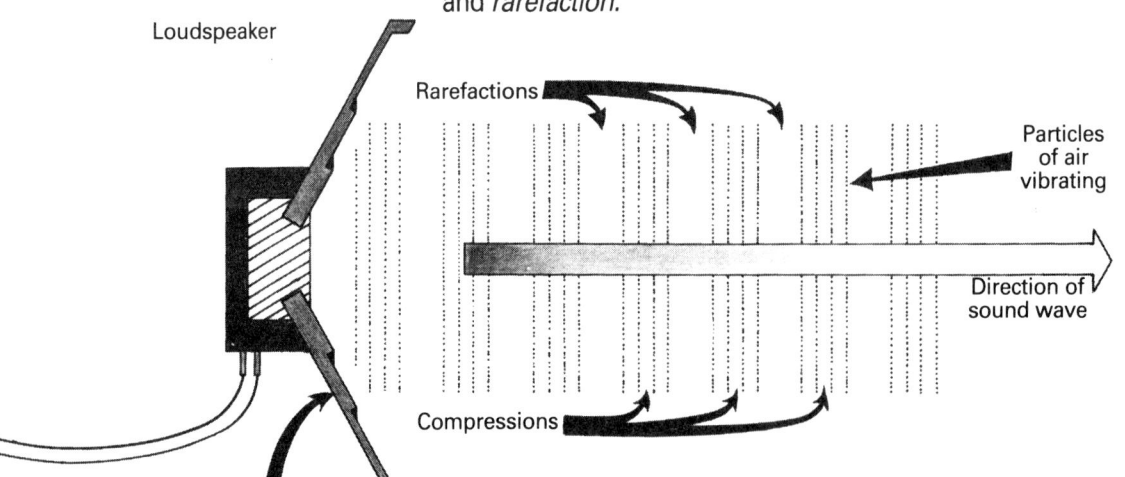

These compressions and rarefactions travel outwards, away from the object vibrating. This is how a sound wave is carried.

Sound waves need a material or *medium* to carry them. They cannot travel in a vacuum. Whenever any medium carries a sound wave the molecules inside it vibrate backwards and forwards. In some parts of the wave the molecules are squashed together. In other parts the molecules are stretched apart. These 'squashes' and 'stretches' carry sound energy from one place to another.

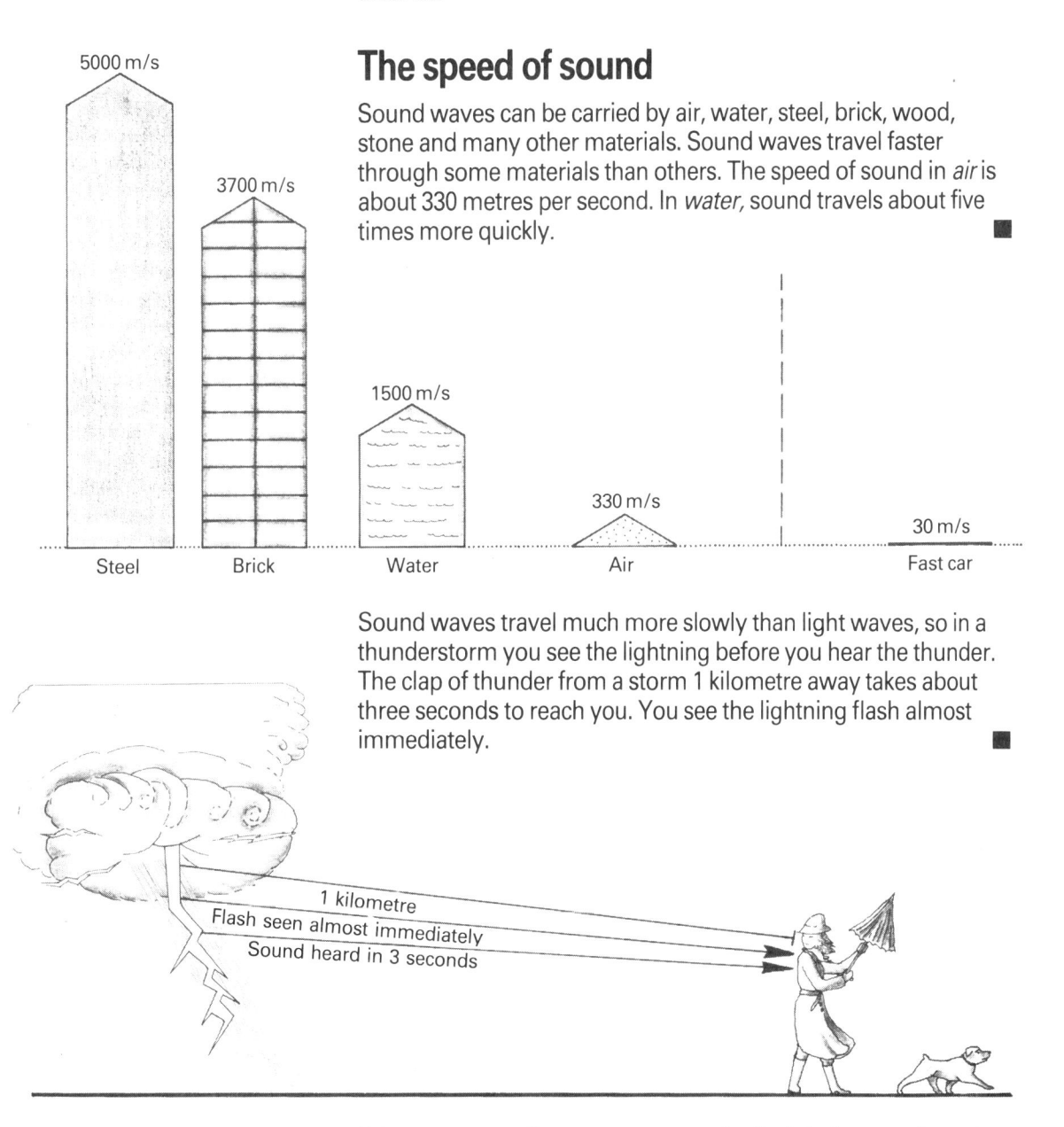

The speed of sound

Sound waves can be carried by air, water, steel, brick, wood, stone and many other materials. Sound waves travel faster through some materials than others. The speed of sound in *air* is about 330 metres per second. In *water,* sound travels about five times more quickly.

Steel	Brick	Water	Air	Fast car
5000 m/s	3700 m/s	1500 m/s	330 m/s	30 m/s

Sound waves travel much more slowly than light waves, so in a thunderstorm you see the lightning before you hear the thunder. The clap of thunder from a storm 1 kilometre away takes about three seconds to reach you. You see the lightning flash almost immediately.

1 kilometre
Flash seen almost immediately
Sound heard in 3 seconds

When someone fires a gun you see the flash before you hear the shot. The sound travels at about 330 m/s, while light travels at 300 million m/s! If the person firing the gun is 330 metres away the time between seeing the flash and hearing the bang is about one second.

Echoes

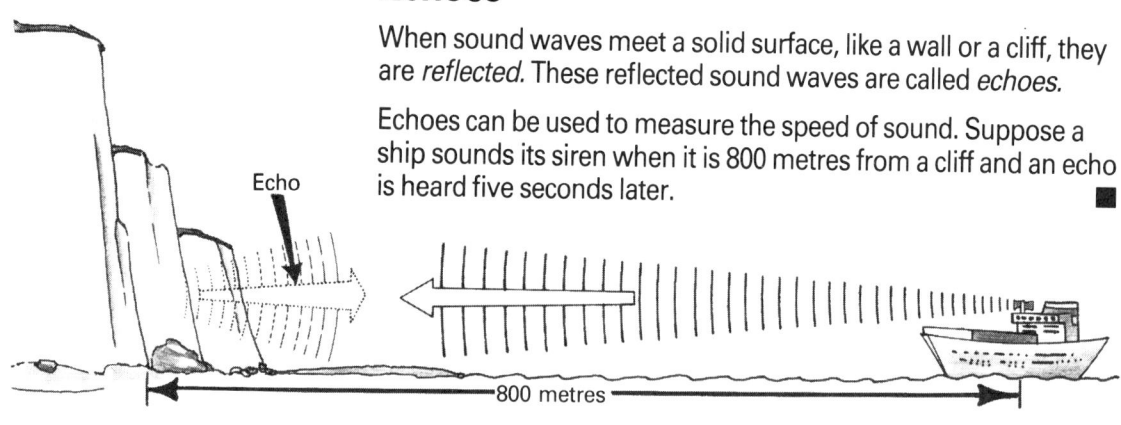

When sound waves meet a solid surface, like a wall or a cliff, they are *reflected*. These reflected sound waves are called *echoes*.

Echoes can be used to measure the speed of sound. Suppose a ship sounds its siren when it is 800 metres from a cliff and an echo is heard five seconds later.

The sound travels 1600 metres, to the cliff and back, in five seconds.

Speed of sound = Distance/Time = 1600 m/5 s = 320 m/s

Echoes can also be used to find the depth of the sea bed underneath a ship. A wave is sent out from the bottom of the ship, bounces off the sea bed, and comes back to the ship. The depth of the sea can be found if we know the time taken for the echo to come back and also the speed of sound in water.

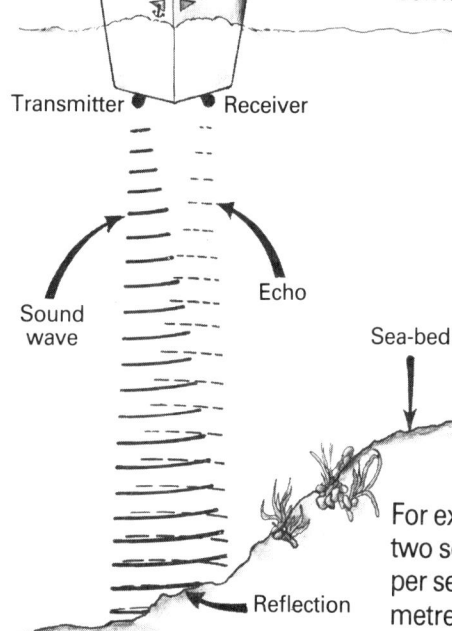

For example, suppose the wave is sent out and the echo returns two seconds later. If the speed of sound in water is 1500 metres per second the sound wave must have travelled 1500 × 2 or 3000 metres. It has to go there and back. So the sea must be 3000 ÷ 2 or 1500 metres deep.

Although echoes can be useful they can sometimes be a nuisance in a room or a hall. Concert halls, theatres and cinemas often have specially padded walls and ceilings. The soft padding *absorbs* the sound and stops sound waves from echoing round the room, interfering with each other. The study of echoes in halls and theatres is called *acoustics*.

Frequency, pitch and loudness of sound

The pitch of a sound wave or a musical note depends on its frequency. High-pitched sounds consist of waves with a high frequency. The waves are closely packed together, with a short wavelength. With a lower pitch the wavelength is longer and the frequency is less.

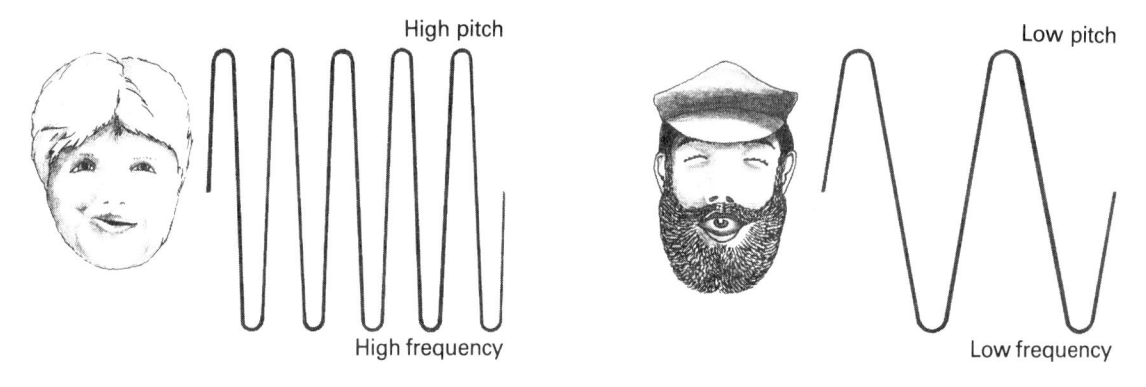

High pitch

High frequency

Low pitch

Low frequency

Frequency is measured in cycles per second, or *hertz* (Hz). People can hear notes as high as 20 000 Hz — while cats and dogs can hear notes, such as a high-pitched whistle, above this frequency.

The loudness of a sound or noise depends on the size or *amplitude* of the waves.

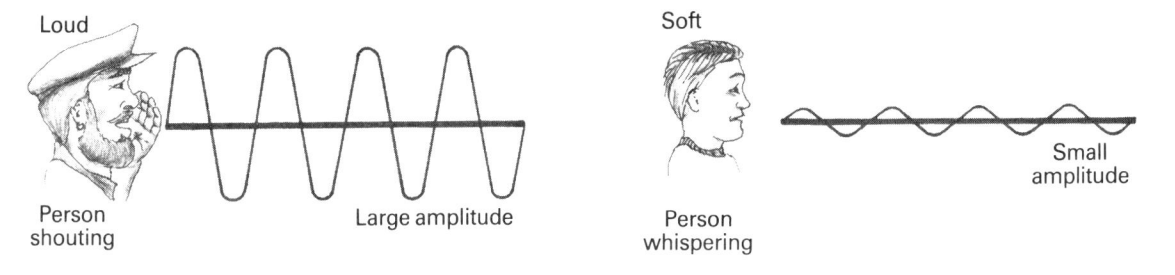

Loud

Person shouting

Large amplitude

Soft

Person whispering

Small amplitude

As the amplitude of the wave increases so does the loudness of the sound. Loudness is measured in *decibels.*

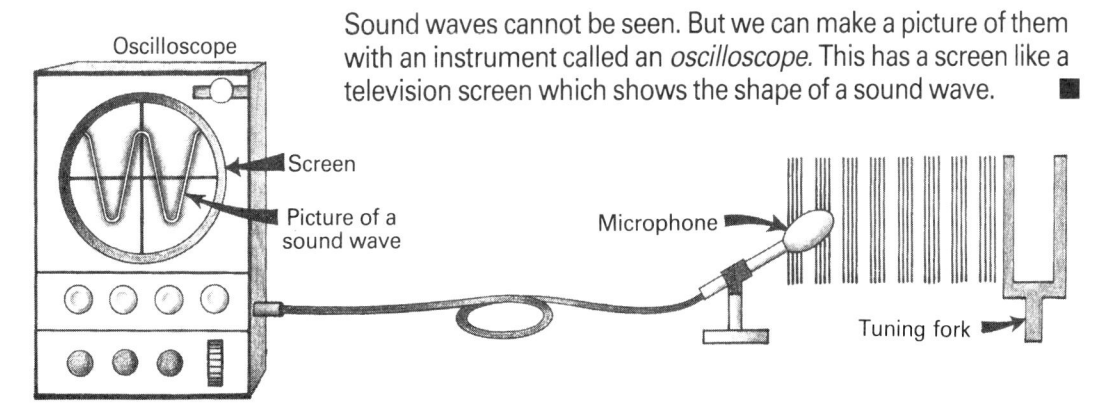

Sound waves cannot be seen. But we can make a picture of them with an instrument called an *oscilloscope.* This has a screen like a television screen which shows the shape of a sound wave.

Oscilloscope

Screen

Picture of a sound wave

Microphone

Tuning fork

Musical notes

Musical notes are formed by:
(a) vibrating strings, e.g. in a guitar, piano or violin,
(b) vibrations in pipes or tubes, e.g. in an organ, flute, trumpet or trombone,
(c) percussion instruments, e.g. bells, gongs or drums.

In a percussion instrument the *surface*, like a drumskin or the gong of a bell, vibrates when you hit it.

The frequency of a note from a string can be changed by altering either its *tension* or its *length*. A short string gives a high note. A longer string gives a lower note. Special screws on the top of a guitar or violin are used for tightening the strings. The tighter the string, the higher the note. ■

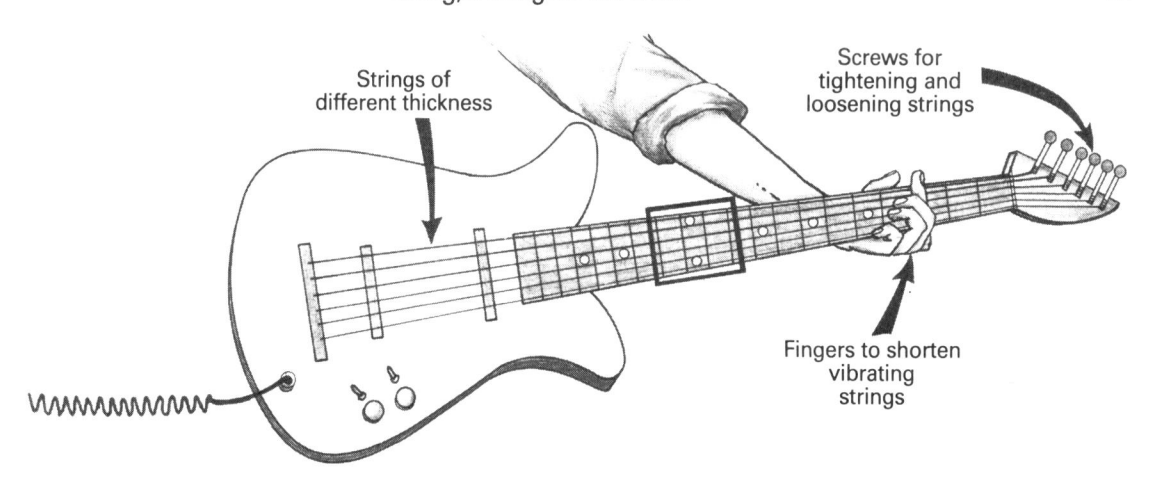

Strings of different thickness

Screws for tightening and loosening strings

Fingers to shorten vibrating strings

Thicker strings give a lower note than the thin strings. ■

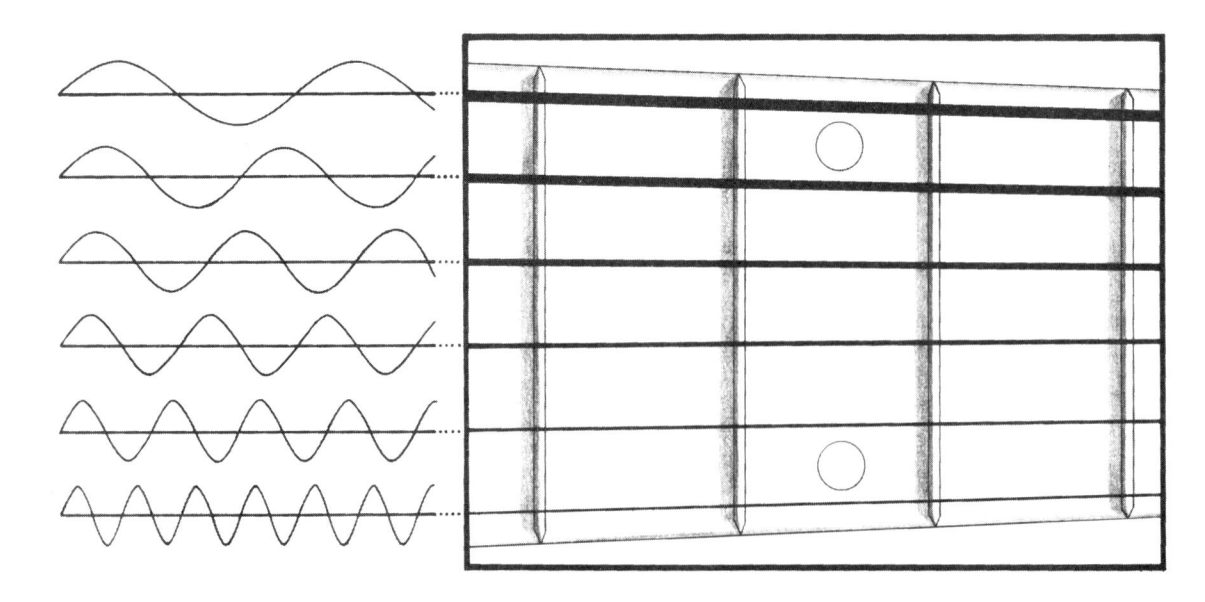

A musical note can be produced in a pipe by blowing into it or across the top of it. Short pipes give high notes. Longer pipes give lower notes. This is used in trumpets, trombones and recorders.

A tuning fork can be used to make the air in a pipe or tube vibrate. A vibrating tuning fork is held above a glass tube, or even a milk bottle.

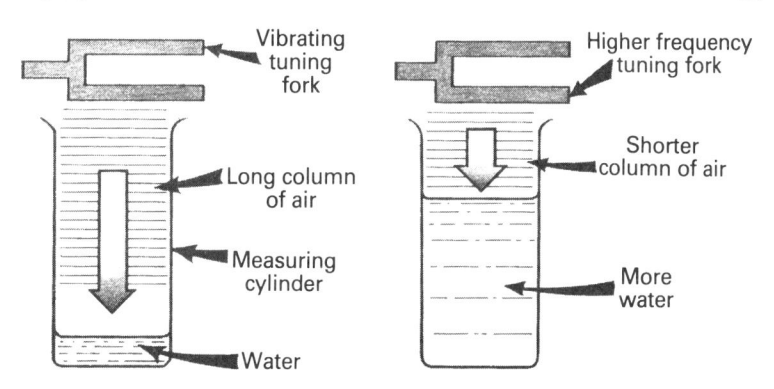

The air in the tube is set into vibration by the tuning fork. If water is slowly added to the tube there comes a time when quite a loud sound is heard. The air in the tube then has exactly the same frequency as the tuning fork. The tuning fork and the air in the tube are vibrating together with the same *natural frequency*. This is called *resonance*. A popular example of resonance is the opera singer who breaks a wine glass, or a window pane, when she reaches a high note. Her voice and the wine glass have the same natural frequency.

Musical notes can be arranged in correct order to make a musical scale. Middle C is a note with a frequency of 256 Hz. A note with double this frequency (512 Hz) is called Top C. It is said to be one *octave* above middle C.

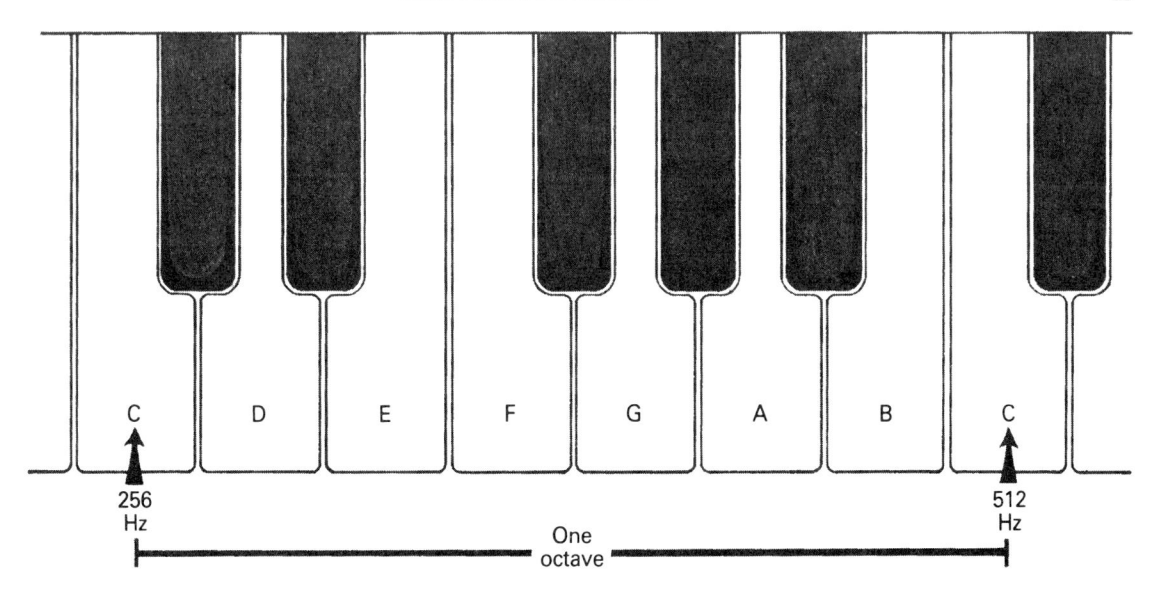

Questions 21

1. Name three materials, or mediums, which sound can travel in. Describe how a sound wave is carried through a material.
2. How far can a sound wave travel in air in:
   (a) 2 seconds   (b) 4 seconds
   (c) 8 seconds   (d) 10 seconds?
   How far would sound travel in water in these times? (Suppose that the speed of sound in air = 330 m/s; the speed in water = 1500 m/s.)
3. A ship sounds its siren when it is 990 metres from a cliff. How long will it be before the echo is heard?
4. The following arrangement would be suitable for measuring the speed of sound.

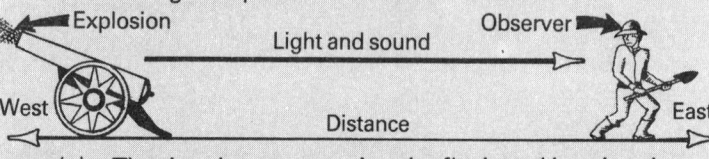

   (a) The time between seeing the flash and hearing the gun is about 5 seconds and the distance between the gun and the observer is 1600 metres. Calculate the speed of sound in air.
   (b) If a wind was blowing from East to West, how would the new value calculated for the speed of sound in air be different from the value in still air?
   (c) If the sound travelled the same distance but through water instead of air, how would you expect the time taken for the sound to travel to a detector to alter?
   (LREB)
5. Here is a list of frequencies of different musical notes:

C	D	E	F	G	A	B	C
256	288	320	341	384	426	480	512 Hz

   (a) Which is the highest note?
   (b) Which has the highest pitch?
   (c) Which has the lowest frequency?
   (d) Which one has the smallest wavelength?
   (e) Why are there two Cs?
6. If a tiny piece of plasticine were stuck on each prong of a tuning fork, what would happen to its frequency?
7. On this graph of a wave mark the amplitude and the wavelength. Sketch the graph of a wave with twice the frequency. Sketch the graph of a sound wave that is much louder.

8. How many complete waves are shown here? What is the wavelength of each?

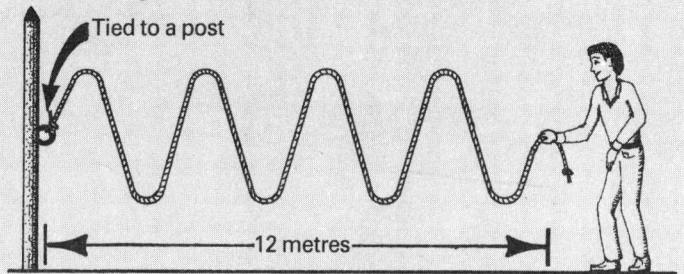

   Tied to a post

   12 metres

9. Most guitars have thick and thin strings. Which strings produce high frequency notes and which low frequency? How else can their pitch be altered?

10. A ship's echo sounder sends short pulses of sound waves down from a sender unit, A, and they are collected by a receiver unit, B. The frequency used is 20 000 Hz. The speed of sound in water is 1500 m/s. It takes 0.1 s for the sound from A to reach B.

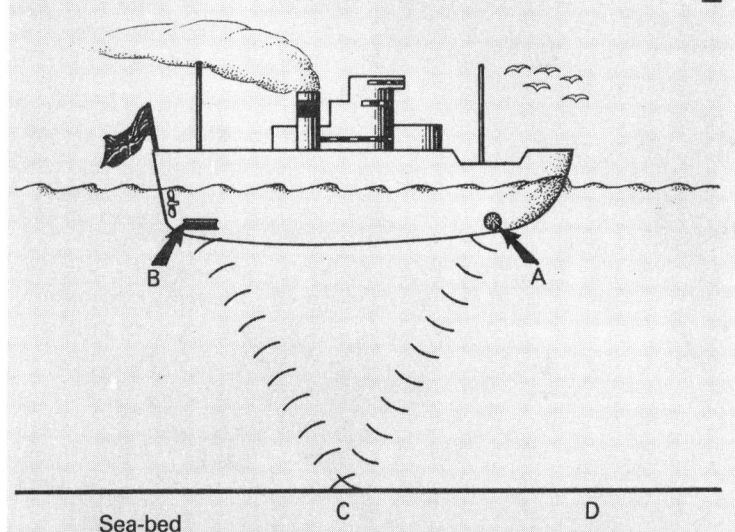

    Sea-bed   C   D

    (a) What is happening to the sound waves at C?
    (b) Calculate the depth of water beneath the ship.
    (c) Calculate the wavelength of these sound waves in water.
    (d) As the sound waves travel from A to C, what changes are there, if any, in:
        (i) their frequency,
        (ii) their amplitude?
    (e) Explain why it would be difficult to use this method to find the depth of water in front of the ship at D.
    (f) In theory, it should be possible for aircraft to use sound echoes to measure their height above the ground. Give one reason why this is not done.

    (YREB)

CROSSWORD 4

Across

5. When two 19 across cancel each other out this is called destructive ___ (12)
8. White light can be formed by mixing red, ___ and 7 down (5)
9. The distance from the lens to 18 across is called the ___ length (5)
10. The ___ taken for sound to travel 320 metres is 1 second (4)
11. The ___ at the back of a camera is inverted (5)
14. It has one convex lens (3)
15. Light enters one type of camera through a pin- ___ (4)
16. You are using your own lenses now, doing this! (7)
18. Where the rays come to one point (5)
19. You may see them in a ripple tank (5)
21. They are used in periscopes (6)
22. Sound waves ___ much more slowly than light waves (6)

Down

1. White ___ is made up of different colours (5)
2. When a disc with seven different colours is spun quickly the colours ___ together to form white light (5)
3. In a ___ wave the vibrations are at right angles to the direction of the wave (10)
4. The ability of the eye to view objects at different distances is called ___ (13)
6. Velocity = ___ × wavelength (9)
7. See 8 across (4)
12. A ___ lens is a diverging lens (7)
13. A mirror can ___ 1 down (7)
17. A ___ is a line at right angles to a mirror (6)
20. Add the three missing letters: ROYG ___ (3)

A radio telescope at Jodrell Bank, Cheshire. This telescope receives and sends messages from satellites in the form of low frequency, long wavelength radio waves. (see page 120)

A satellite in orbit. This satellite sends and receives messages to radio telescopes like the one mentioned. (see page 120)

Modern cameras in action. (see page 111)

A total solar eclipse photographed in Kenya in 1980. The white corona is shaped by magnetic forces. (see page 97)

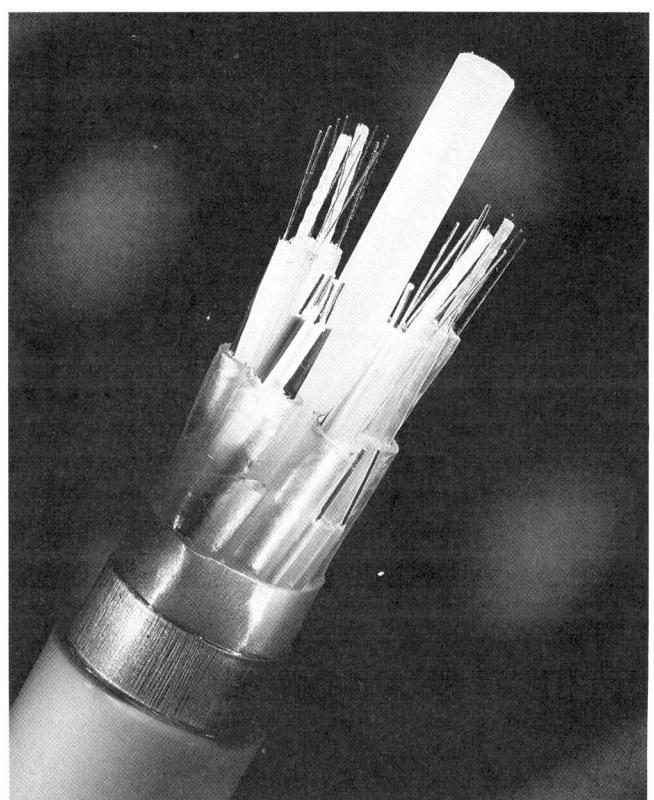

A fibre-optic cable used in a telephone network — this fibre carries pulses of light.

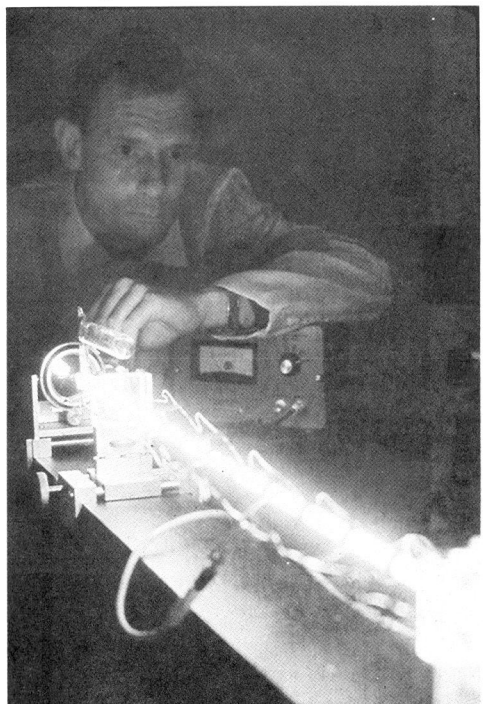

A helium-neon laser producing an intensive beam of light.

Musical instruments on Broadway, New York City. (see page 132)

A photograph of southern Britain taken by a crewman of Skylab 3.

Part 5

Electrical Energy

Chapter 22
Making electricity

Electricity is always made by changing one of the other types of energy into electrical energy.

The simple cell

In a cell or battery *chemical energy* is changed into electrical energy. (People often call a single cell a *battery*. But really a battery is a group of two of more cells.)

The simplest kind of cell uses two metal plates, one copper and one zinc, dipping into weak sulphuric acid. It is called the *simple cell* and makes about 1½ volts, but only for a few minutes. After that the cell stops working because hydrogen gas bubbles collect on the copper plate. These bubbles stop the electric current.

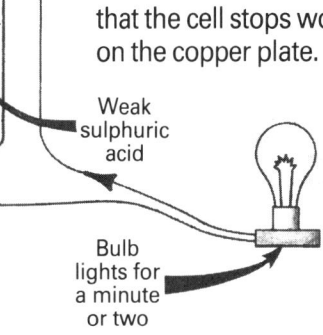

The dry Leclanché cell

A special chemical, called *manganese dioxide,* is used to get rid of these hydrogen bubbles in the cells that we use in torches, radios or lamps. These cells are called *dry cells* because they use a *paste* of ammonium chloride instead of a liquid. A carbon rod is used instead of copper as the positive pole of the cell.

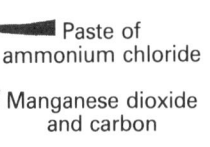

The first cell of this type was made by a Frenchman called Georges Leclanché in 1866. One cell gives about 1½ volts, but after some time its chemical energy is used up and it is thrown away.

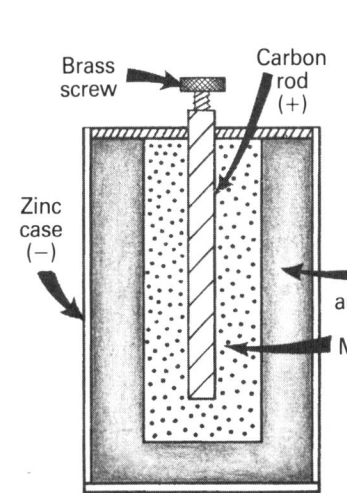

The lead-acid accumulator

One type of cell can be charged up again after it has run down. This cell is called the *lead-acid cell,* or the *lead accumulator.* It is made by putting two thick lead plates into a solution of sulphuric acid.

One of the lead plates becomes a positive plate with a brown coating of lead dioxide. The other lead plate is negative. When new the cell gives about 2 volts, but as it runs down this gets less and less. It can be 'charged up' by feeding a steady electric current into it for several hours.

The acid must be kept at a certain level by 'topping up' with distilled water. These cells are used in car batteries by putting six in a row to make a total of 12 volts. Lead-acid cells can supply a much larger current than dry cells, for a much longer time.

All these cells change chemical energy into electrical energy. But most of the electricity used in homes and factories is made by generators in power stations. Different power stations use different forms of energy: chemical energy from coal, atomic energy or the energy of moving water. This energy is used to make a coil of wire spin inside huge magnets. Electricity is generated in the coil. Generators will be described in Chapter 25.

Static electricity

Electricity can be made simply by rubbing a plastic comb on a cloth. The comb can be used to pick up a small piece of paper.

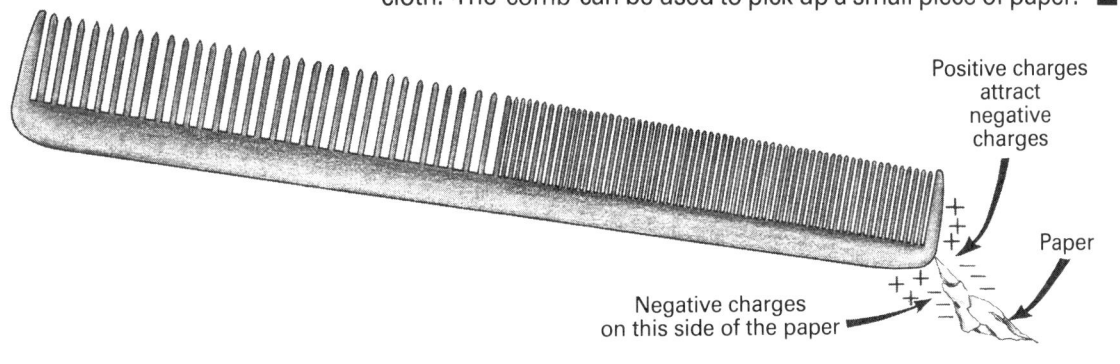

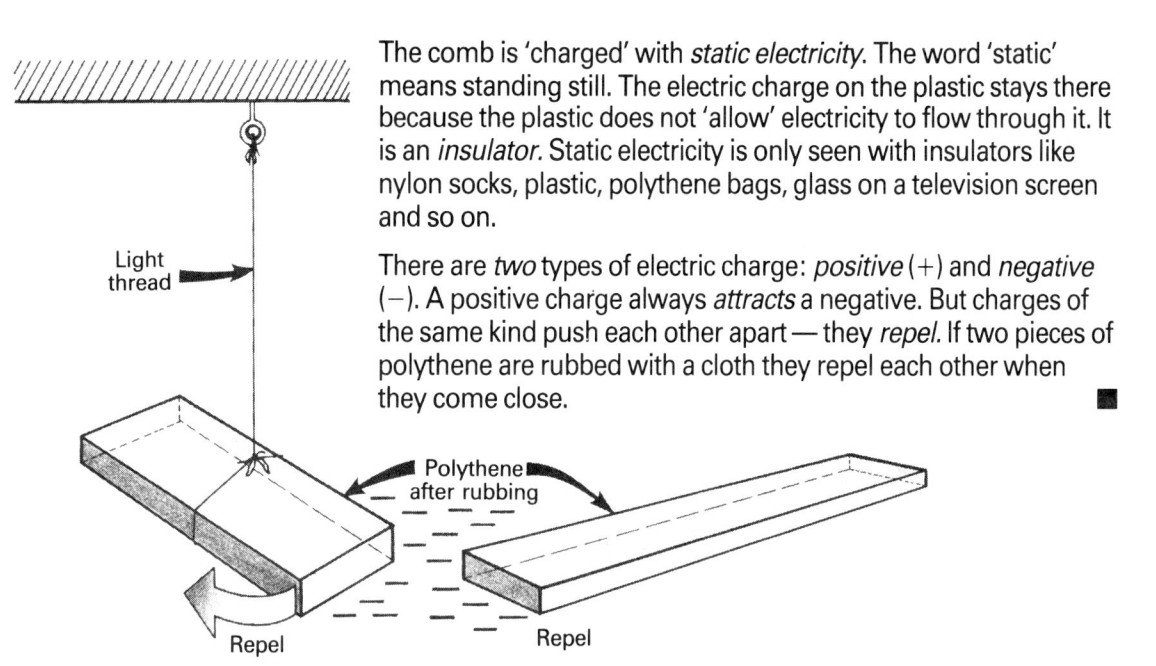

The comb is 'charged' with *static electricity*. The word 'static' means standing still. The electric charge on the plastic stays there because the plastic does not 'allow' electricity to flow through it. It is an *insulator*. Static electricity is only seen with insulators like nylon socks, plastic, polythene bags, glass on a television screen and so on.

There are *two* types of electric charge: *positive* (+) and *negative* (−). A positive charge always *attracts* a negative. But charges of the same kind push each other apart — they *repel*. If two pieces of polythene are rubbed with a cloth they repel each other when they come close.

Both pieces of polythene carry a negative charge. The two negative charges repel each other.

What is static electricity?

To understand electric charge and static electricity you need to know how atoms are made up (see Chapter 27). Every atom has a centre called the *nucleus,* which carries a positive charge. Tiny particles called *electrons* travel round and round this central nucleus. These carry a *negative* charge.

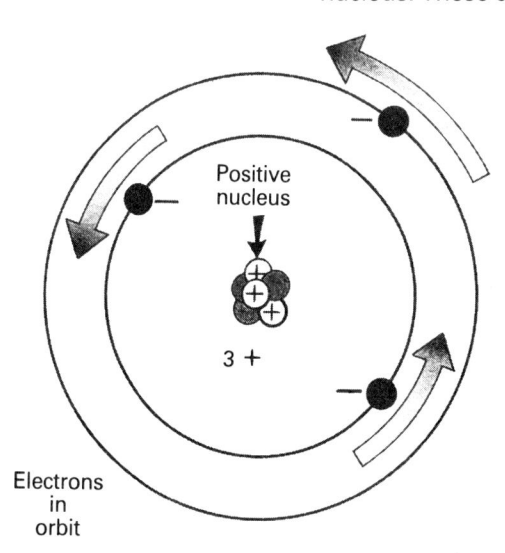

Every atom has the same number of + and − charges. But when a piece of polythene is rubbed with a cloth it gains electrons from the cloth. These extra electrons give the polythene a negative charge. The charge stays there because polythene is an insulator.

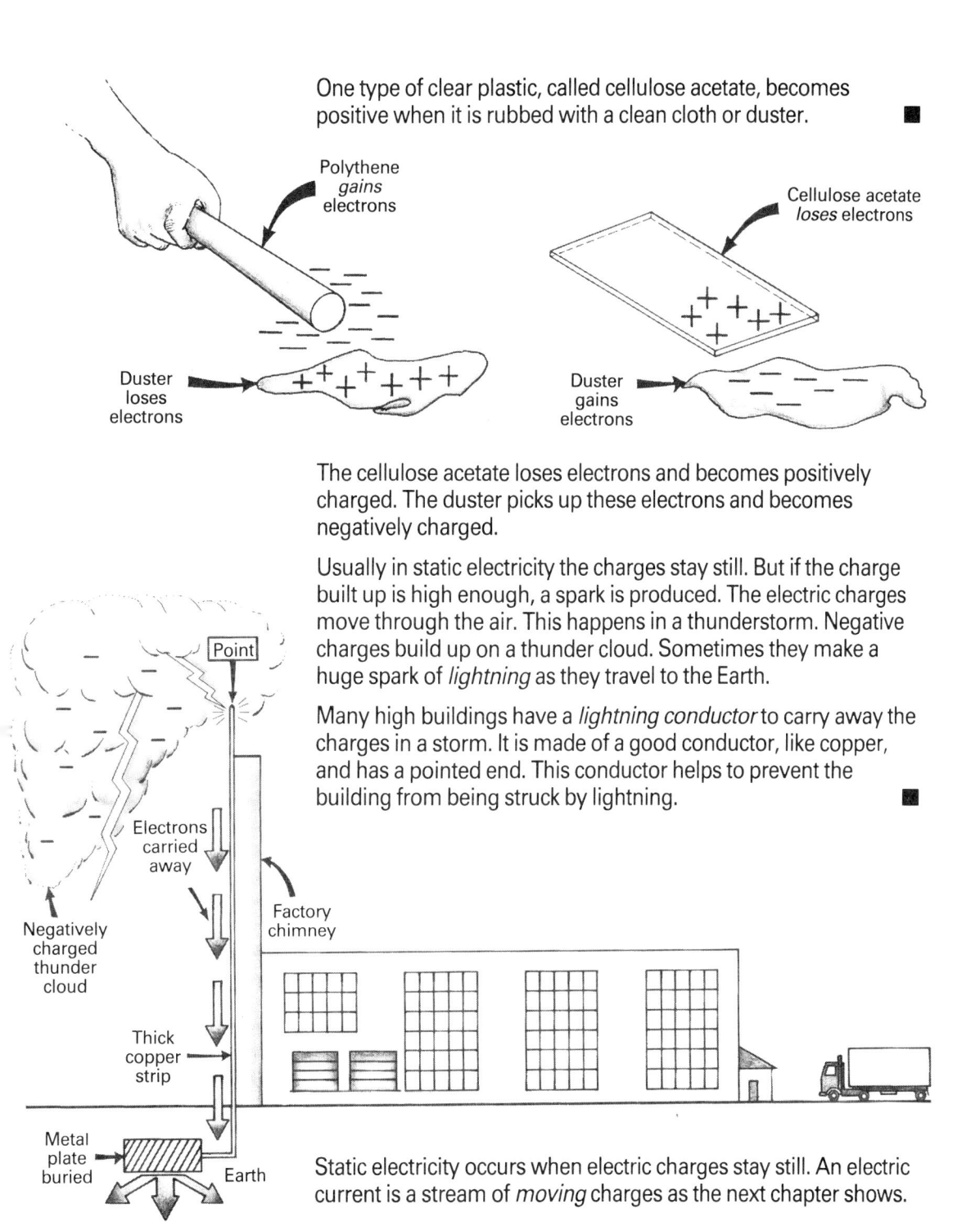

One type of clear plastic, called cellulose acetate, becomes positive when it is rubbed with a clean cloth or duster.

The cellulose acetate loses electrons and becomes positively charged. The duster picks up these electrons and becomes negatively charged.

Usually in static electricity the charges stay still. But if the charge built up is high enough, a spark is produced. The electric charges move through the air. This happens in a thunderstorm. Negative charges build up on a thunder cloud. Sometimes they make a huge spark of *lightning* as they travel to the Earth.

Many high buildings have a *lightning conductor* to carry away the charges in a storm. It is made of a good conductor, like copper, and has a pointed end. This conductor helps to prevent the building from being struck by lightning.

Static electricity occurs when electric charges stay still. An electric current is a stream of *moving* charges as the next chapter shows.

Questions 22

1. Fill in the missing words:

   'A dry cell produces ___ volts. Dry cells can be used in ___ and ___. Two or more cells joined together form a ___. A lead-acid cell produces about ___ volts. It uses two ___ plates dipping into a solution of ___ acid. The acid level should be topped up using ___ ___. All cells change ___ energy into ___ energy.'

2. This diagram shows a type of cell used widely in torches, radios, etc.

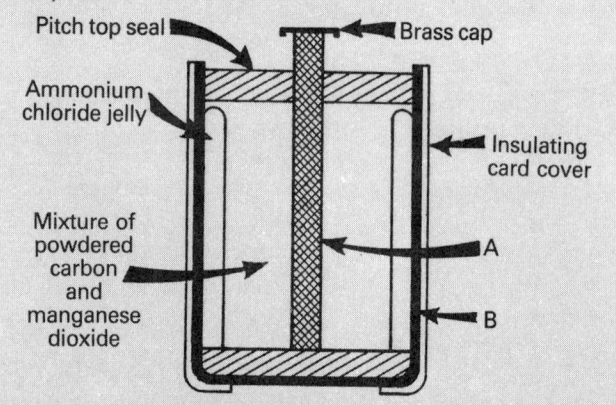

   (a) What is the name given to this type of cell?
   (b) What is the rod A made of?
   (c) What is the outer case B made of?
   (d) Which part of the cell is the *negative* electrode?
   (e) State two advantages a lead-acid accumulator has over this cell. (EMREB)

3. What is *static electricity?* What kinds of material collect static electricity?

4. A polythene rod can be electrically charged by rubbing it with a woollen duster.
   (a) What type of charge will the polythene rod have?
   (b) What name is given to the type of material which does not allow electrical charges to pass through it?
   (c) What name is given to the type of material which does allow charges to pass through it?
   (d) Which of the above two types is polythene? (EMREB)

5. (a) Why is a lead-acid accumulator used in a car battery and not a dry Leclanché cell?
   (b) Give two advantages that lead-acid cells have over dry cells.
   (c) Give one advantage that the dry cell has over the lead-acid cell.

6. In terms of *electrons* describe why a piece of polythene becomes charged when it is rubbed with a duster.

Chapter 23

Electric circuits

What is electricity?

Most people know what electricity is used for, how it is made, and how it is carried. But what is an electric current?

An electric current is a stream of tiny moving particles, called *electrons,* which can travel in a wire. All substances are made up of atoms, and all atoms contain electrons. In certain metals, especially copper and silver, some electrons are *free* from their atoms and are able to travel along the metal. Materials like these are called *conductors*.

A force is needed to push these electrons along a conductor. This is called an *electro-motive force,* e.m.f. for short. This e.m.f. can come from a cell or a battery. Electrons carry a *negative* charge. So they are always pushed away from the negative side of a battery and attracted towards the positive side.

Electric currents must always travel on a complete path or *circuit*. If the circuit is broken the current stops.

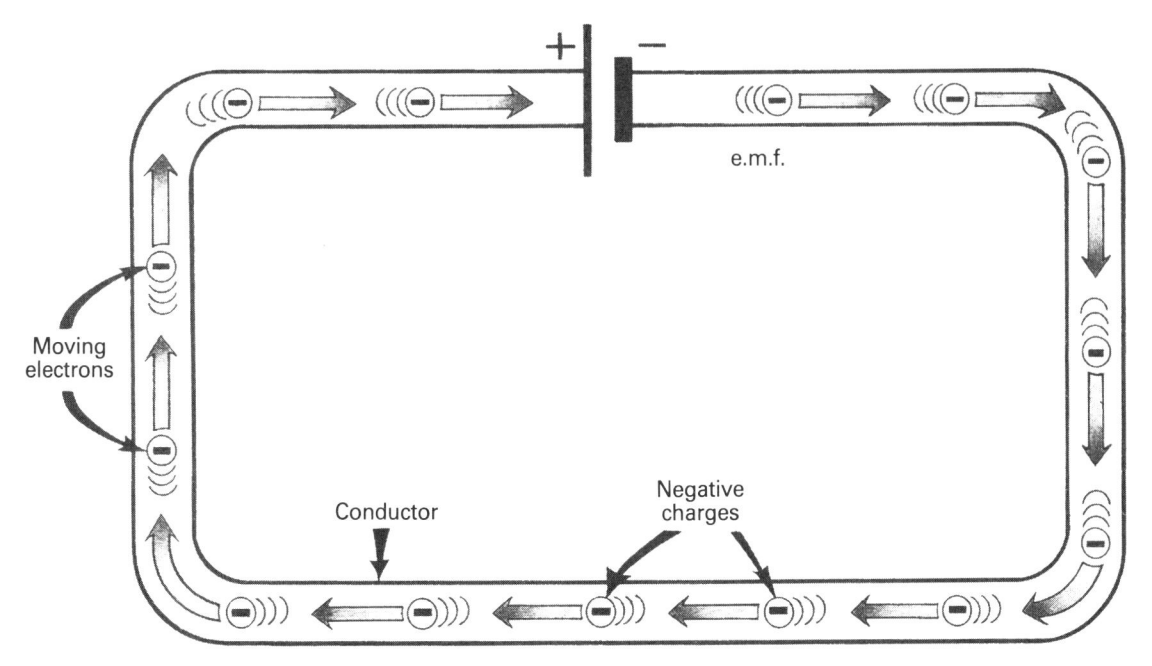

Circuit diagrams

Every electric circuit needs two things: an electro-motive force to drive the current, e.g. from a cell, battery or a dynamo; and something to carry the current in a complete circuit.

An electric circuit can be broken using a switch. This is the *symbol* for a switch: ―――/―•―

Here are some simple electric circuits, with different symbols.

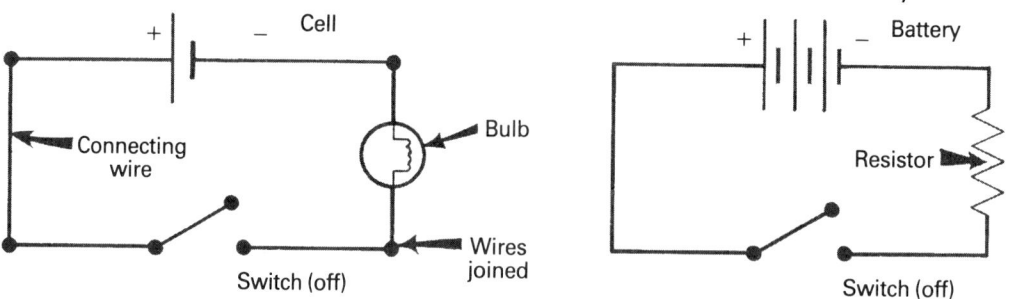

Scientists have agreed that the *direction* of the current will always be drawn travelling from + to −. This is called the *conventional current* (the word 'convention' means 'agreement'). In fact the electrons travel in the opposite direction.

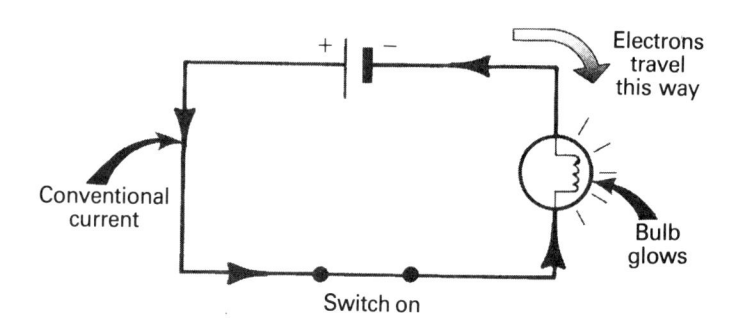

A resistor is a wire or any other material that carries a current, but offers *resistance* to it. A long, thin wire has a higher resistance than a short, thick wire. The more resistance a circuit has the less current it will carry. By increasing or decreasing the resistance in a circuit the current can be changed. This is done by using a variable resistor, called a *rheostat*.

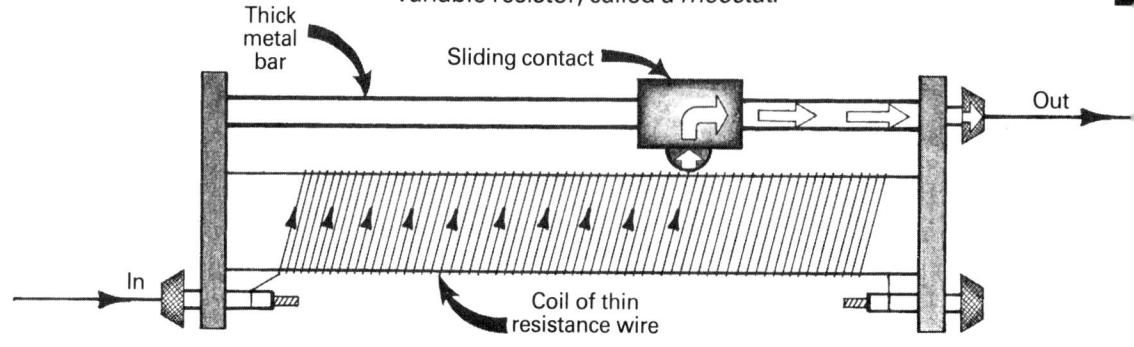

The rheostat changes the length of wire that the current has to travel through. Rheostats are used in *dimmer switches* to control the brightness of a light.

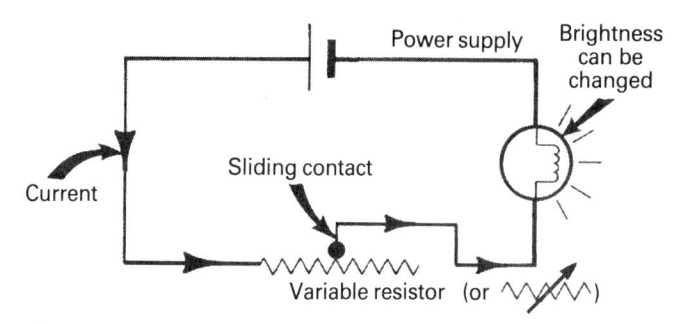

They are also used for volume controls on radios, TVs, record players, and so on.

Series and parallel

Parts of an electric circuit can be connected in two different ways called *series* and *parallel*.

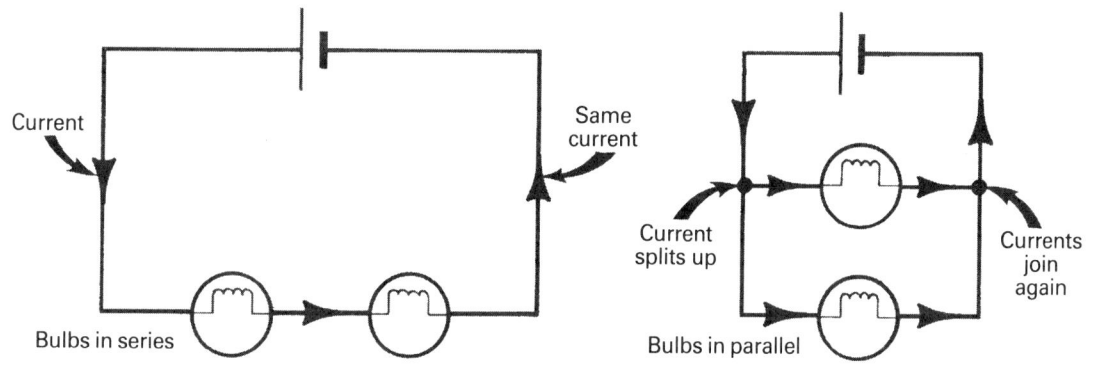

In series both bulbs carry the same current. In parallel the current splits up. If both bulbs are exactly the same, half the current goes through one bulb and half through the other. But if one bulb has *less resistance* than the other it carries more current. If two bulbs are connected in series and one bulb breaks, the circuit is broken and the other one goes off. In parallel, if one breaks the other bulb is still part of a circuit and so it stays on. Christmas-tree lights are sometimes connected in parallel so that if one bulb breaks the other bulbs stay on.

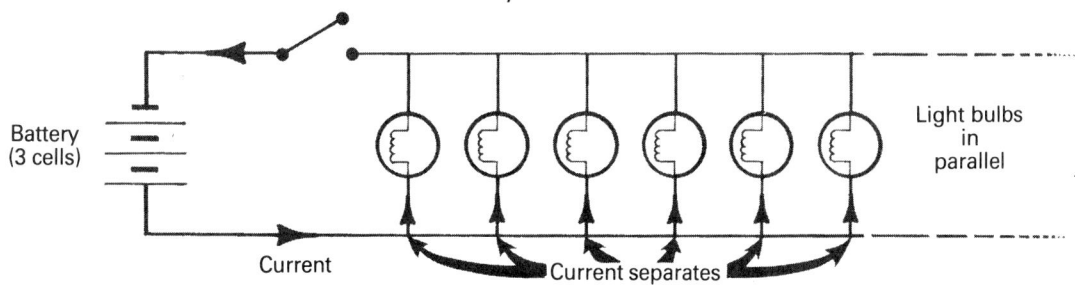

Measuring electricity

The electro-motive force of a circuit is measured in *volts* (V in short).

The current flowing in a circuit is measured in amperes. Amperes are often called *amps* and can be abbreviated to A.

The resistance of a circuit is measured in *ohms*. Ohms are sometimes written as Ω, which is a capital Greek letter (called an omega).

Electricity is measured with three main types of meters: *galvanometers, voltmeters* and *ammeters.* Galvanometers are much too sensitive for ordinary use. They must be changed, or 'protected', to measure larger currents and voltages.

(a) *Voltmeter.* This is a galvanometer with a high resistance connected to it, so that it cannot carry a large current. Voltmeters are always connected in *parallel* in a circuit. They measure the voltage across certain parts of a circuit, like a resistor or a bulb. ∎

The voltage is called the *potential difference* across the resistor, bulb, cell or other part of a circuit. This potential difference, p.d. for short, is measured in volts.

(b) *Ammeter.* This is a galvanometer connected to a *shunt.* The shunt has a low resistance and carries most of the current itself so that the galvanometer is protected. Ammeters are always connected in *series* so that they measure the current flowing round the circuit. ∎

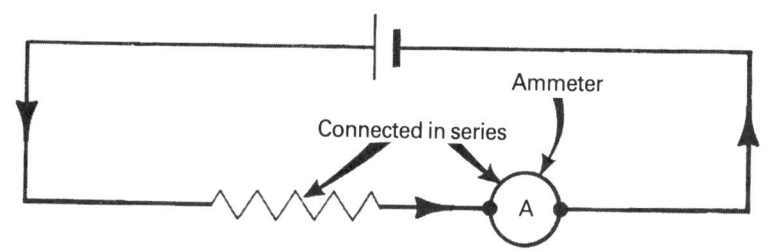

An ammeter will give the same reading at any part of a simple series circuit. ∎

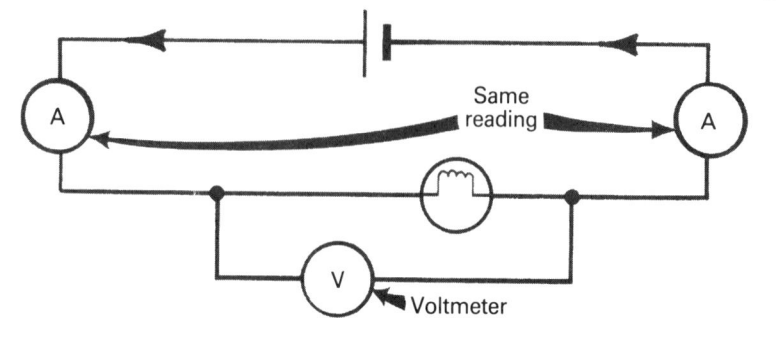

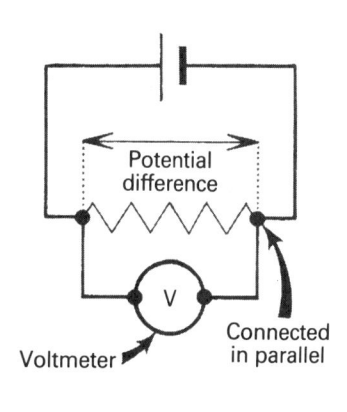

Ohm's Law

In 1826 a German scientist called Georg Ohm discovered an important rule: as the voltage across a conductor is increased the electric current running through it increases in *proportion.* If the voltage is doubled the current doubles, if the voltage is trebled the current is trebled, and so on. This rule applies as long as the conductor's temperature stays the same. It is called *Ohm's Law*.

The voltage, current and resistance of an electric circuit are connected by a simple formula:

$$\frac{\text{Voltage}}{\text{Current}} = \text{Resistance}$$

The three quantities can be placed in a triangle.

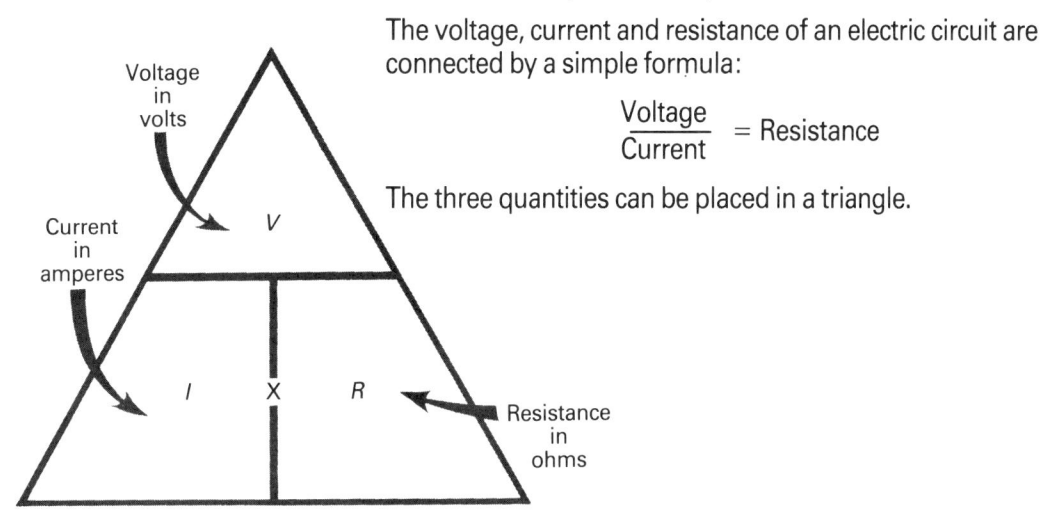

For example, if voltage = 6V, current = 2A,

then resistance = 6/2 = 3 ohms.

This formula is very useful in electric circuits.

Resistors in series and parallel

Resistors can be connected in either series or parallel. If two resistors are connected in series their total resistance increases. To find the total resistance just add the two separate resistances.

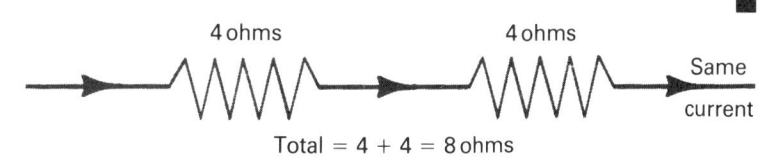

Total = 4 + 4 = 8 ohms

In parallel the total resistance gets less.

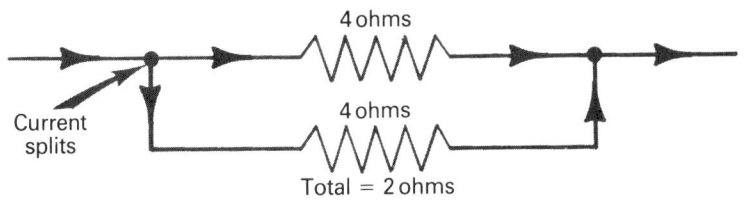

Total = 2 ohms

Two resistances of 4 ohms make a total resistance of 2 ohms when they are joined in parallel. It is like joining two thin wires to make one thicker wire.

149

Ohm's Law can still be used when a circuit has two or more resistances. The total resistance must be found and then the formula can be used. In parallel the same rule is used.

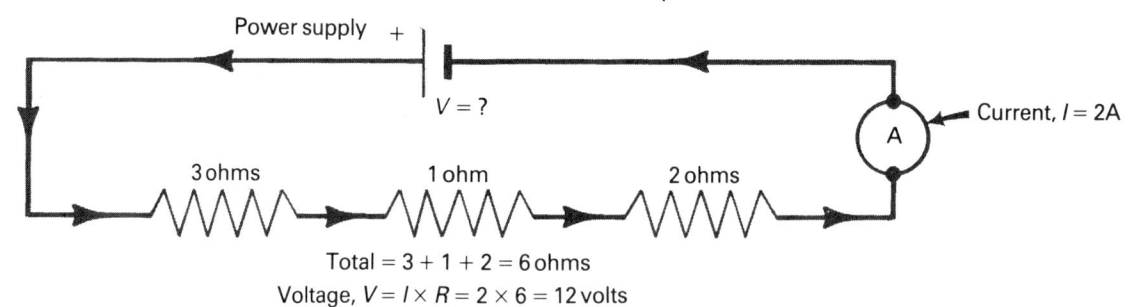

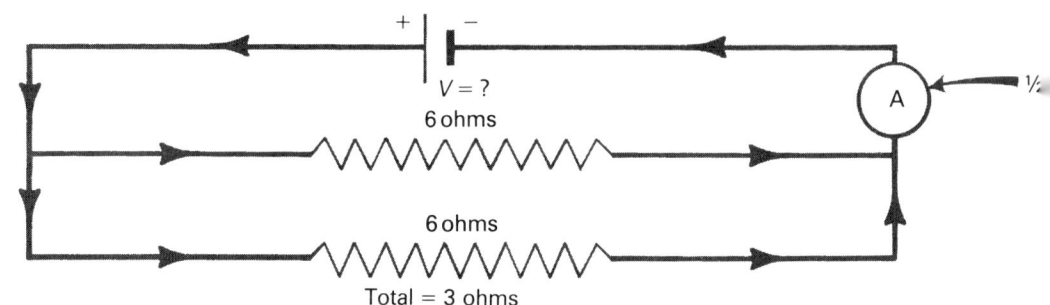

Total = 3 + 1 + 2 = 6 ohms
Voltage, $V = I \times R = 2 \times 6 = 12$ volts

Total = 3 ohms
Voltage, $V = I \times R = \frac{1}{2} \times 3 = 1\frac{1}{2}$ V

Power

Power is measured in *watts* (W) or *kilowatts* (kW). 1000 W = 1 kW. The power of an electric circuit or instrument measures how much electrical energy it uses up every second. If 100 J of energy are used every second, the power is 100 W; 1000 J/s is 1 kW and so on.

A simple formula can be used to find the power in watts of a circuit or instrument:

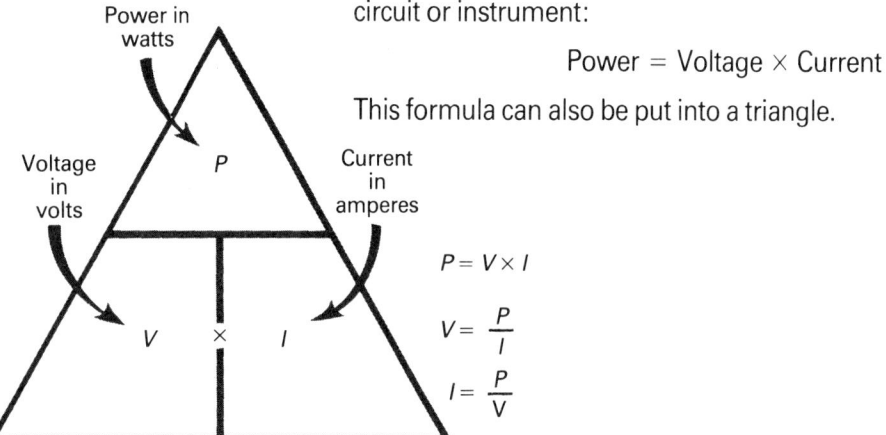

$$\text{Power} = \text{Voltage} \times \text{Current}$$

This formula can also be put into a triangle.

$P = V \times I$

$V = \frac{P}{I}$

$I = \frac{P}{V}$

For example, if a current of 3 A is used by a heater at 240 V,

Power of the heater = $V \times I = 240 \times 3 = 720$ W

(There will be more on power in Chapter 26.)

Questions 23

1. What is an electric current?
2. Write down three materials which carry electrons and three which do not (insulators).
3. Draw a table with e.m.f., current, resistance and power showing what unit each one is measured in and what it means.
4. Draw an electric circuit containing a cell, a bulb, a switch and a rheostat. What is the rheostat used for?
5. Draw a circuit diagram showing two bulbs in series, and then two bulbs in parallel. Which type of connection is best for Christmas-tree lights?
6. (a) What are the names of the three meters used for measuring electricity?
   (b) What does each one measure?
   (c) Draw a diagram to show how two of the meters are connected to a resistor in an electric circuit.
   (d) How can these meters be used to find the *resistance* of a resistor?
7. (a) What is the name of component P in this diagram?
   (b) What might it be used for in the circuit?
   (c) With the switch closed, the ammeter reads 1.5 A and the voltmeter reads 6 V. What value does this give for the resistance of device Q?
   (d) What is device Q?
   (e) With the switch closed, what is the effect, if any, on the ammeter reading if the ammeter is placed between the switch and battery?   (EMREB)
8. Use the triangle containing V (voltage), I (current) and R (resistance) to find the missing quantity:
   (a) $V = 6$ volts, $R = 2$ ohms, $I = ?$
   (b) $V = 50$ volts, $I = 5$ amps, $R = ?$
   (c) $I = 3$ amps, $R = 10$ ohms, $V = ?$
   (d) $V = 240$ volts, $R = 80$ ohms, $I = ?$
9. An electric kettle works at 240 volts. Its resistance is 30 ohms. What current does it carry? What is the power of the kettle? How many joules of energy does it use in one minute?

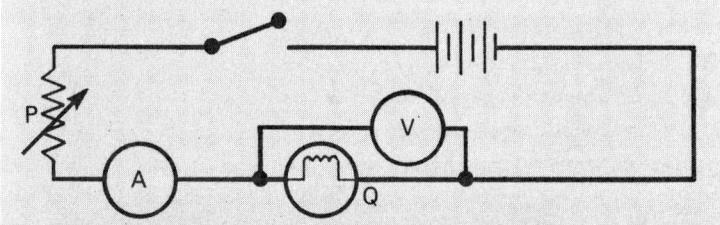

10. (a) The diagram below shows three 3 W lamps connected in parallel to a battery. Each of the ammeters A_1, A_2 and A_3 reads 0.5 ampere.

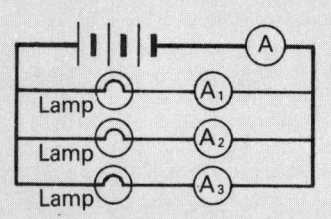

    (i) What is the reading on the ammeter A?
    (ii) How many joules of energy are converted by one of the lamps in 5 seconds?
    (iii) What would happen to the brightness of the other two lamps if one of the lamps burned out?

(b) Three lamps are placed in series with a battery as shown in the diagram below.

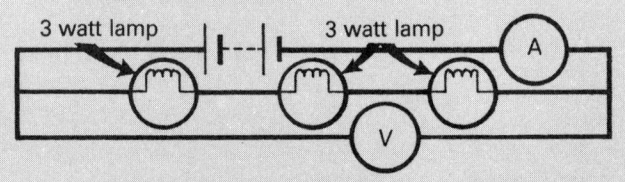

    (i) What would happen to the other lamps if one lamp burned out?
    (ii) If the ammeter reading is 1.5 A, what is the voltmeter reading?

(c) The diagram shows part of the lighting circuit for one room using two 60 W lamps.

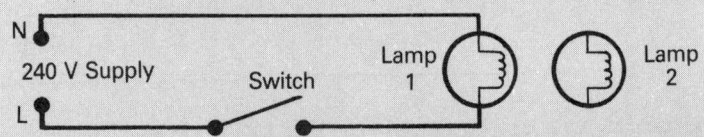

    (i) By drawing lines on the diagram join lamp (2) to lamp (1) so that both are on at the same time at equal brightness.
    (ii) Mark with an X on the diagram the place where you would include a fuse in the circuit.*
    (iii) Give a reason for using a fuse in the circuit.
    (iv) Calculate the current flowing when both lamps are switched on.
    (v) What will be the current in the circuit if one of the lamps burns out?
    (vi) What will be the voltage across the bulb that is still working?
    (vii) What will be the voltage across the bulb which has burnt out?
    (LREB)

11. Use the triangle connecting power, voltage and current to find the missing quantity:
    (a) $V = 60\,V$, $I = 2\,A$, Power = ?
    (b) $V = 240\,V$, $I = 4\,A$, Power = ?
    (c) Power = 2000 watts, $I = 8\,A$, voltage = ?
    (d) Power = 4 kW, $I = 16\,A$, voltage = ?
    (e) Power = 60 watts, voltage = 240 V, current = ?

12. In an experiment to measure the resistance of a wire the following apparatus is used:

    a battery, an ammeter, a voltmeter, a switch, the wire under test and connecting wires.
    (a) Draw a circuit diagram to show how the apparatus would be set up.
    (b) If, when the switch is closed, the voltmeter reading is observed to be 6 V and the ammeter reading is 0.5 A, write down the resistance of the wire.
    (c) If another identical resistance wire is added in series with the above wire, what would the resistance of the combination be?
    (d) What then would be the ammeter reading?   (LREB)

13. The diagram below shows a simple electric circuit.

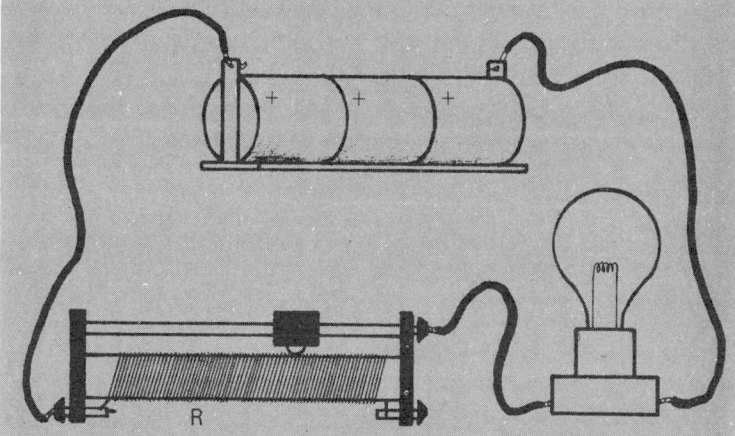

    (a) What is the name of the instrument labelled R?
    (b) What can it be used for? Explain briefly how it works.
    (c) Draw a *circuit diagram* of the electric circuit above including an *ammeter* in the circuit. Use the correct *symbols* for each part of the circuit i.e. battery, lamp, ammeter etc.
    (d) What is the ammeter used for? Is it connected in series or parallel? Why?
    (e) Now add a voltmeter to your circuit diagram (using the correct symbol) so that it can measure the potential difference across the lamp. How is this connected?

* Fuses are described on p. 170.

Chapter 24

Magnetism

■■■■■■■■■■■■■■
Making magnets

The first magnets were made over 2000 years ago from a type of rock called *lodestone.* Nowadays we usually think of a magnet as a piece of steel which attracts other steel or iron objects towards it, and also points North when it is allowed to swing. ■

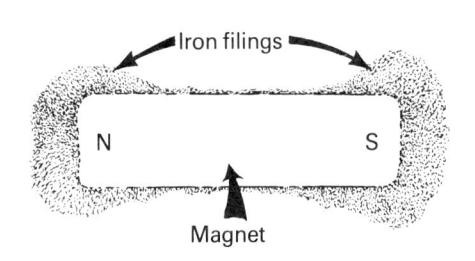

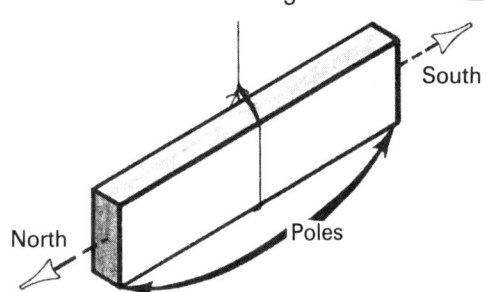

The ends of a magnet are called its North and South poles. When the pole of one magnet is close to the pole of another they either *attract* each other or push each other apart. ■

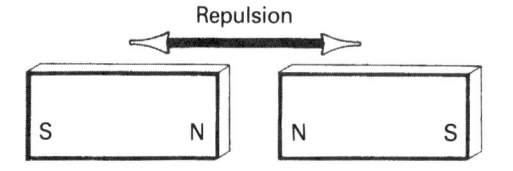

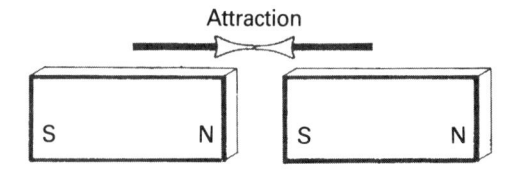

A good way of making a magnet is to wrap a long coil of wire, called a *solenoid,* around an iron or steel bar and pass a direct current through the coil. ■

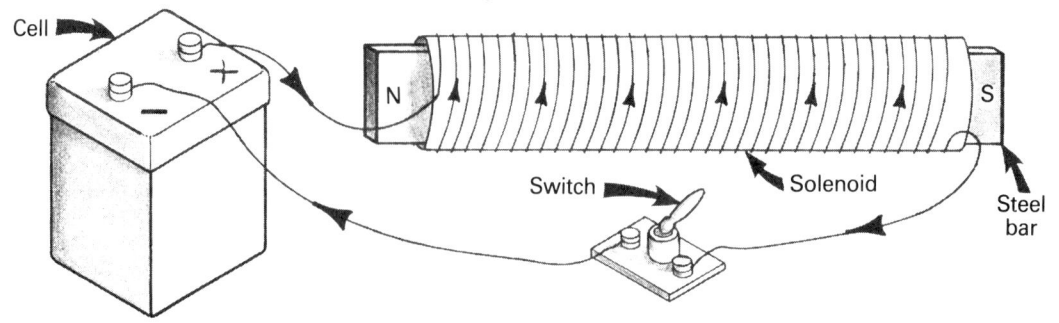

154

With a steel bar a *permanent* magnet is made. When the current is switched off the bar is still magnetic, and keeps its magnetism well. But a soft iron bar loses its magnetism as soon as the current is switched off (soft iron is best for *temporary* magnets).

Another way of making a permanent magnet is by 'stroking' a steel bar, or even a steel knitting-needle, with a strong magnet. After the steel has been stroked it becomes a magnet itself with its own North and South poles.

Wide circle

Magnet

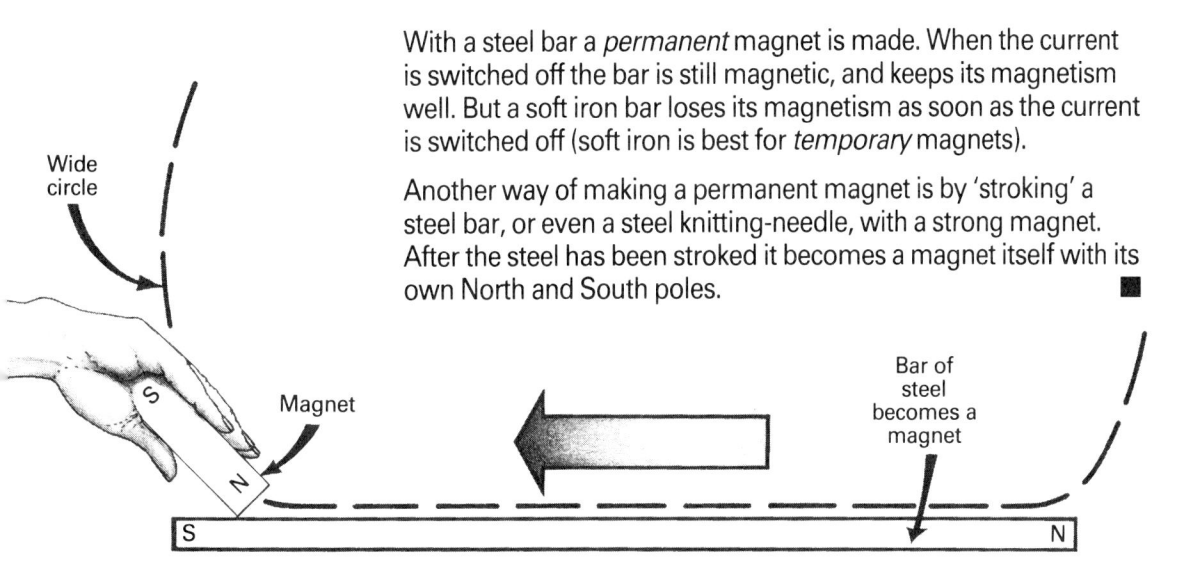

Bar of steel becomes a magnet

Once a magnet has been made from a piece of steel it keeps its magnetism well unless it is dropped or hammered, or heated up to 'red heat'. The magnet is then *de-magnetised*.

Magnetic fields

Every magnet is surrounded by a *magnetic field*. This is the name given to the region around a magnet where its magnetic force acts. The field around a bar magnet has a special shape which can be drawn by using a small compass needle. The compass needle always points along the lines of the magnetic field, and so the field can be drawn on paper.

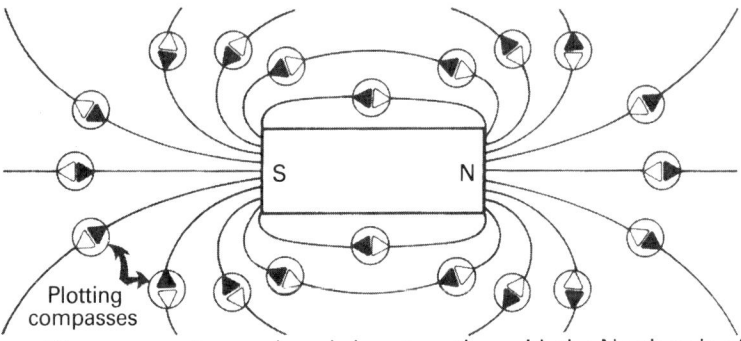

Plotting compasses

If two magnets are placed close together with the North pole of one facing the South pole of the other, the magnetic field lines join. The lines are always drawn pointing North to South.

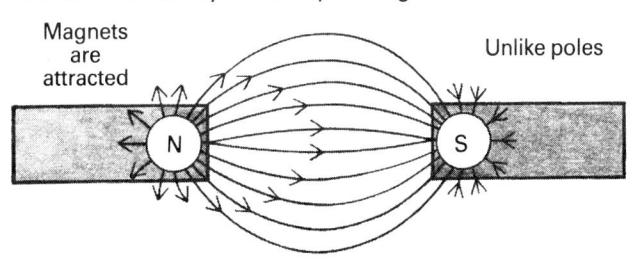

Magnets are attracted

Unlike poles

When the North poles of the two magnets face each other the magnets repel and the lines of the two fields never meet. Between the two magnets there is one point where the two magnetic fields cancel each other out. This is called a *neutral point*. At this point there is no magnetic force. ■

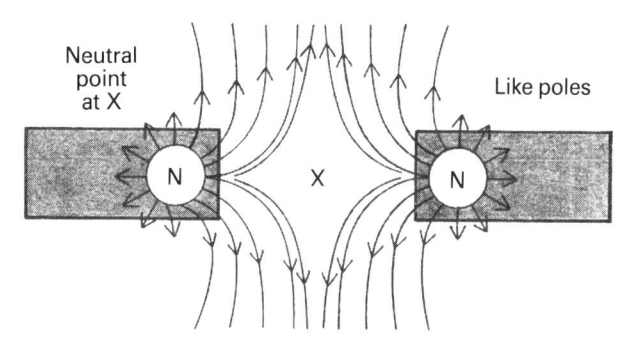

The shape of magnetic fields can also be seen by using tiny pieces of iron called 'iron filings'. The magnet is placed under a piece of paper and iron filings are shaken on to it. The filings follow the lines of the field when the paper is tapped gently. ■

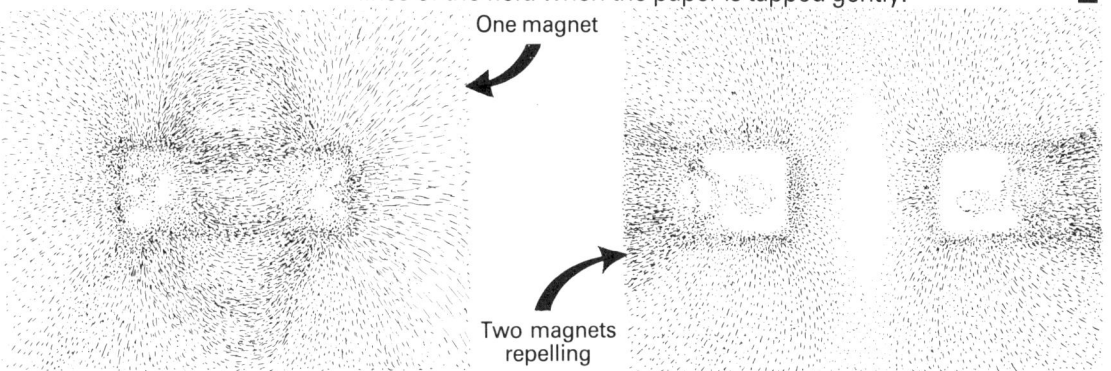

The Earth's magnetic field

Men have known for centuries that a magnetic needle always points North when it is free to swing. Nowadays we know that the Earth itself behaves like an enormous magnet. Imagine that there is a huge magnet in the middle of the Earth. The *magnetic* North pole of this magnet points towards the geographic South pole. ■

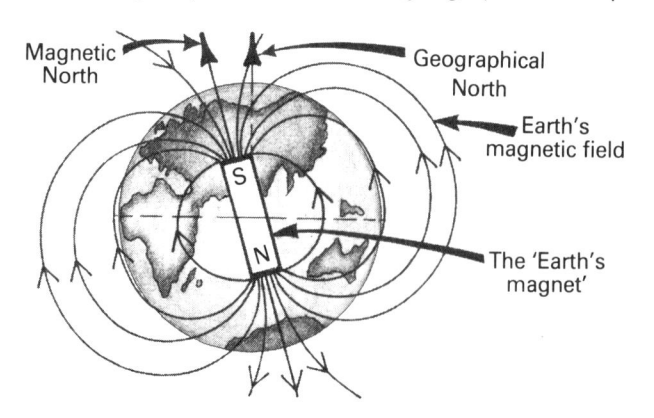

The Earth's *magnetic* South pole actually points towards the *geographic* North pole. The North pole of a compass needle always follows the Earth's magnetic field, and is drawn towards the Earth's magnetic South pole, or geographic North.

At most places on the Earth a compass needle does not point exactly towards true North. There is usually a small angle between *magnetic North* and *geographic North.* This angle is called the *declination.* In Britain the angle is about 7°.

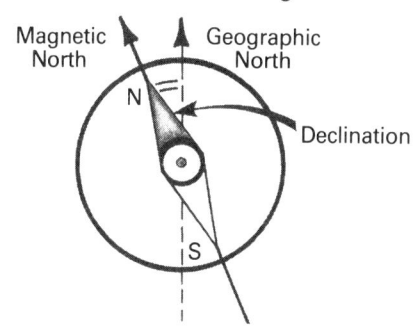

The Earth's magnetism is still a mystery to scientists, since we know that the centre of the Earth is extremely hot and red heat destroys magnetism. If we imagine that somehow there is a large magnet at the centre of the Earth we can explain why a compass needle *dips* when it is allowed to swing either up or down.

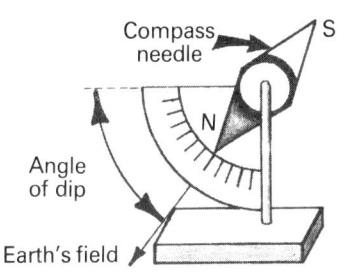

In Britain a compass needle dips by about 65°. This is called the *angle of dip.* At the magnetic North Pole the needle points directly downwards — the angle of dip at the two Poles is 90°. Finally, at the magnetic equator a compass needle does not dip at all because the Earth's magnetic field there is horizontal — the angle of dip is zero.

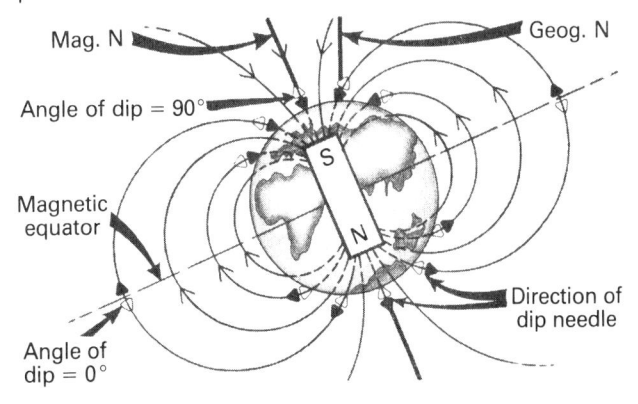

157

What is magnetism?

When a magnet is brought close to a piece of steel, a pin for example, we know that the pin itself becomes a magnet and is pulled towards it.

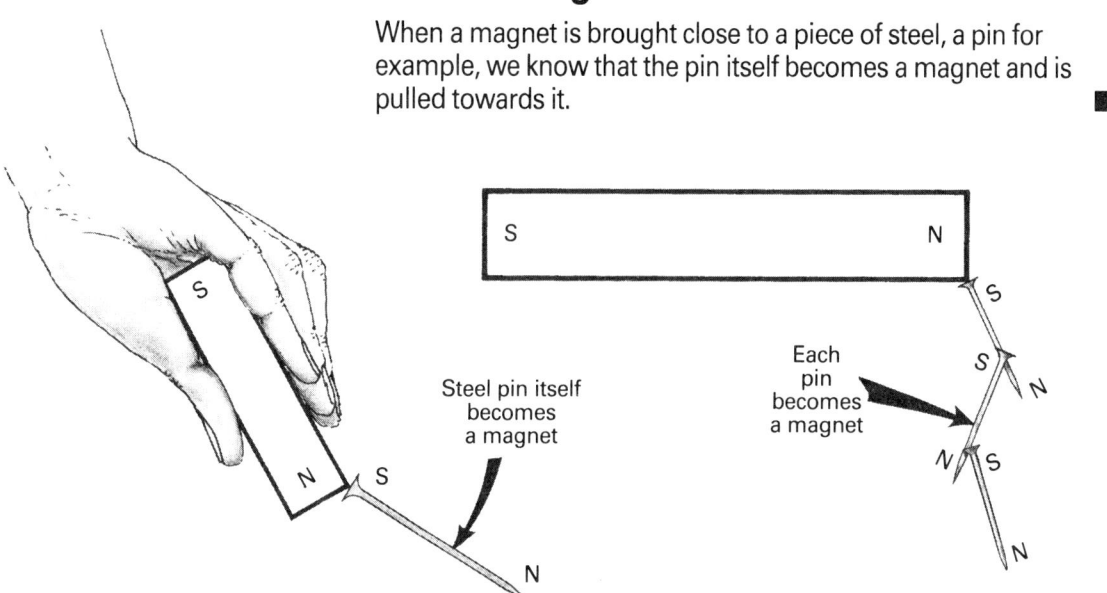

Steel pin itself becomes a magnet

Each pin becomes a magnet

This still does not tell us what magnetism is. One theory which scientists have, says that iron and steel contain tiny magnetised regions called *domains*. When a steel bar is de-magnetised all the domains point in different directions. But when the bar is magnetised, say by stroking it with another magnet, all the domains are pulled into the same direction. They all point the same way.

Domains point in *every* direction

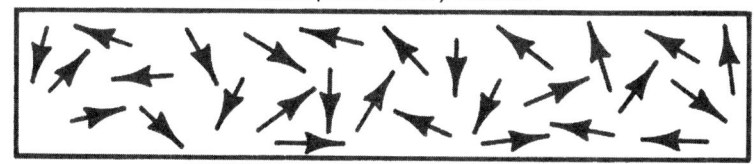

Demagnetised

Domains point in *one* direction

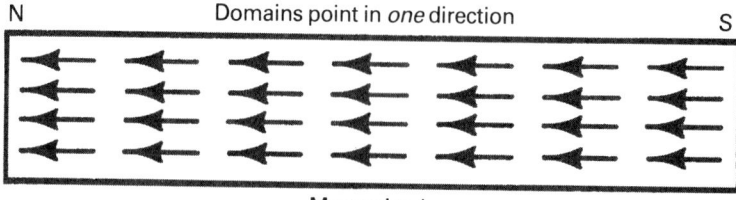

Magnetised

If the bar is heated the domains are 'shaken up' and point in different directions again. The bar is then de-magnetised. This is called *the domain theory of magnetism*. But it still does not tell us what magnetism really is.

Questions 24

1. Describe two ways of making a magnet from a piece of iron or steel. Which material is best for permanent magnets?
2. How can a magnet lose its magnetism?
3. Draw a sketch of the magnetic field between two magnets when the North pole of one faces the South pole of the other.
4. The diagram represents part of a magnetic field.

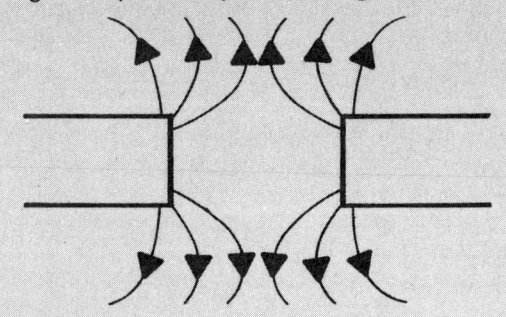

    (a) What are the lines with arrows called?
    (b) What do the arrows show?
    (c) Mark on the diagram with an N or an S any magnetic poles which may be present.
    (c) Mark with a cross a neutral point in the magnetic field.
    (YREB)
5. This diagram shows a permanent magnet being used to magnetise a steel rod.

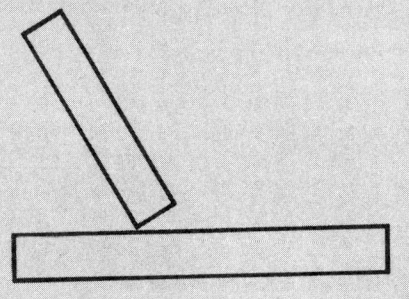

    (a) Label the magnet and the rod.
    (b) Draw arrows on the diagram to show the direction of any movement that takes place.
    (c) Label the magnetic poles on both the magnet and the rod.
6. (a) Describe how the Earth's magnetic field can be helpful in navigation.
   (b) What is meant by the angle of dip of a compass needle? What is the angle of dip in Britain? What is the angle of dip at the Equator?

7. Describe what happens when a magnet attracts a steel pin.
8. What is meant by the *domain theory of magnetism?*
9. (a) The diagram shows a magnet supporting a row of *iron* tacks.

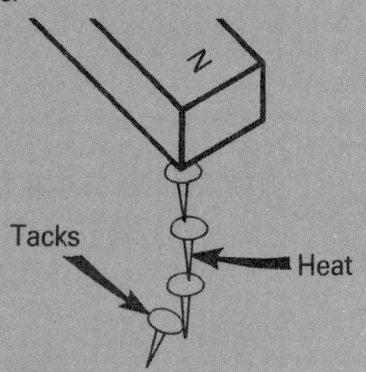

    (i) Describe what happens when the middle tack is heated.
    (ii) Why does this happen?
   (b) Two identical, cylindrical magnets are held as shown in the diagram.

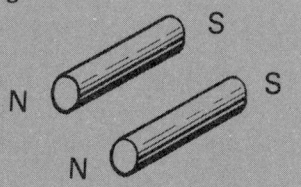

    (i) What happens when they are released?
    (ii) Why does this happen? (YREB)
10. The drawing below shows two permanent magnets suspended by threads.

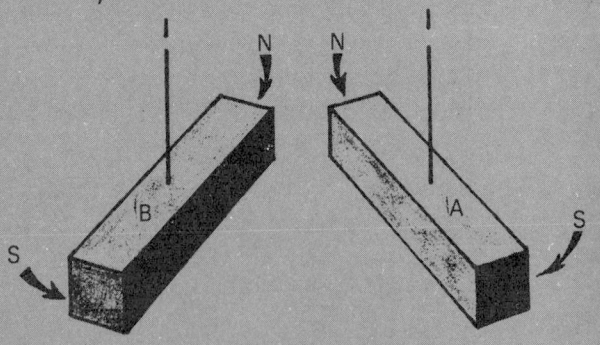

    (a) What do the letters N and S stand for?
    (b) What will happen if magnet A is brought closer to B? Explain why.
    (c) Suppose the other end of B is brought nearer to magnet A. What will happen? Why?
    (d) What are 'permanent magnets'?

Chapter 25

Electricity and magnetism

In this chapter you will see how a magnet can be made from electricity, and also that electricity can be made by using a magnet.

Electromagnets

A simple electromagnet can be made by winding copper wire around a large nail.

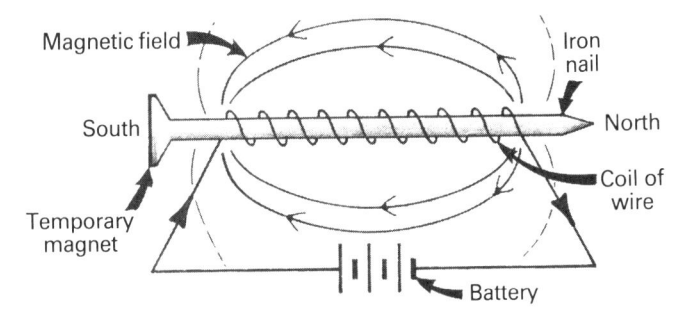

When electricity flows through the wire the nail becomes a magnet. It will attract small iron and steel objects, and even has a magnetic field around it like any bar magnet.

Electromagnets are *temporary* magnets. When the current stops they are no longer a magnet. They can be made in all shapes and sizes, and have very many uses: in the telephone, the electric bell, in a loud-speaker, or for lifting heavy iron objects in a scrap-yard.

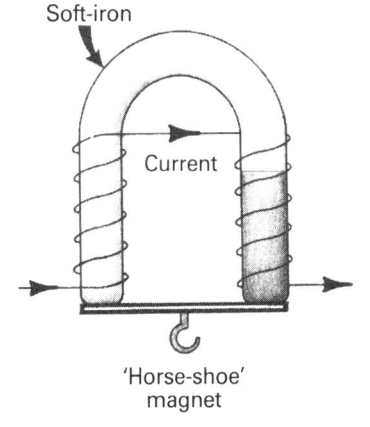

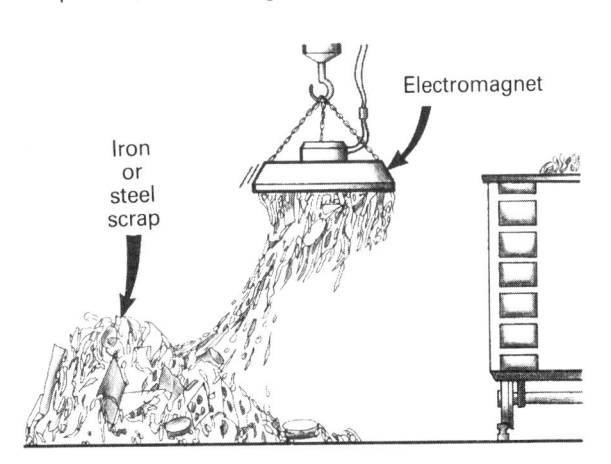

Making electricity with a magnet

When a magnet is moved in and out of a coil of wire an electric current is made. This current can be seen on a sensitive meter called a *galvanometer*. As the magnet is pushed into the coil the needle on the meter moves one way. When the magnet is removed the needle moves the other way.

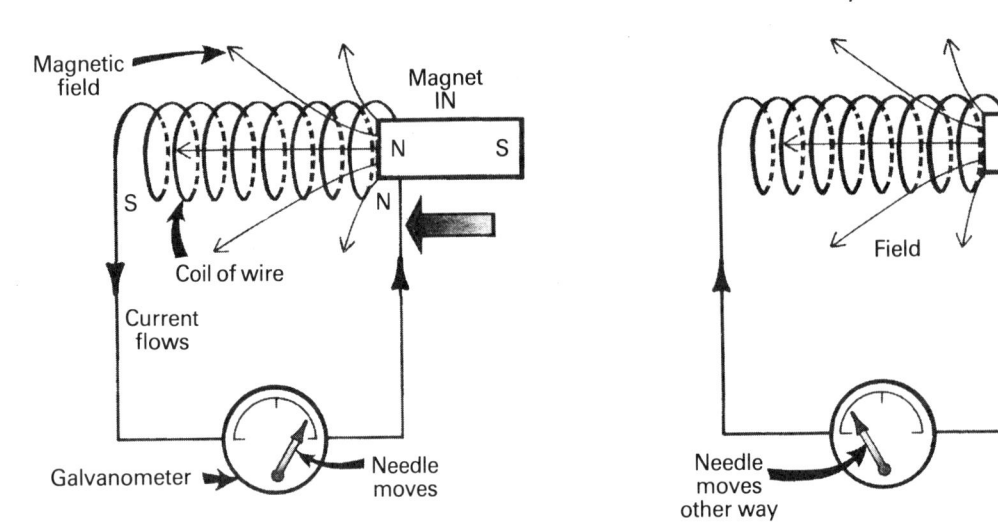

Whenever a magnet is moved near a wire in a circuit an electric current is produced. This is called *electromagnetic induction*.

Dynamos

Electricity can also be made by moving a coil of wire near a magnet which stays still. This is done in a *dynamo*. A coil of wire is held between the two poles of a magnet. When the coil spins an electric current is generated.

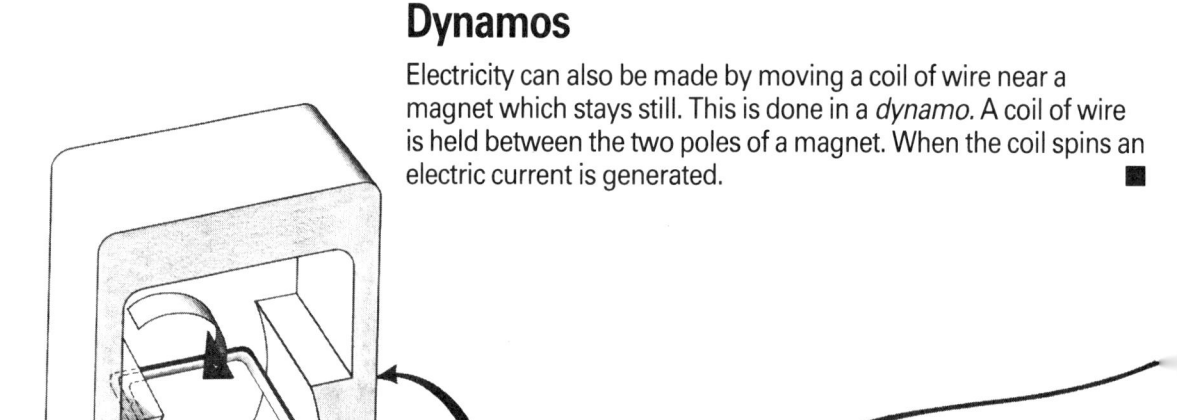

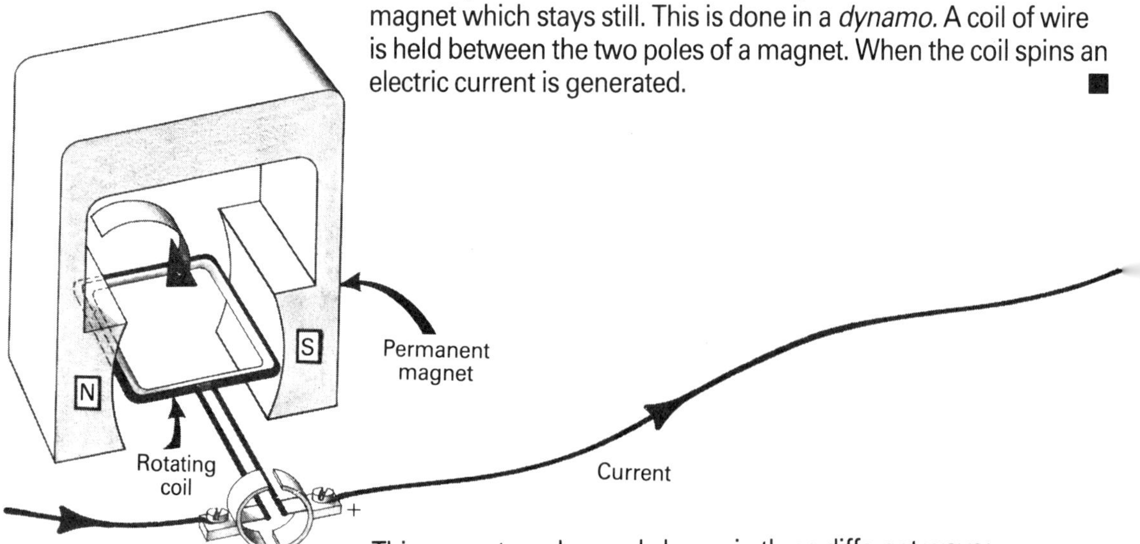

This current can be made larger in three different ways:
(a) by spinning the coil faster,
(b) by using a stronger magnet,
(c) by using a larger coil, with more wire on it.

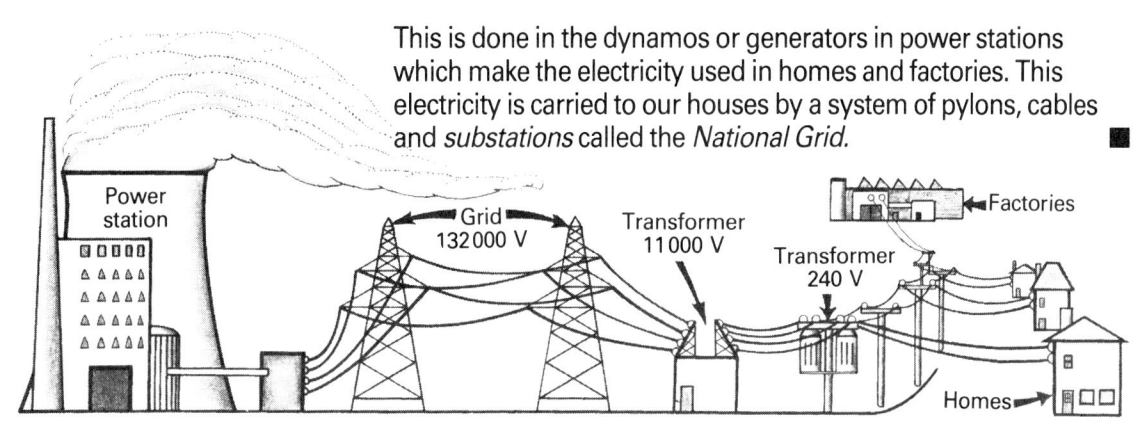

This is done in the dynamos or generators in power stations which make the electricity used in homes and factories. This electricity is carried to our houses by a system of pylons, cables and *substations* called the *National Grid*.

Every power station needs a supply of energy: there are coal, oil, nuclear and hydro-electric power stations. This energy provides the *work* needed to make the coil spin inside the magnet. The work done on the coil is changed to *electrical energy*.

Electric motors

Whenever a wire carries an electric current inside a magnetic field a *force* acts on it. This is sometimes called the *motor force*. The wire is 'catapulted' out of the magnetic field.

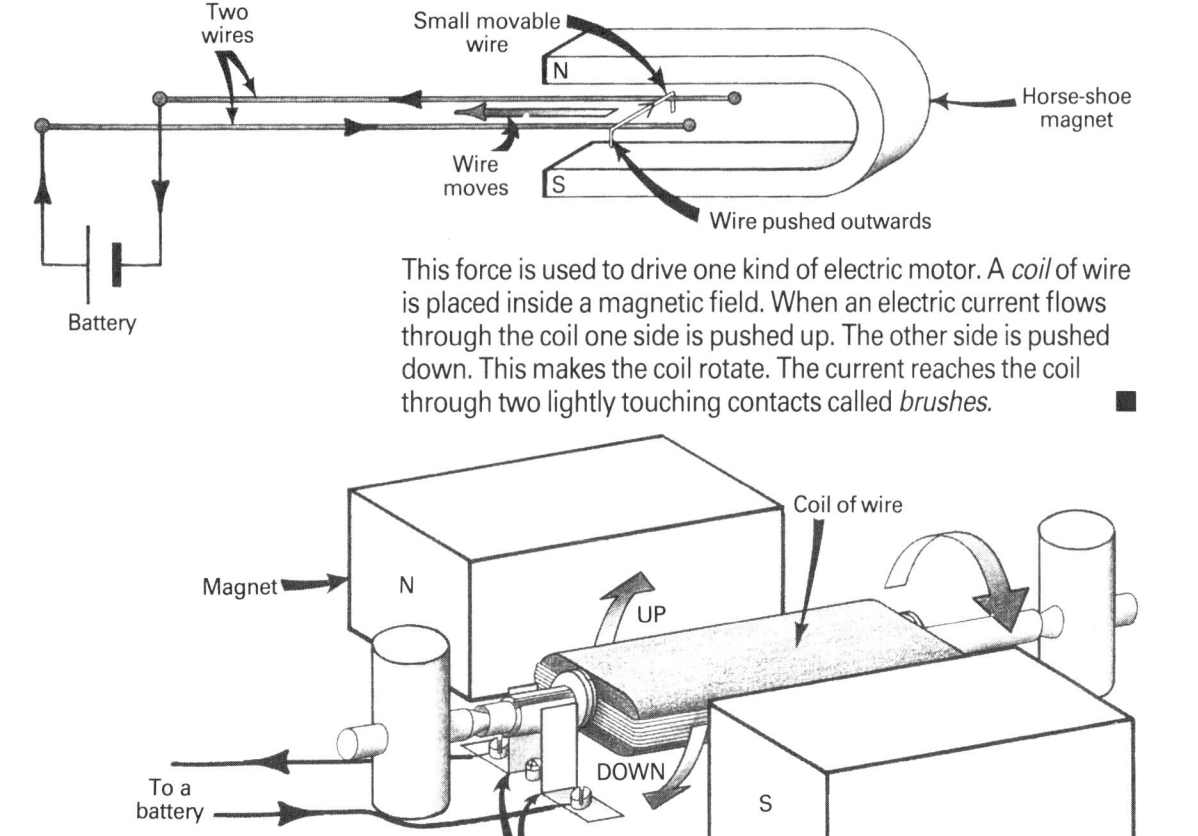

This force is used to drive one kind of electric motor. A *coil* of wire is placed inside a magnetic field. When an electric current flows through the coil one side is pushed up. The other side is pushed down. This makes the coil rotate. The current reaches the coil through two lightly touching contacts called *brushes*.

Electric motors are used to do many useful jobs of work: in vacuum cleaners, washing machines, drills, trains, lifts, milk floats, and so on. In a way the motor does the opposite to a dynamo, although they both use a coil inside a magnetic field. A motor uses electrical energy to do work — work has to be done on a dynamo to make electrical energy.

Current meters

Current meters also use the 'motor force'. A meter can be made by placing a coil of wire, wrapped round a soft iron 'core', between the poles of a magnet. The coil is attached to a spring. When a current travels in the coil it turns and moves a pointer that is attached to it. The larger the current, the more the coil turns.

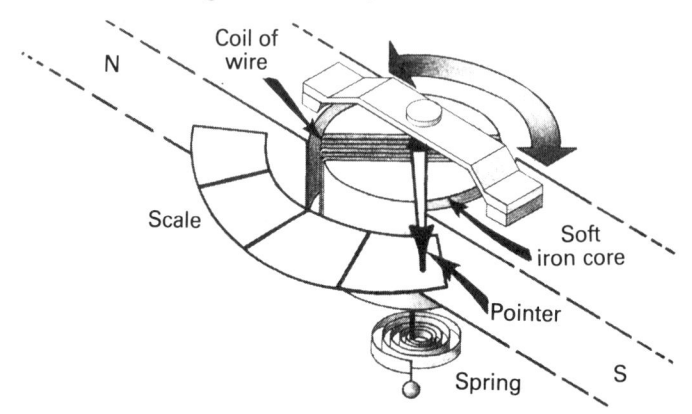

Very sensitive *moving-coil* meters are called *galvanometers.* These can be made into either ammeters or voltmeters (see Chapter 23).

AC and DC

There are two kinds of electric current: *alternating current* (a.c.) and *direct current* (d.c.). An alternating current flows first in one direction and then the other. A direct current flows in one direction only.

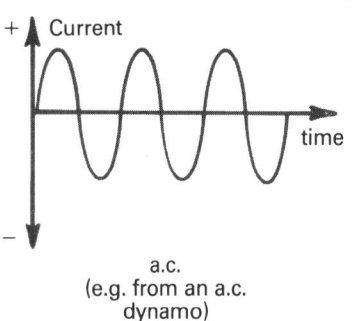

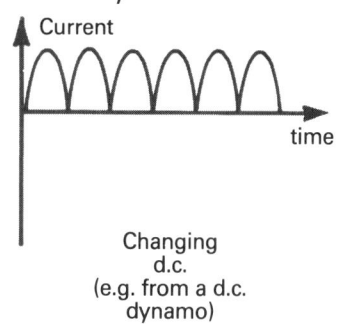

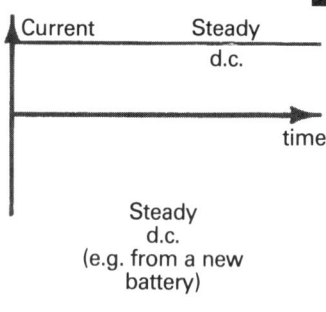

a.c. (e.g. from an a.c. dynamo)

Changing d.c. (e.g. from a d.c. dynamo)

Steady d.c. (e.g. from a new battery)

The mains electricity we use is a.c. — it changes direction 100 times every second. The current from a battery is *direct* — it always travels in the same direction.

Dynamos can be made to produce either a.c. or d.c.

Questions 25

1. Fill in the blanks:

   'When a ____ is moved into a coil of wire it makes an electric ____, which can be detected by a ____. This is called electro-magnetic ____. In a ____, a coil of wire spins between two poles of a magnet. The faster the coil spins the ____ the electric current produced.'

2. What are the main parts of a dynamo? Describe three ways of changing a dynamo to make it generate a larger current.

3. This diagram shows an electromagnet.

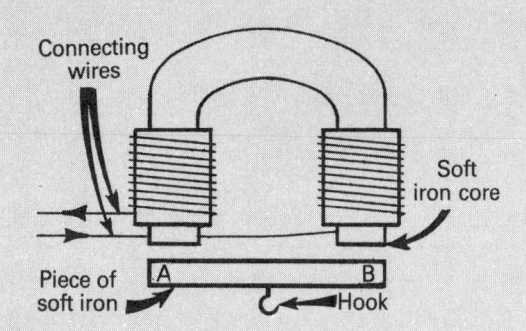

   (a) (i) Show, at the right-hand side, the circuit to which it must be connected in order to make the electromagnet work. The circuit should contain a cell, a switch and a variable resistance (in order to vary the current).

   (ii) When no current passes through the electromagnet, would the piece of soft iron, AB, be attracted? Give a reason.

   (iii) With the circuit connected and a small current flowing, the maximum weight which can be supported on the hook is 10 newtons. Give two alterations each of which could be made in order to make the electromagnet stronger.

   (iv) What difference would it make to the electromagnet if the coil were wound on a wooden core instead of a soft iron one?

   (b) (i) If the electromagnet were wound on a steel core and the current were switched on, would AB still be attracted?

   (ii) What would happen if the current were then switched off again?

   (iii) Give two reasons why the core of an electromagnet is usually soft iron. (LREB)

4. Name three instruments or machines that use electric motors. In what ways is an electric motor very much like a dynamo. How are they different?

5. What are the two types of electric current? Explain how they are different.

6. (a) The diagram shows the shape of the magnetic field around a pair of bar magnets.

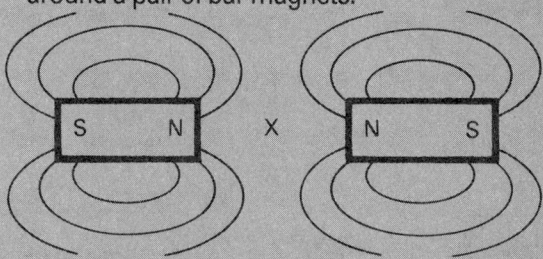

   (i) On the diagram, by means of arrows, show the directions of two separate lines of force.
   (ii) What is point X called?
   (iii) Is the force between the two bar magnets when arranged as shown in the diagram attractive or repulsive?

   (b) (i) Name the material from which permanent magnets are made.
   (ii) Name a material which is suitable for use as the core of an electromagnet.
   (iii) Give a reason for your answer to (b)(ii).
   (EMREB)

7. An electromagnet is made by winding a coil of wire on a soft iron rod.

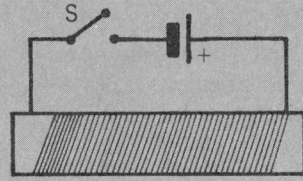

   (a) When a current flows in the coil, what happens to the soft iron rod?
   (b) Why is hard steel not suitable for the *core* of the electromagnet?

8. The diagram below shows an electro-magnetic relay, which is a type of switch using an electromagnet.

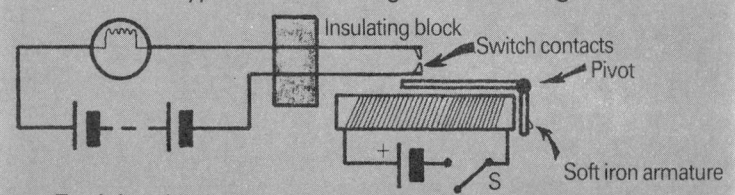

   Explain why the lamp lights when the switch S is closed.
   (Reproduced from LEAG GCSE Physics specimen paper 2)

Chapter 26

Using electrical energy

Electrical energy is probably the most useful form of energy because it can easily be changed into other forms, e.g. heat energy, light energy, kinetic or sound energy. The uses of electricity depend on three *effects* of an electric current: the heating effect, the magnetic effect and the chemical effect.

Heating and lighting

When an electric current flows through a *resistance* wire, heat is produced. A coil of wire inside an electric fire, kettle, iron or cooker which heats up when a current travels through it is called a *heating element.*

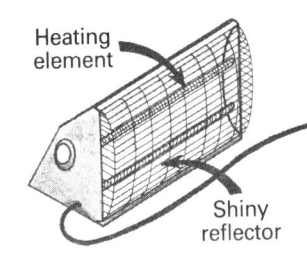

An electric iron has a heating element which can be switched on or off by a bi-metallic strip, or thermostat. The thermostat can be altered by a control knob — this can be set to switch the element off at a certain temperature.

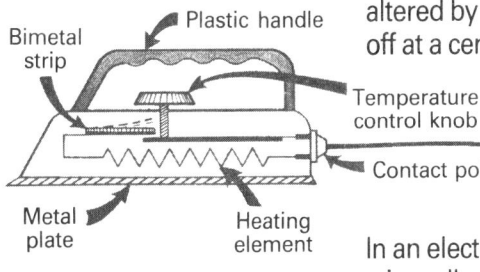

In an electric light bulb, electric current flows through a very thin wire called a *filament*. This filament is made of tungsten, which becomes 'white hot' and glows to produce light and heat energy. Light bulbs are filled with a special gas called argon, which stops the filament from burning as it would do in air.

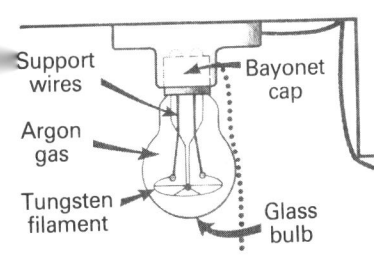

Light energy can also be made in a fluorescent lamp or tube, when electric current travels through a gas.

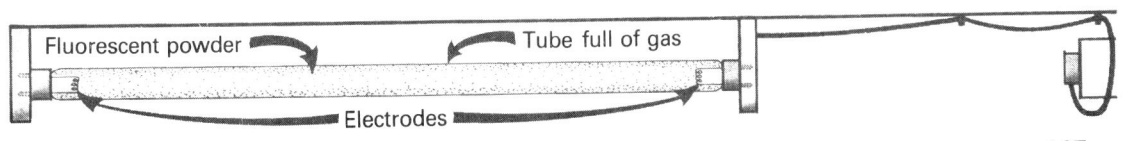

Magnetic effect of an electric current

You saw in Chapter 25 that a coil of wire with an iron bar inside it becomes an electromagnet when it carries an electric current. This is an example of the *magnetic effect*. It was discovered in Denmark by Hans Oersted in 1820.

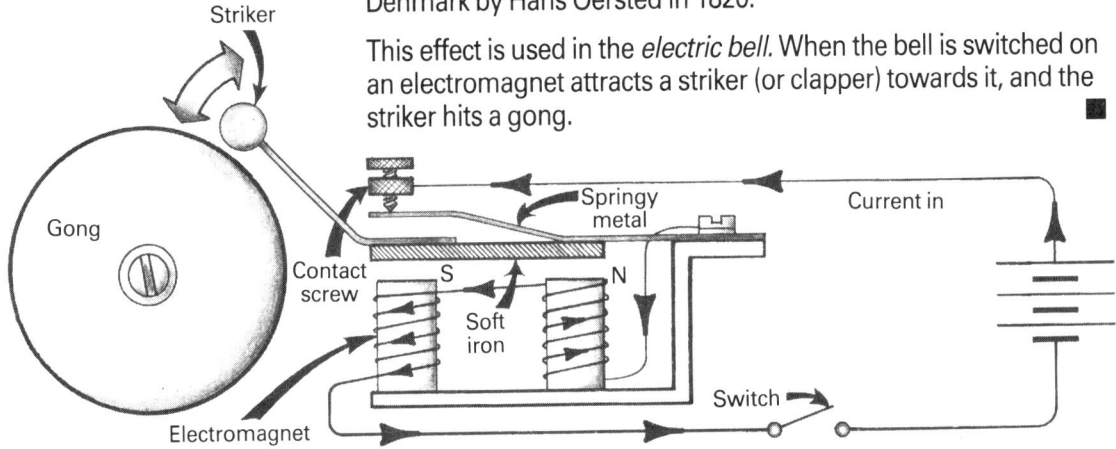

This effect is used in the *electric bell*. When the bell is switched on an electromagnet attracts a striker (or clapper) towards it, and the striker hits a gong.

As the striker moves across, the contact with a special screw is broken and the current is switched off. The electromagnet loses its magnetism. Then the striker springs back, makes contact with the screw again and the current is switched on. The current makes an electromagnet again, the striker is pulled across, and the whole process is repeated. This happens many times every second, and so the bell rings.

Electromagnets are used in telephone earpieces and loudspeakers, as well as the bell. They all change electrical energy into *sound energy*.

Electricity in chemicals

The third effect of electricity is the *chemical effect*. Certain liquids such as salt solution (salt dissolved in water) or acid solution will carry an electric current when two metal plates, or electrodes, are dipped into them. The current goes in through the positive electrode (the *anode*), travels through the liquid, and leaves through the negative electrode (the *cathode*). A liquid which carries electricity is usually called an *electrolyte*.

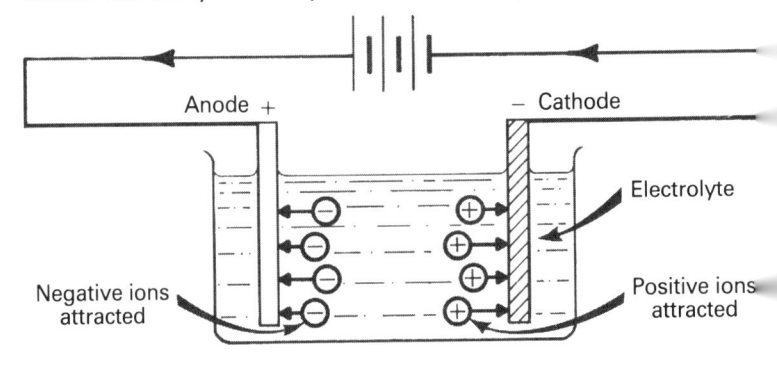

Sometimes a liquid can be split up, or separated, into different chemicals when electricity travels through it. This 'splitting up' of a liquid is called *electrolysis.*

When electricity travels through water with a little sulphuric acid in it, the water is split into *hydrogen* and *oxygen.* Hydrogen gas collects above the cathode, oxygen gas collects over the anode. This is a useful way of making hydrogen and oxygen.

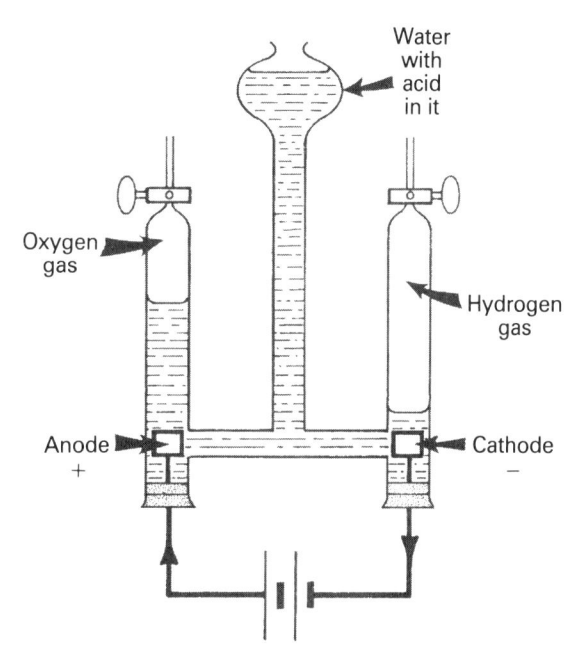

Another use for electrolysis is in *electro-plating,* e.g. copper plating, zinc plating, silver plating, chrome plating, and so on. A spoon can be copper plated by putting it inside a solution of copper sulphate (blue crystals). The spoon is connected to the *negative* terminal of a battery. Gradually, a thin layer of copper covers the spoon as more and more electric current travels through the copper sulphate solution.

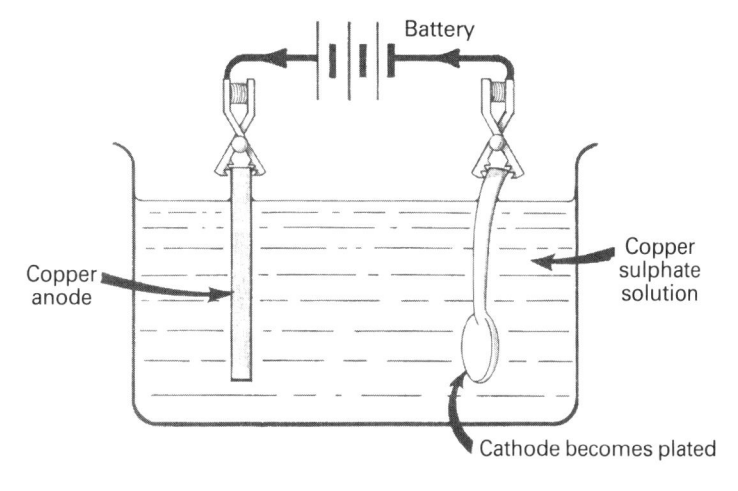

Using electricity at home

The 'mains' electricity you use at home has a voltage of 240 V. This makes it dangerous. There are two main dangers from electricity: *shock* and *fire.* There are two ways of making it safer: fuses and earth wires.

(a) *Fuses.* A fuse is made from a thin piece of wire which can only carry a certain current, e.g. 3 amps, 5 amps, 13 amps and so on. If the current goes above this limit the wire melts or 'blows'. ■

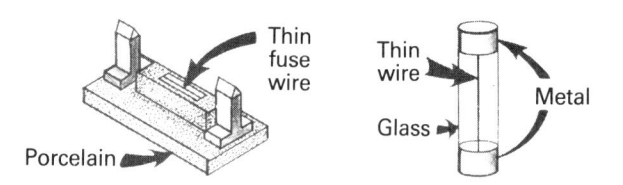

(The word 'fuse' means 'melt'.) The fuse is part of the electric circuit — if it melts the current is switched off before the rest of the wires can overheat and catch fire.

The 'fuse box' is usually placed where the mains electricity enters the house. Each of the electric circuits in the house is protected by a fuse inside this box. The electric sockets in a house are usually arranged in a ring which starts, and ends, at this fuse box. Each socket on the ring has three connections: *live, neutral* and *earth.* ■

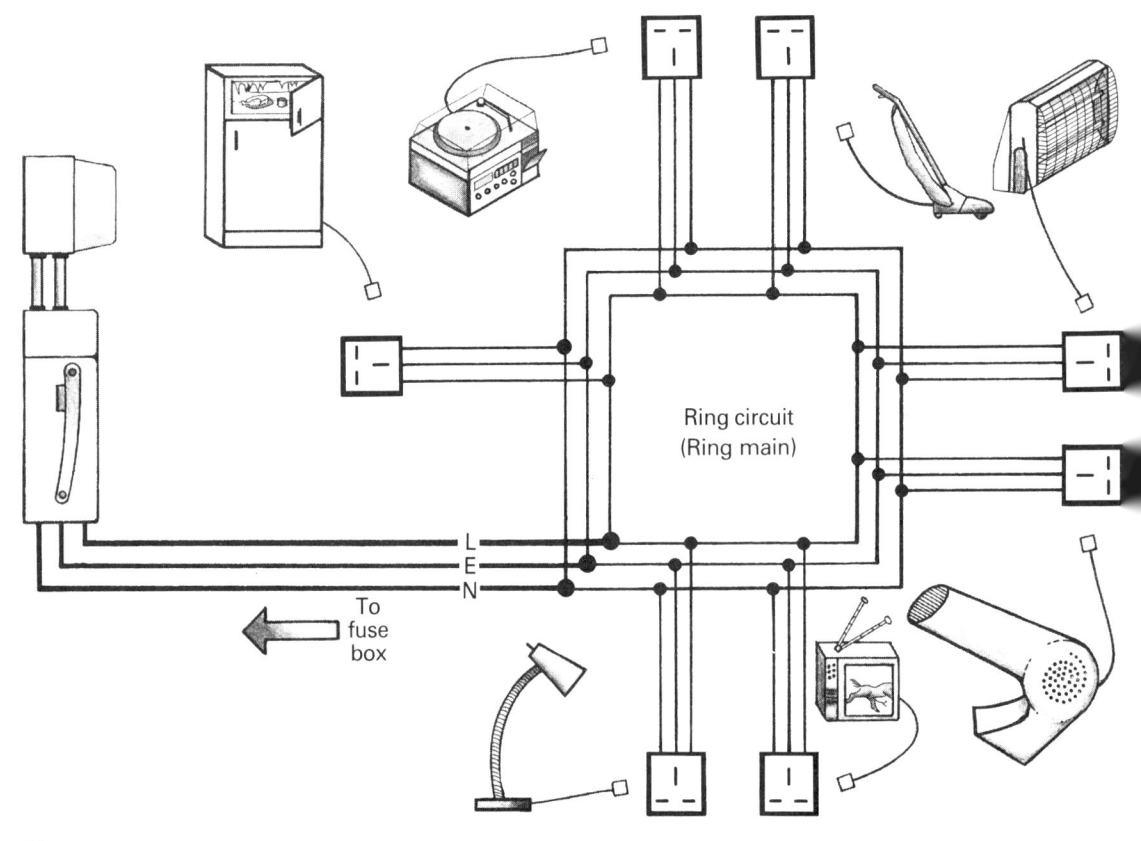

The plugs that go into these sockets also have three connections. Electric cables have a different coloured wire for each one. ■

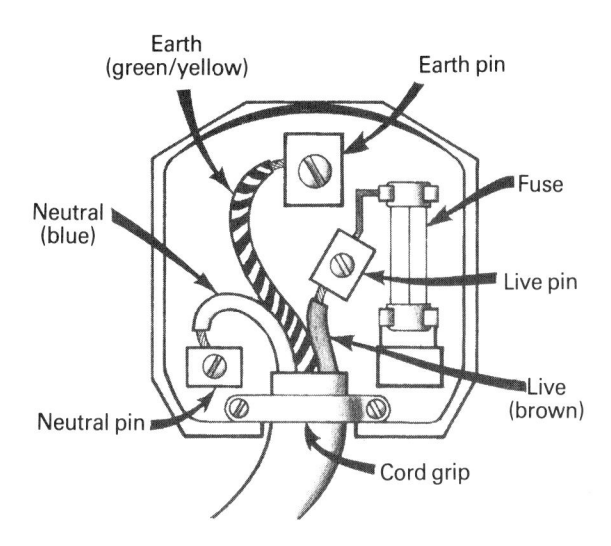

Every plug has its own fuse, always thinner than the one in the fuse box. Two sizes are commonly used: ■

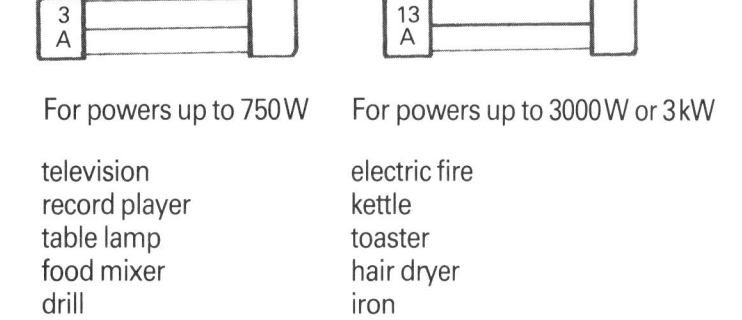

For powers up to 750 W

television
record player
table lamp
food mixer
drill

For powers up to 3000 W or 3 kW

electric fire
kettle
toaster
hair dryer
iron

Nowadays some houses use *circuit-breakers* instead of fuses. These are made from a spring loaded switch on an electromagnet. If the current rises too high the electromagnet becomes strong enough to open the switch. This breaks or 'trips' the circuit. If a fuse has 'blown' or a circuit-breaker has 'tripped' it is important to find the fault and put it right before trying to switch on again.

(b) *Earth wires.* The job of the earth wire is to protect you against electric shock. This wire is usually connected to a metal plate buried in the earth. Suppose you are using a device with a metal case, an electric kettle for example. If the kettle was damaged and the live wire touched this case it would become 'live' and dangerous. The kettle should be 'earthed' by connecting the metal case to the earth wire. Current then flows safely to earth instead of through you. This current should blow the fuse and switch the kettle off.

Paying for electricity

Different electrical appliances use different amounts of electricity. The amount of electrical energy used depends on their *power*. An iron with a power of 750 W uses 750 J of electrical energy every second — a 60 W light bulb uses 60 J of energy every second.

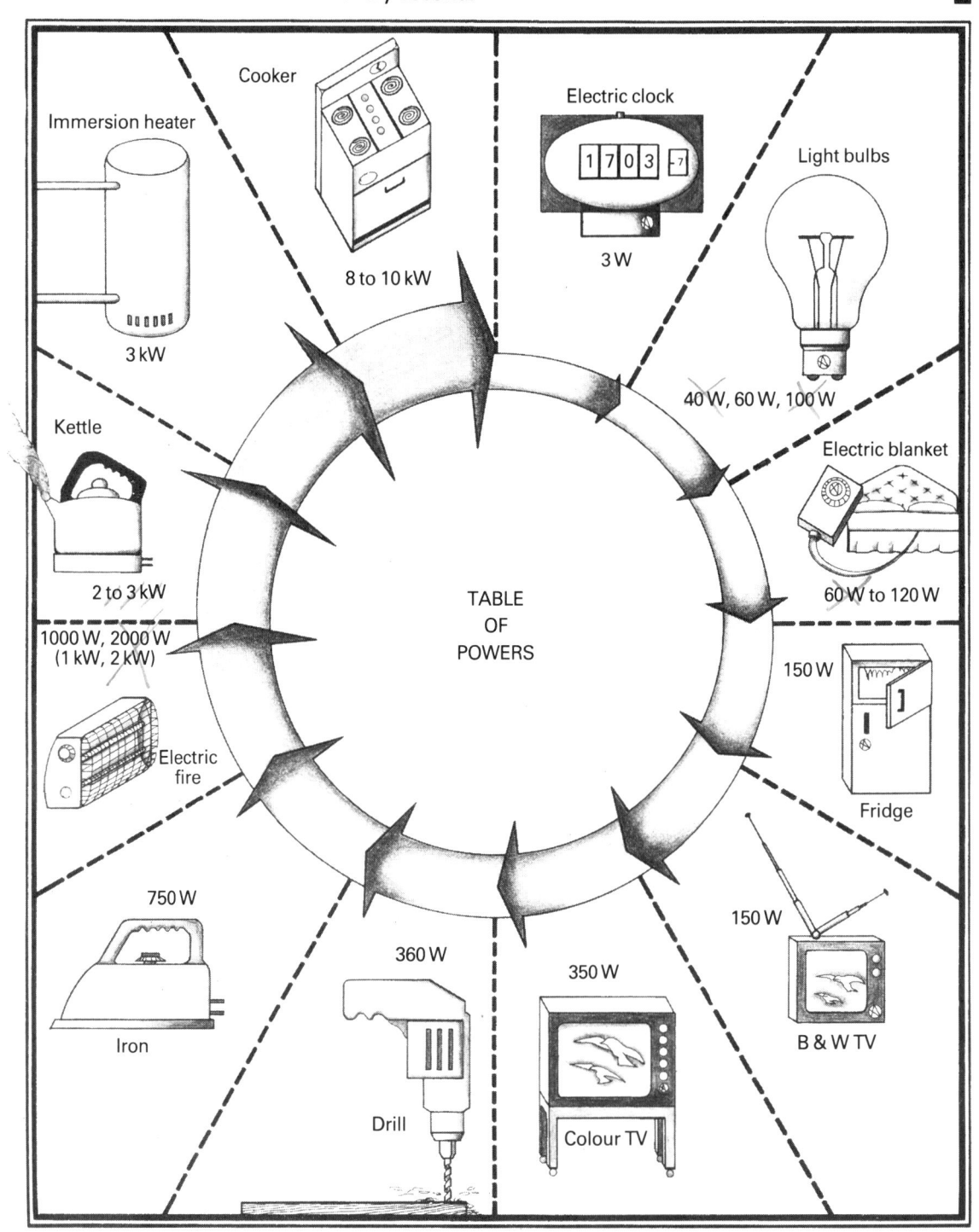

TABLE OF POWERS

- Immersion heater — 3 kW
- Cooker — 8 to 10 kW
- Electric clock — 3 W
- Light bulbs — 40 W, 60 W, 100 W
- Electric blanket — 60 W to 120 W
- Kettle — 2 to 3 kW
- Electric fire — 1000 W, 2000 W (1 kW, 2 kW)
- Fridge — 150 W
- Iron — 750 W
- Drill — 360 W
- Colour TV — 350 W
- B & W TV — 150 W

The more electrical energy you use, the more you pay. One joule is a very small amount of energy, so the electricity used in homes is measured by a meter in units called *kilowatt-hours*.

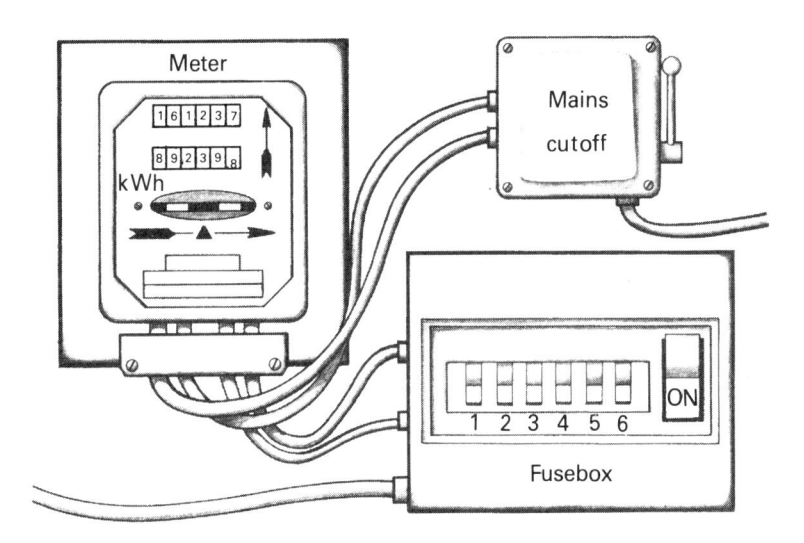

A kilowatt-hour (kWh) is the amount of electrical energy used by a device with a power of *one kilowatt* if it is left on for *one hour*. An iron with a power of 1 kW uses *two* kilowatt-hours of energy if it is used for *two* hours. A 3 kW electric fire left on for 2 hours uses 6 kWh of energy; a 4 kW fire, on for 3 hours, uses 12 kWh of energy:

Number of kWh used = Power in kW × number of hours used

Our electricity bills depend on how many kilowatt-hours, or 'units', we use. Suppose each kWh, or unit, costs 5 p. A 2 kW electric fire left on for 4 hours uses 8 kW, or 8 units. This will cost 8 × 5 p or 40 pence. The more units used, the higher the bill!

Questions 26

1. What are the three effects of electric currents?
2. Name three instruments that use the heating effect of a current.
3. Label this diagram of a light bulb.

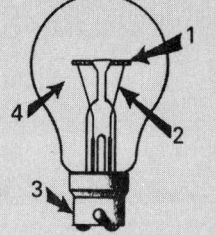

    (a) Why is tungsten used for the filament?
    (b) Why is the bulb filled with argon?
4. This apparatus would be suitable for copper plating.

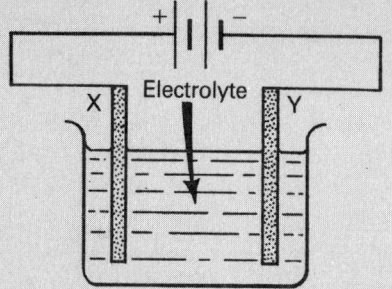

    (a) What are the electrodes X and Y called?
    (b) What electrolyte is used?
    (c) Which electrode would be plated with copper?
    (d) Draw the diagram and show the direction of the electric current with an arrow.
5. This diagram shows a 13 amp plug.

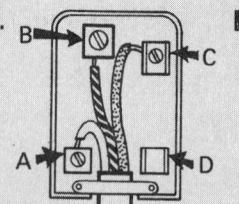

    (a) Which wires are joined to A, B and C?
    (b) What is the colour of each wire?
    (c) Where is the fuse placed?   (LREB)
6. In a domestic ring circuit what is the purpose of the earth connection? Why are fuses placed in every plug?
7. This diagram shows an electric current being passed through acidified *water*.

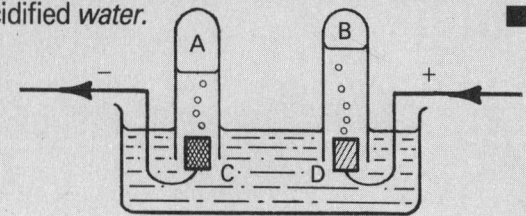

(a) What gases are present at A and B?
(b) What are the electrodes C and D called?

8. Suppose that one unit (1 kWh) of electrical energy costs 5 p. How much will it cost for:
   (a) a 2 kW fire to be left on for 3 hours,
   (b) a 2 kW kettle to be used for 6 hours,
   (c) a 750 W iron (¾ kW) used for 2 hours,
   (d) a 100 W light bulb (¹⁄₁₀ kW) left on for 30 hours?

9. The diagram shows an incorrectly wired 13 A plug.

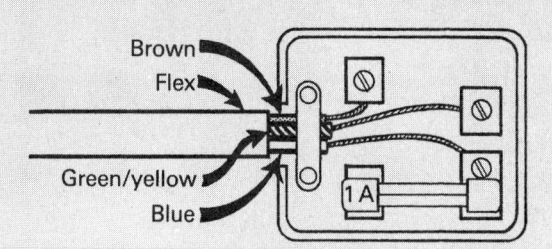

   Brown
   Flex
   Green/yellow
   Blue
   1 A

   (a) What is incorrect in the connections made?
   (b) State two other faults shown in the diagram
   (c) An appliance has a plug which is wired as above. A fault in the appliance causes it to take 20 A of current. Explain what will happen, and say why the appliance is made dangerous because of the way the plug is wired. (SWEB)

10. An electric iron is shown in the diagram below.

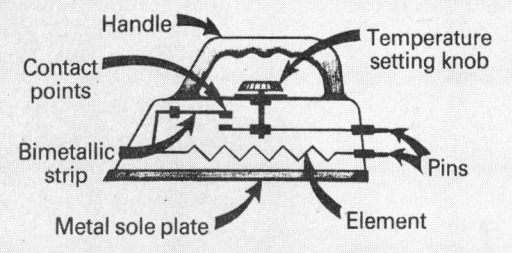

    Handle
    Contact points
    Bimetallic strip
    Metal sole plate
    Temperature setting knob
    Pins
    Element

    (a) What is the purpose of the element?
    (b) To what part of the iron would the earth lead be connected?
    (c) Why do you think a layer of asbestos is placed above the element and a layer of metal is placed below it?
    (d) What material could be used for the handle of the iron? Give reasons.
    (e) State the purpose of the bimetallic strip.
    (f) How does the bimetallic strip achieve this purpose?
    (LREB)

CROSSWORD 5

Across

1. A current can be produced by moving a magnet near a wire in a circuit. This is called ___ induction (15)
8. An electric light can be made dimmer using a ___ (8)
9. A simple 10 across makes about ___ and a half volts (3)
10. A simple one uses copper, 15 across and sulphuric acid (4)
12. An electric current can make a filament very ___ (3)
14. Resistance is measured in ___ (4)
15. See 10 across (4)
17. The live wire going into a plug is covered with ___ insulation (5)
18. It makes electricity (6)
21. A safety device in an electrical circuit (4)
22. The voltage across a 20 ohm resistor is 180 volts. What is the current in amps? (4)
24. The gas inside an electric bulb (5)
25. He discovered the magnetic effect of an electric current (7)
26. Something electrical used in the kitchen (6)

Down

1. The three connections in an electric plug are live, neutral and ___ (5)
2. It moves to produce an electric current (8)
3. A 3 kW electric fire uses electricity at a faster ___ than a 1 kW fire (4)
4. They use electrical energy to do work (6)
5. One of the two colours on the 1 down wire (5)
6. The amount of electrical energy used by an electric fire depends on the number of kilowatts it uses and the ___ it is left on (4)
7. In a dynamo a ___ of wire is held between the two poles of a magnet (4)
11. He first made a particular type of 10 across (9)
13. A metal ___ electricity (8)
16. A magnetic material (4)
18. If you touch a live electric circuit, you may finish up being this! (4)
19. The positive electrode (5)
20. The number of electrodes in a simple cell (3)
23. If you touch an electric circuit, the current may pass through your ___ to your heart (3)

Top left. An Electromagnet. When the electric current is turned off, all the metal will fall. (see page 161)

Top right. Domestic wiring.

Using electricity: foundryman at work with an electric arc furnace, used to produce crude steel.

An oil-fired power station in Dorset.

Lightning strikes. (see page 143)

Insulators in a CEGB sub-station with pylons in the background.

Huge dynamos in a power station. (see page 162)

Part 6

Atomic Physics

Chapter 27

The atom and radiation

The inside of the atom

In the last century scientists believed that *atoms* were like hard, indestructible balls which could not be broken down into smaller parts (the word 'atomos' meant 'unsplittable' in ancient Greece). In this century the atom has been split. We know that atoms are made up of three parts: *electrons, protons* and *neutrons.*

The simplest atom of all, hydrogen, has only one proton and one electron. The proton stays at the centre of the atom while the electron travels round and round it, rather like the Moon orbits the Earth. The proton has a *positive* charge, the electron has an exactly equal *negative* charge.

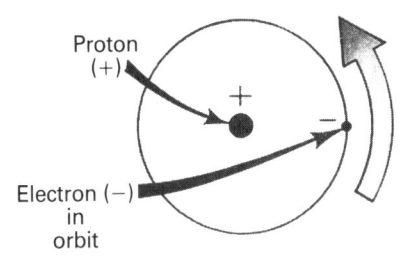

Larger atoms have neutrons as well as protons at the centre, or nucleus, of the atom. Neutrons are not positive or negative but *neutral.*

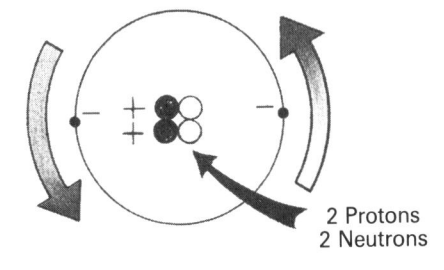

As atoms get bigger and bigger they contain more and more electrons, protons and neutrons. They always contain exactly the same number of protons as they do electrons. This is called the *atomic number.*

The total number of protons and neutrons in the nucleus of an atom is called the *mass number.* This number tells you the mass of an atom compared with the mass of a hydrogen atom. Electrons are very, very small compared with protons — their mass can be ignored. For example, the mass number of hydrogen is 1, and its atomic number is 1. The mass number of helium is 4, its atomic number is 2.

Elements and their symbols

Some substances contain only one sort of atom — these are called *elements.* Copper is an element. It contains only copper atoms. Iron contains only iron atoms, helium contains only helium atoms, carbon contains only carbon atoms, and so on. These are all elements.

Each element has a different atom, with different numbers of protons, neutrons and electrons, e.g. carbon atoms have 6 protons, 6 electrons and 6 neutrons. Every element has its own *symbol:* H (hydrogen), He (helium), Cu (copper) and Ge (germanium) are a few examples. Over 100 elements have been discovered.

The mass number and atomic number are usually written next to the symbol, e.g. $^4_2$He, $^1_1$H. This is a quick way of showing what you need to know about the atom of an element. ■

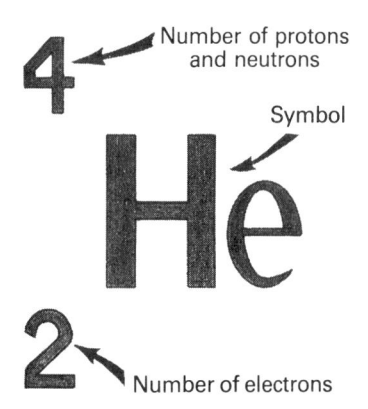

^{4} ← Number of protons and neutrons

He ← Symbol

$_2$ ← Number of electrons

Element	Symbol	Its atom is made up of ...		
		Protons	Electrons	Neutrons
Hydrogen	$^1_1$H	1	1	0
Helium	$^4_2$He	2	2	2
Carbon	$^{12}_{6}$C	6	6	6
Oxygen	$^{16}_{8}$O	8	8	8
Copper	$^{63}_{29}$Cu	29	29	34
Lead	$^{208}_{82}$Pb	82	82	126

Isotopes

Not all atoms of an element are exactly the same. Some atoms of the same element may have more neutrons in them than others. For example, all carbon atoms have six electrons and six protons. But some carbon atoms have six neutrons, while others have eight neutrons. These two types of carbon atom are called *isotopes*.

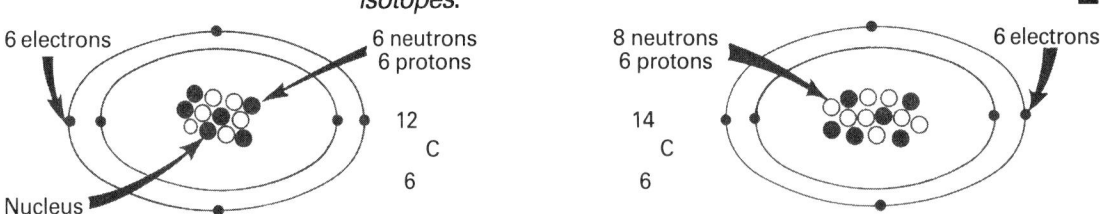

$^{12}_{6}C$ — 6 electrons, Nucleus, 6 neutrons, 6 protons

$^{14}_{6}C$ — 8 neutrons, 6 protons, 6 electrons

The atoms of most elements are *stable*. This means that their atoms do not break up easily. But some elements have isotopes that are *unstable*. These are usually larger atoms, with a lot of protons and neutrons in their nucleus. They are called *radio-isotopes*. Two well-known radio-isotopes are radium and uranium. The nucleus of their atoms can suddenly break up, i.e. *disintegrate*. Small particles, and sometimes dangerous rays, fly off when this happens. These rays and flying particles are called *radioactivity*.

Different types of radioactivity

There are three main types of radioactivity from atoms: *alpha, beta* and *gamma* radiation.

(a) *Alpha (α) particles.* This is simply a particle which flies off at high speed from the nucleus of an atom. It is made up of two protons attached to two neutrons — in other words, the nucleus of a helium atom. Alpha particles can only travel about a metre in air and can be stopped by a thin sheet of paper, or human skin.

(b) *Beta (ß) particles* are just fast-moving electrons. They can travel further than α particles but can be stopped by a thin sheet of metal, like aluminium foil.

(c) *Gamma (γ) rays* are very dangerous. They can only be slowed down by very thick lead sheets, or concrete. They are electromagnetic waves like X-rays, but they have a higher frequency and are much more penetrating and dangerous.

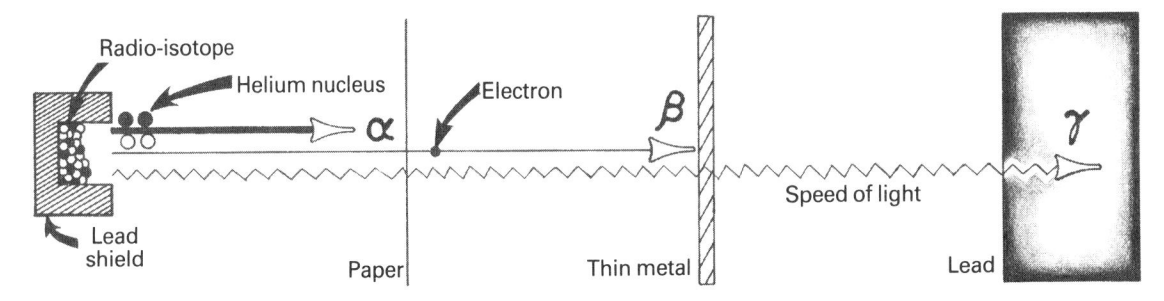

All three types of radiation can damage human skin and tissue. Gamma rays can even cause cancer.

Finally, it has been discovered that two of these types of radiation can be bent, or deviated, by a magnetic field. The path of alpha particles is deviated one way, while beta rays are deviated the other way by a magnet. Gamma rays go straight through a magnetic field.

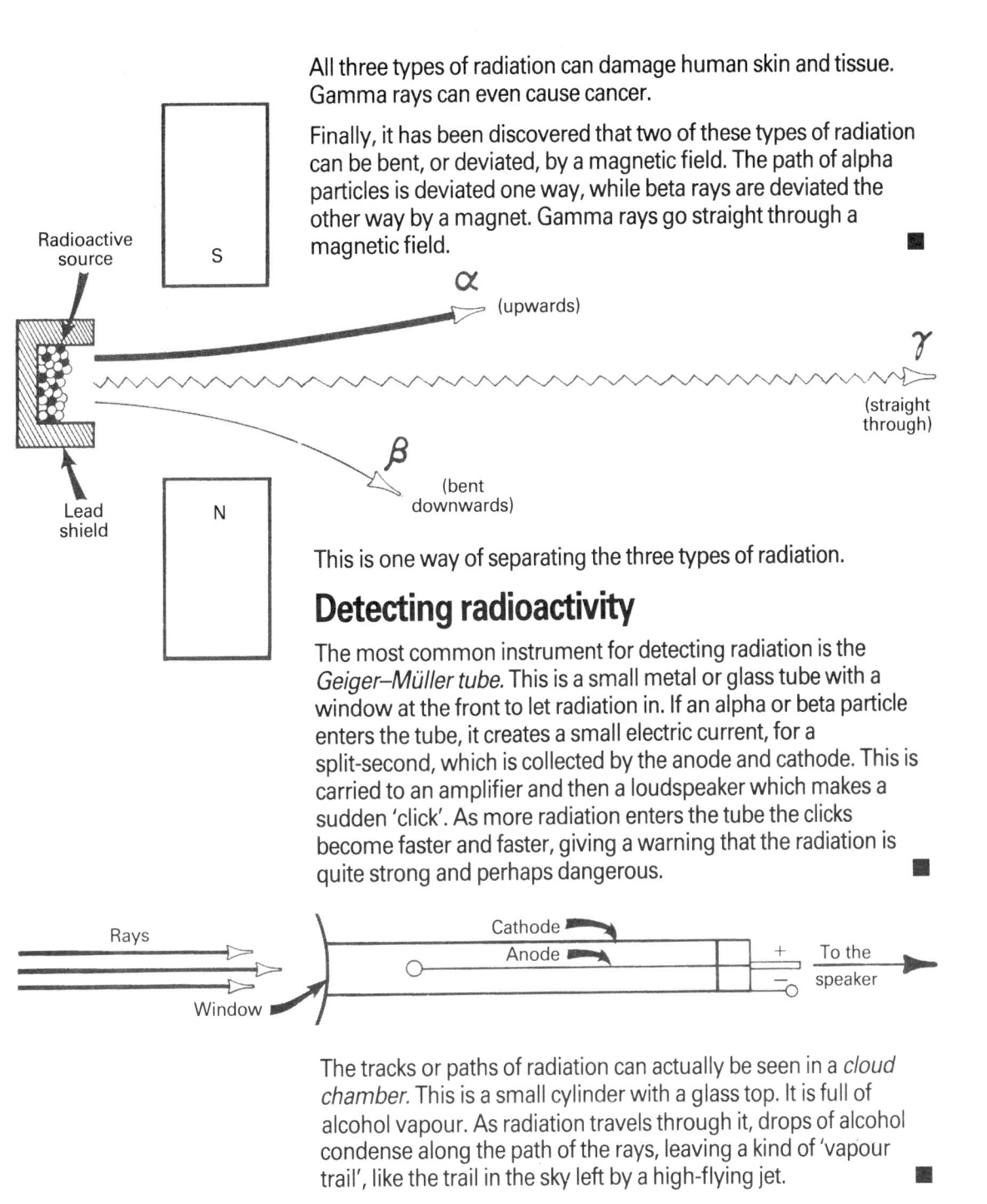

This is one way of separating the three types of radiation.

Detecting radioactivity

The most common instrument for detecting radiation is the *Geiger–Müller tube.* This is a small metal or glass tube with a window at the front to let radiation in. If an alpha or beta particle enters the tube, it creates a small electric current, for a split-second, which is collected by the anode and cathode. This is carried to an amplifier and then a loudspeaker which makes a sudden 'click'. As more radiation enters the tube the clicks become faster and faster, giving a warning that the radiation is quite strong and perhaps dangerous.

The tracks or paths of radiation can actually be seen in a *cloud chamber.* This is a small cylinder with a glass top. It is full of alcohol vapour. As radiation travels through it, drops of alcohol condense along the path of the rays, leaving a kind of 'vapour trail', like the trail in the sky left by a high-flying jet.

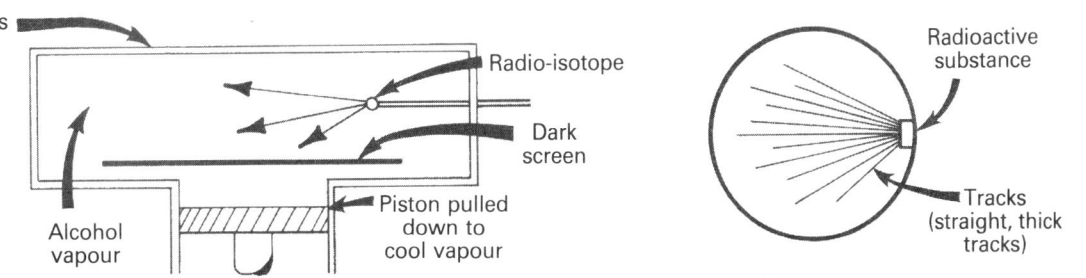

Questions 27

1. Draw diagrams of the atoms of hydrogen and helium. Label the parts, showing the charge on each one.
2. Aluminium is an element. The symbol for its atom can be written as $^{27}_{13}Al$.
   (a) What do the numbers 27 and 13 stand for?
   (b) How many *neutrons* are there in the nucleus of an aluminium atom?
   (c) How many electrons are there outside the nucleus?
3. What is meant by an isotope? Give one example. What is a *radio-isotope?*
4. The following are five particles.

    proton; neutron; electron; atom; molecule.

    Which of the above:
   (a) has the smallest mass?
   (b) has a positive charge?
   (c) is to be found in the nucleus of an atom but has no charge?
   (d) moves with rapid, random motion in the gaseous state? (EMREB)
5. Which type of radioactivity:
   (a) is the most penetrating?
   (b) is stopped by a sheet of paper?
   (c) has a negative charge?
   (d) is not deviated by a magnetic field?
   (e) travels at the speed of light?
   (f) has a positive charge?
   (g) is a high frequency wave?
   (h) is a helium nucleus?
6. (a) Name each of the atomic particles described below.
      (i) It has a negative charge and almost zero mass.
      (ii) It has a mass of one atomic unit and no charge.
      (iii) It contains all the positive charge and almost all the mass of the atom.
   (b) Two kinds of radiation from radioactive materials are called alpha and gamma. Give a brief description of each. (EMREB)
7. How is radiation detected?
8. The stable atoms of potassium have 19 electrons, 19 protons and 21 neutrons. Atoms of a radioactive type of potassium have 19 electrons and 22 neutrons and give off beta (β) radiation.
   (a) Give the atomic number of potassium.
   (b) Give the atomic mass number of the stable atom of potassium.

(c) How many protons has the radioactive atom of potassium?
(d) In what part of an atom are the protons situated?
(e) What name is given to these different forms of potassium?
(f) Give three properties of beta radiation (i.e. three facts about beta radiation). (YREB)

9. Look at the table on page 181
   (a) The number of protons in each atom is often called the *proton number*. For each atom write down the proton number next to the symbol.
   (b) The total number of neutrons *and* protons in the nucleus of an atom is often called the *nucleon number*. Write down the nucleon number for each atom.
   (c) What can you say about the proton number and the number of electrons in a neutral atom?
   (d) Which number is *different* for different isotopes of the same element?

10. One type of atom can change into another type when it gives out an alpha particle. This is called *alpha decay*. For example, radium 226 can decay into radon 226. The decay can be shown as a kind of equation:

    $$^{226}_{88}Ra \longrightarrow {}^{222}_{86}Rn + {}^{4}_{2}He$$

    (a) What do the symbols Ra and Rn stand for?
    (b) What are their proton numbers?
    (c) What is the nucleon number of radium? . . . and of radon?
    (d) What is the difference between their nucleon numbers? What is the difference between their proton numbers?
    (e) What do you notice about the numbers on both sides of the equation?

Chapter 28
Using radioactivity and atomic energy

Using radioactivity

Radioactivity has many uses in medicine and in industry:

(a) *Medicine.* Gamma rays can be used to cure cancer. A dose of γ-radiation can kill cells in the body that have been affected by cancer. X-rays are used to photograph the inside of the human body, e.g. in looking for broken bones.

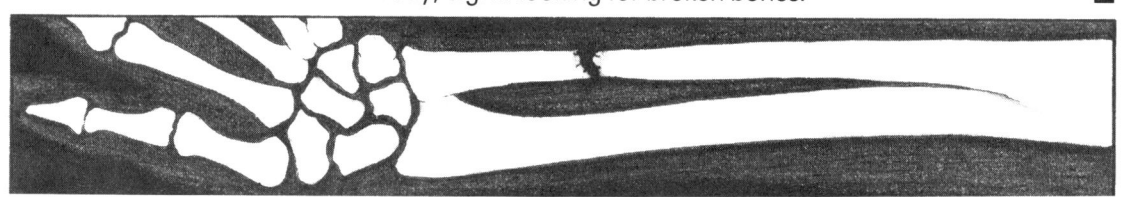

In a similar way gamma rays can be used to take pictures, called *radiographs,* of metal instruments, tanks or boilers when looking for cracks.

(b) *Tracers.* Some radioactive substances are used as 'tracers'. A harmless radio-isotope is sometimes added to food so that the passage of food through a body can be watched or *traced* by the radiation it gives off. Small doses of a radio-isotope can also be fed to plants and animals. Their passage through the plant, or through an animal's bloodstream, can be traced and studied.

(c) *Measuring thickness.* A radio-isotope can be used to check the thickness of a moving sheet of material, such as metal, plastic or paper.

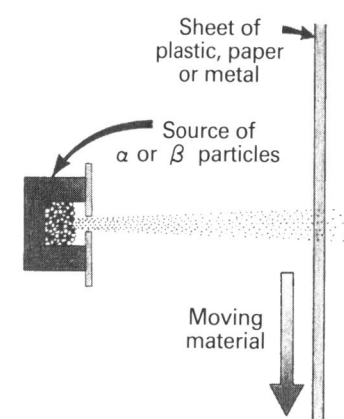

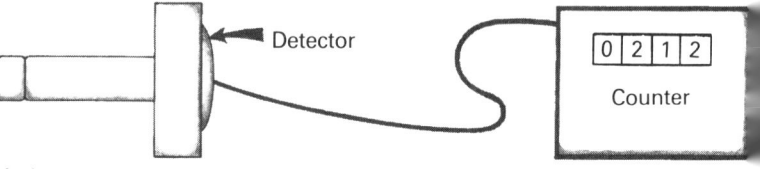

A detector, such as a Geiger–Müller tube, is used to collect the radiation on the other side of the sheet. It *counts* the amount of radiation coming through. If the count is steady then the sheet is the same thickness all the way along. If the count gets less, the sheet must be getting thicker — if the count gets more, the sheet must be getting thinner, as more radiation gets through. In this way the thickness can be quickly checked.

Atomic energy

In 1911 Ernest Rutherford discovered that atoms have a nucleus, and later that this nucleus can be split. This splitting of atoms, called *nuclear fission,* was first used in 1945 to make the atom bomb.

Nowadays, uranium atoms are split to produce atomic energy. Uranium is an element which has two types of atom: $^{235}_{92}U$ and $^{238}_{92}U$. These are called *U-235* and *U-238.* Less than one atom in a hundred is a U-235 atom. But these are the most useful. They suddenly break up and send out flying neutrons.

If enough U-235 atoms are put together they can make a *chain reaction.* It is started by one neutron which splits one uranium atom. This gives off two neutrons which go on to split two more uranium atoms. Four more neutrons fly off which split more uranium atoms, and so on. The result is called a *chain reaction.*

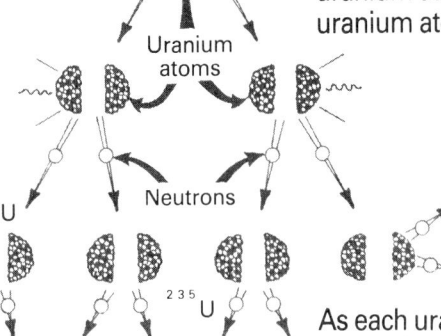

As each uranium nucleus is split a great deal of heat and light energy is produced. This could build up to make an atomic explosion. But if the chain reaction is slowed down by stopping some of the flying neutrons, nuclear fission can be used to produce a steady supply of heat energy. This is done in *nuclear reactors.*

Making electricity from atomic energy

Nuclear reactors use specially prepared uranium rods (containing more U-235 atoms than natural uranium) as their fuel. *Control rods* are used to soak up some of the flying neutrons and slow down the chain reaction. The reactor is closed in by a thick concrete or lead shield to stop dangerous radiation from escaping.

The heat energy from the reactor is used to make steam in a special 'heat exchanger' — this steam can then be used to drive turbines to generate electricity. In Britain there are several atomic power stations generating electricity from atomic energy. Unfortunately the waste products from a reactor are very dangerous and difficult to dispose of.

One other way of making atomic energy is by forcing two hydrogen atoms together at a very high temperature (about 10 million °C). This is called *nuclear fusion.* When hydrogen atoms are joined, or 'fused', a great deal of energy is given out, even more than from nuclear fission. This energy has been used to make the hydrogen bomb (or H-bomb) and we now know that the Sun's heat comes from nuclear fusion.

The dangers of radioactivity

Radioactivity is extremely dangerous because we can receive a harmful dose of radiation without realising it. It probably caused the death of Marie Curie, the person who first isolated radium.

Strong doses of radiation can burn the skin. But a greater danger is the effect of gamma radiation on body tissues, bones and blood cells deep inside the body. Gamma radiation may even lead to cancer or leukaemia (cancer of the blood) in later life.

When radio-isotopes are used in hospitals or in industry many safety precautions are taken, such as: protective clothing, lead or concrete shielding, and handling with long mechanical tongs.

Half-life

The activity of a piece of radioactive material gradually gets less and less with time. It is very difficult to know when a material has lost all its radioactivity. So instead we measure the time taken for radioactivity to fall by *half.* This is called its *half-life.*

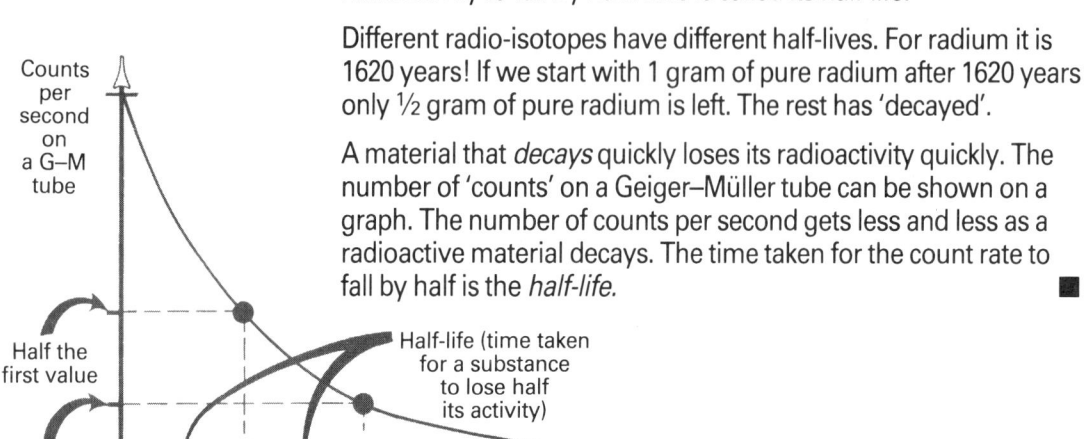

Different radio-isotopes have different half-lives. For radium it is 1620 years! If we start with 1 gram of pure radium after 1620 years only ½ gram of pure radium is left. The rest has 'decayed'.

A material that *decays* quickly loses its radioactivity quickly. The number of 'counts' on a Geiger–Müller tube can be shown on a graph. The number of counts per second gets less and less as a radioactive material decays. The time taken for the count rate to fall by half is the *half-life.*

Here are the 'half-lives' of some other substances:

Thoron (a gas)	Radon	Polonium	Carbon-14
52 seconds	4 days	140 days	5600 years

The isotopes used in medicine have short half-lives. The greatest danger often comes from radio-isotopes with very long half-lives. These are present in radioactive waste from atomic power stations. The disposal of this waste is one of the big problems for the future because it stays dangerous for so many years.

Atoms for war

Atomic bombs (or A-bombs) use fission, the splitting of large atoms of uranium or plutonium. The first A-bomb was tested in a desert in 1945 releasing dust and debris in the shape of a mushroom cloud. Shortly afterwards a second A-bomb was dropped by an American plane on the Japanese port of Hiroshima, killing about 100 000 people and causing terrible injuries to thousands more.

First A-bomb test, July 16, 1945

Mushroom cloud

The Hiroshima bomb used a piece of U-235 about the size of a grapefruit. The uranium was probably 'squeezed together' by a small explosion first. This started an uncontrolled chain reaction leading to an atomic explosion. A second A-bomb was dropped on Nagaski, another Japanese city. This used plutonium and about 50 000 died. These two A-bombs came at the end of the Second World War. No A-bomb has been used in war since.

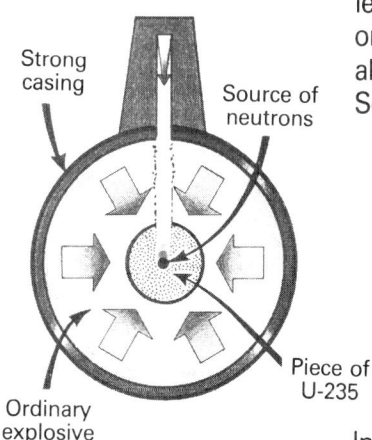

Strong casing
Source of neutrons
Piece of U-235
Ordinary explosive

In 1952 the Americans tested a hydrogen bomb (or H-bomb) in the Pacific Ocean. This uses fusion. Two types of hydrogen atom are forced together to make helium. As they join tremendous energy is released.

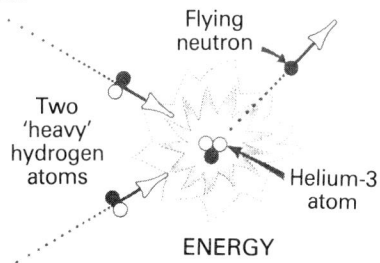

Flying neutron
Two 'heavy' hydrogen atoms
Helium-3 atom
ENERGY

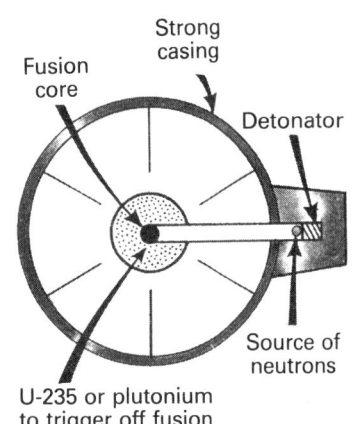

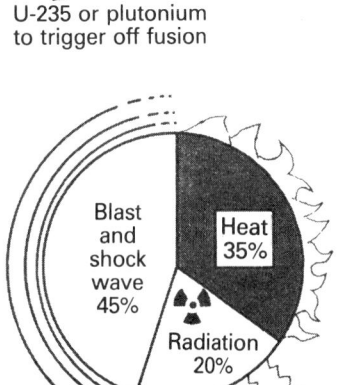

But first the hydrogen atoms must reach a temperature of about 10 000 000 °C. This is reached by exploding an A-bomb. Heat from the fission then triggers off fusion.

The largest H-bombs today can release about 4000 times as much energy as the Hiroshima bomb. This energy is released as a huge blast or shock wave, terrific heat in a fireball, and deadly radiation.

Bombs exploded near the ground suck up dirt and ashes and make them radioactive. These ashes eventually fall again as radioactive fall-out. This fall-out carries many dangerous radio-isotopes, including carbon-14.

Small H-bombs, called nuclear warheads, are now placed inside missiles. Since 1952 scientists have made these missiles faster and much more accurate, using satellites and computers to guide them. About 8000 nuclear missiles are now ready for use worldwide.

A very small H-bomb has recently been made called the neutron bomb. This is designed to produce a lot of radiation (flying neutrons) but a very small blast. It can kill people but with less damage to buildings or tanks. If ever used, it might increase the chance of a war developing into a nuclear war.

Questions 28

1. What is a *radiograph*?
2. Describe how radio-isotopes can be used as tracers.
3. Describe what is meant by a *chain reaction*.
4. What is the difference between nuclear fusion and nuclear fission? Describe how nuclear fission is used to make electricity.
5. This diagram shows a nuclear reactor.

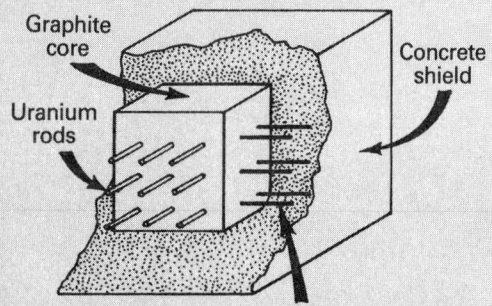

    (a) What is the fuel?
    (b) What are the control rods used for?
    (c) Why does it have a concrete shield?
    (d) Why is the disposal of waste such a problem?
6. Describe some of the dangers of radiation. What safety precautions can be taken?
7. Read the following passage and write notes to explain the meaning of the five terms in italics:

    Radio-isotopes can be used as *tracers* to study the movement of sand in the River Thames. The radio-isotope is introduced to *label the sand* and its movement can be studied by using *Geiger counters*. A radio-isotope is used which has a short *half-life*. (LREB)
8. This graph shows how the activity of a radioactive substance gets less and less with time.

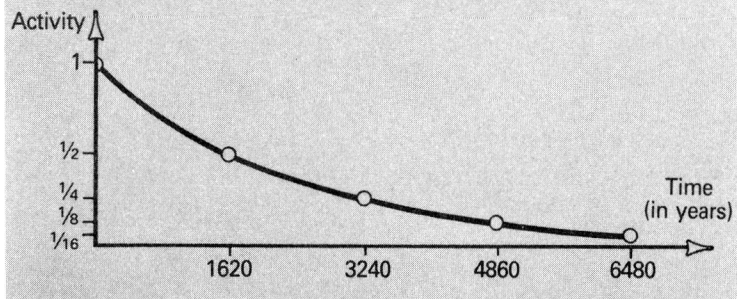

    (a) How long does it take to lose half its activity?
    (b) What is this time called?
    (c) What substance could it be?

191

Chapter 29
Electrons and electronics

Electricity in solids, liquids and gases

An electric current in a metal wire is just a stream of moving electrons carrying a negative charge. In a *liquid* (an electrolyte) an electric current consists of *negative ions* and *positive ions* moving in opposite directions. A *positive ion* is just an atom with an electron *missing;* a *negative ion* is an atom with an extra electron. The negative ions are attracted to the anode, and the positive ones to the cathode.

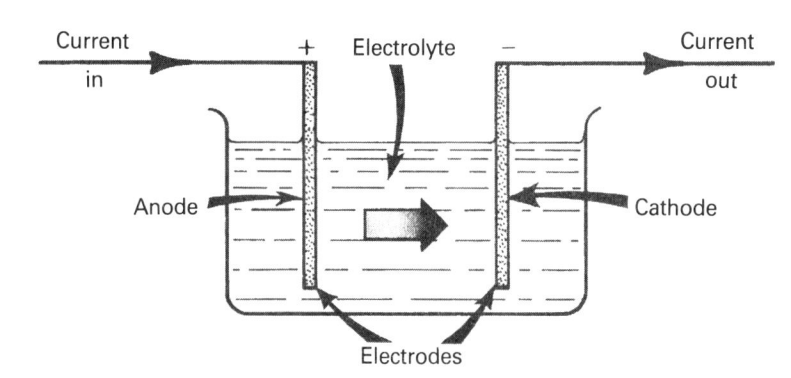

Electricity can also travel through a gas at very low pressure in a *discharge tube.* A stream of electrons travel from the negative plate in the tube (the cathode) towards the positive plate (the anode). This stream of electrons can be bent by a magnet. The moving electrons are often called *cathode rays.*

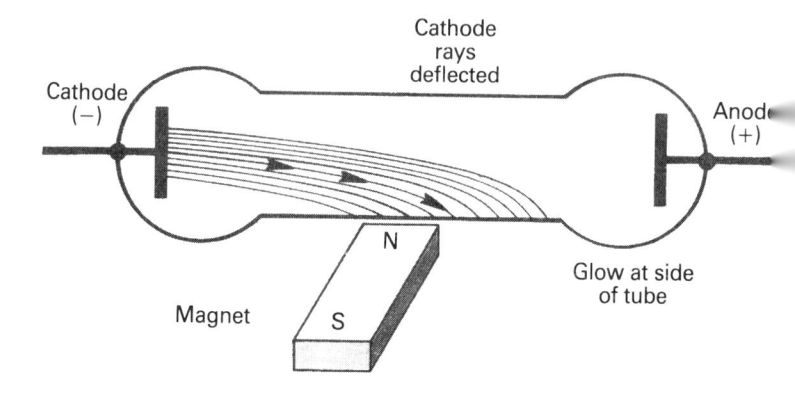

The cathode ray tube

In a *cathode ray tube* a stream of electrons comes from a *hot cathode.* These are attracted by a positive anode which is part of an *electron gun.* The electrons come out of this gun at a high speed in a narrow beam. At the other end of the tube they strike a *fluorescent screen* and make a bright spot. ■

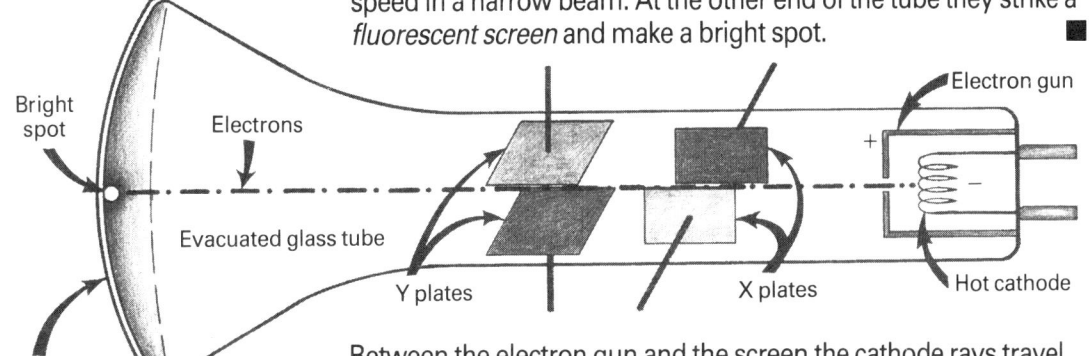

Between the electron gun and the screen the cathode rays travel between two sets of plates called *X plates* and *Y plates.* The Y plates can be used to deflect the beam either up or down. If the top plate has a positive charge it attracts the negative electrons and the beam is pulled upwards. But if the bottom plate has a positive charge the beam is deflected downwards. ■

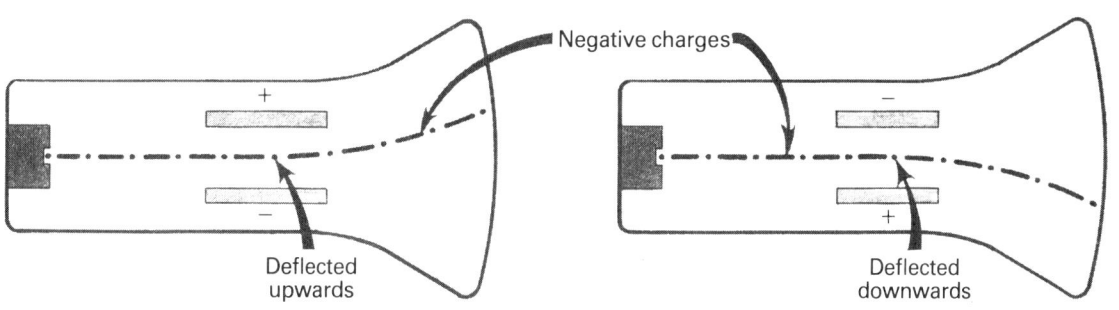

The Y plates can be used to move the beam up or down. The X plates are used to pull the beam from side to side — they pull the cathode rays backwards and forwards across the screen.

Cathode ray tubes are used in science for showing waves and wave forms on a screen in an important instrument called a *cathode ray oscilloscope* (CRO for short). ■

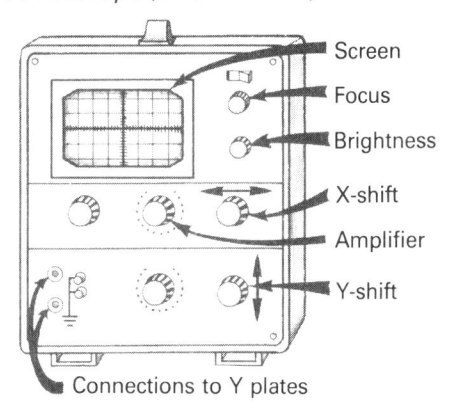

The screen can be used to display the sound wave from a tuning fork or a person's voice, the way that an alternating current changes, or even a person's heartbeat.

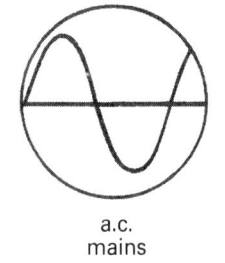

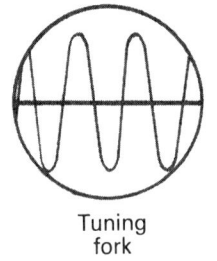

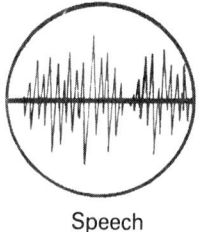

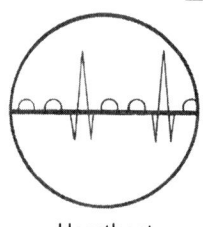

a.c. mains

Tuning fork

Speech

Heartbeat

A cathode ray tube is also the main part of a television. In a TV the beam of electrons sweeps from side to side, and down, hundreds of times every second. This makes a pattern of tiny 'glows' on the screen which you see as a TV picture. A colour TV has three electron guns: one for *green* dots, one for *blue,* and one for *red* dots (the three primary colours).

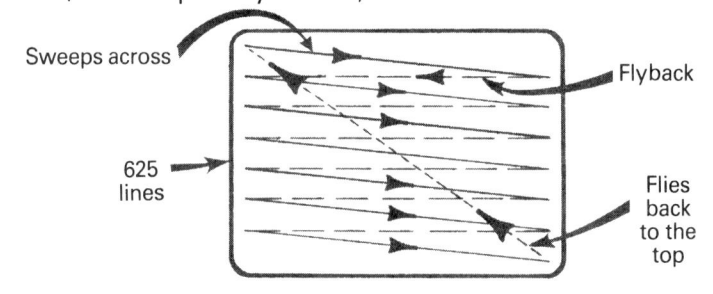

Sweeps across

Flyback

625 lines

Flies back to the top

The diode

In 1904 an invention was made which led to the development of radio: the *diode valve.* A valve carries an electric current in a tube in one direction only. It has a cathode that is heated by a filament and gives off, or *emits,* electrons. These travel across the valve to the anode.

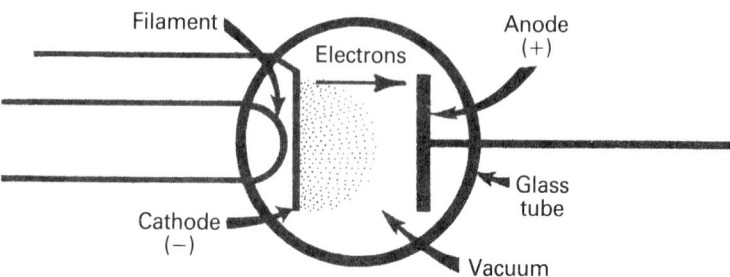

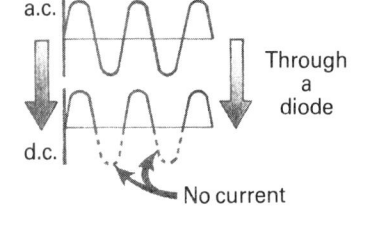

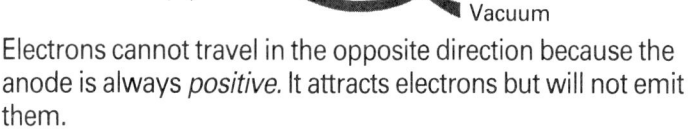

Filament

Electrons

Anode (+)

Cathode (−)

Glass tube

Vacuum

a.c.

d.c.

Through a diode

No current

Electrons cannot travel in the opposite direction because the anode is always *positive.* It attracts electrons but will not emit them.

If a supply of alternating current (a.c.), which is constantly changing direction, is connected to the diode it is changed to a current that flows one way only. Only one half of the alternating current passes through. The a.c. is changed to d.c. — it is *rectified.* This is an important part of radio reception.

Solid-state diodes and transistors

Nowadays diodes are not made from valves, but from solid materials called *semiconductors.* These are substances, such as germanium and silicon, which can carry an electric current but do not conduct as well as copper or brass.

(a) *Diodes.* Some semiconductors are made so that they contain too many electrons. They have an *excess* number of electrons and are called *n-type* materials. The other type of semiconductor is short of electrons — it has gaps or *holes* in it waiting to be filled by electrons from somewhere else. These are called *p-type* materials.

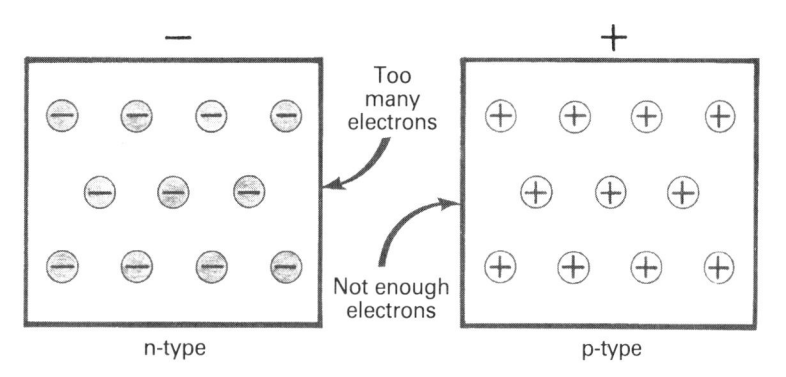

When a piece of n-type is joined to a piece of p-type material, electrons can travel from the n-type to fill the holes in the p-type (this is the same as the electrons in a diode valve travelling from the cathode to the anode). Joining n-type and p-type semiconductors produces a *junction diode.* This will only carry current in one direction, because electrons can only travel from n to p.

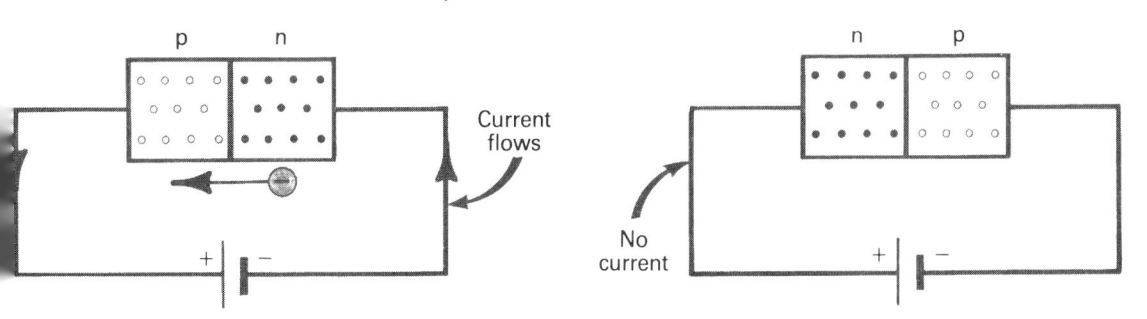

These diodes, called *solid-state diodes,* are used in radios nowadays instead of valves. They can be made very small.

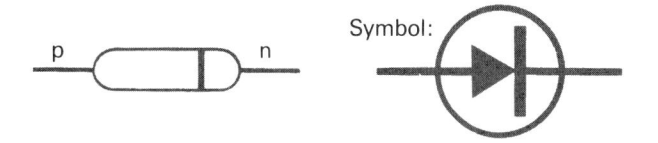

Symbol:

(b) *Transistors.* Another important device made from semiconductors is the transistor. There are two types of transistor: *n–p–n* and *p–n–p* types.

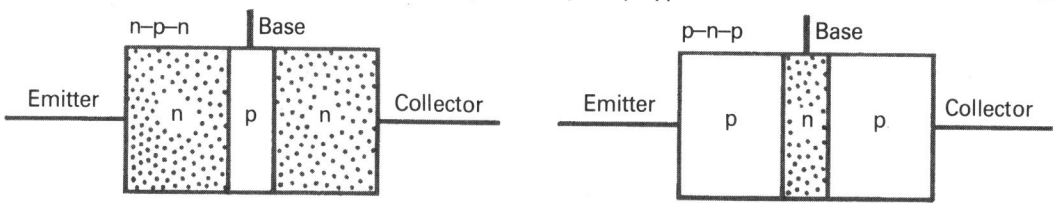

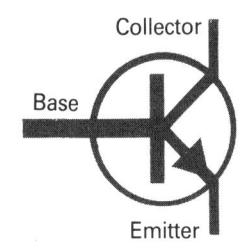

Every transistor has three connections called the *emitter*, the *base* and the *collector*.

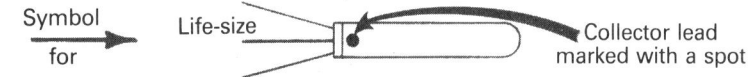

Details of how a transistor works are too complicated to explain here. Its main use is for *amplifying* (making larger) small electric currents or signals. Amplifiers containing transistors are widely used in televisions, record players and radios. Transistors are also used in special switches, e.g. a *photo-transistor* is switched on when light falls on it.

Uses of electronics

Electronics has led to radio, television, hi-fi systems, digital watches, calculators and many other modern devices and instruments. Nowadays electronics is so enormous and widespread that it is a subject on its own.

One interesting branch of electronics is *radio*. Radios use electronic devices like the diode, the transistor, *capacitors* and *inductors*.

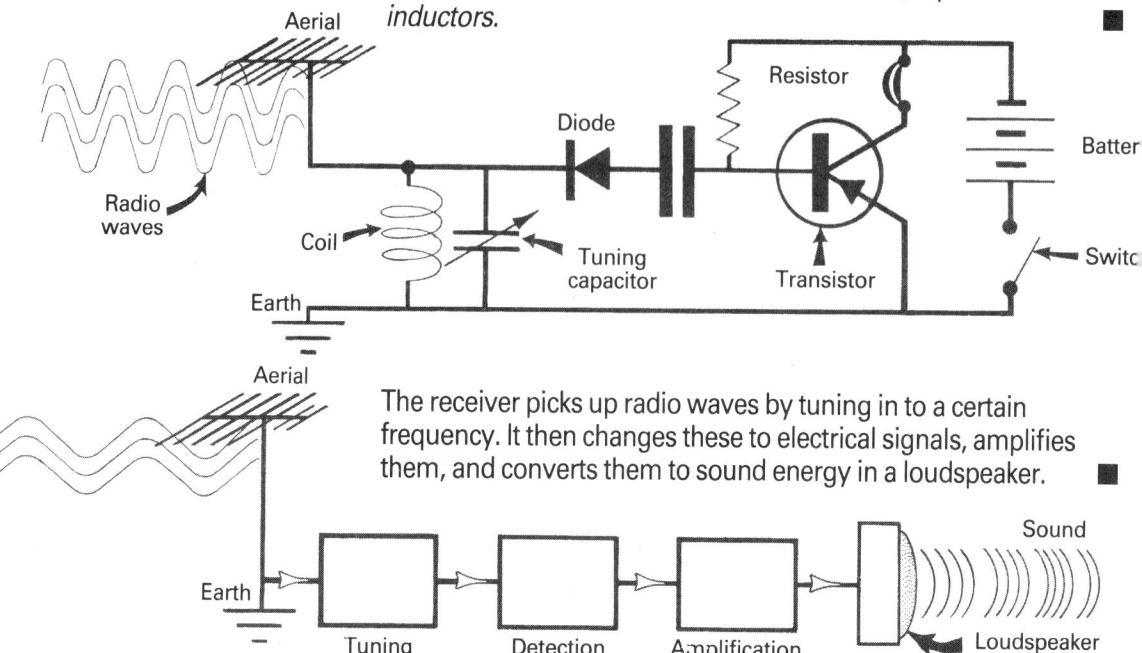

The receiver picks up radio waves by tuning in to a certain frequency. It then changes these to electrical signals, amplifies them, and converts them to sound energy in a loudspeaker.

Questions 29

1. Fill in the missing words:
   'An electric current in a wire is a stream of moving ____, each carrying a ____ charge. A liquid that carries electricity is called an ____. Electricity can travel through a gas in a ____ tube. Electrons travel from the ____ to the ____. Cathode rays can be deflected with a ____.'

2. Describe how electric current is carried in:
   (a) a metal wire, (b) a liquid, (c) a gas.

3. This diagram shows a cathode ray tube.

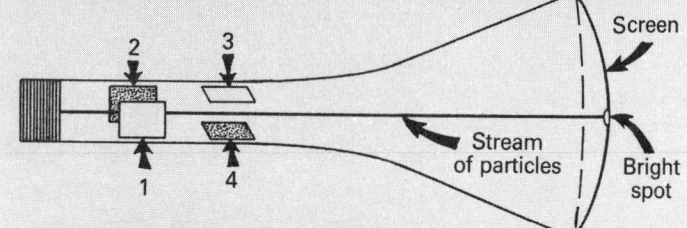

   (a) What is the stream of particles?
   (b) What happens when these particles hit the screen?
   (c) What are the plates 1 and 2, and 3 and 4 used for?
   (d) What are cathode ray tubes used in?

4. (a) What do labels 1 to 5 stand for on this diode valve?

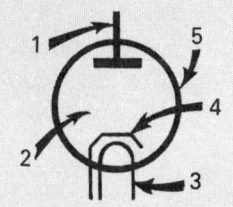

   (b) Which way do the electrons travel?
   (c) Explain how a diode is used to rectify an alternating current.

5. What are n-type and p-type materials? Explain how they can make a *junction diode*.

6. Draw the symbols for a diode and a transistor. What are transistors used for?

7. This diagram represents a cross-section of a cathode ray tube seen from the front. E is the electron beam coming towards you. A, B, C and D are metal plates inside the tube which are used for electrostatic deflection of the beam.

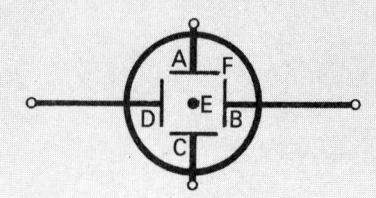

(a) Why is it called a *cathode ray tube?*
(b) What kind of electric charge do electrons have?
(c) If plate D is connected to the positive terminal of a battery and plate B is connected to the negative terminal of the same battery;
  (i) What will happen to the electron beam E?
  (ii) Explain your answer to (c)(i).
(d) Which two plates are the Y plates?
(e) Describe how one or more batteries may be connected to the plates in order to deflect the electron beam E in the direction of F. (YREB)

8. (a) Draw this diagram of a cathode ray tube and label:

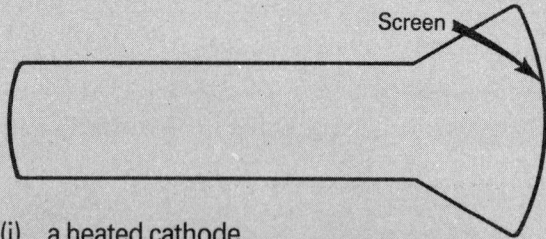

  (i) a heated cathode,
  (ii) an anode,
  (iii) a pair of Y deflector plates.
(b) Describe the function of (a)(i), (ii) and (iii).
(c) Why is it necessary to have a vacuum in a cathode ray tube? (YREB)

9. Describe how electronics has affected our everyday lives.

CROSSWORD 6

Trace this grid on to a piece of paper before working out the answers.

Across

1. Part of an atom (7)
4. A control ___ is used in a nuclear reactor (3)
5. A radioactive material may ___ and lose its radioactivity (5)
8. A type of transistor (1-1-1)
9. Our most important nuclear reactor! (3)
10. A charged particle (3)
12. The chemical symbol for germanium (2)
14. A gap in a semiconductor which is filled by an electron (4)
15. A radioactive element (6)
16. A Geiger- ___ tube is used to detect radiation (6)
17. ___ particles are fast-moving electrons (4)

Down

2. Its atoms are split to produce atomic energy (7)
3. A radioactive element (5)
4. They may be gamma or X (4)
6. Marie ___ was the first person to isolate 15 across (5)
7. Another type of transistor (1-1-1)
8. The mass ___ of helium is 4 (6)
11. Diode ___ carry electric currents in one direction only (6)
12. ___ radiation is very dangerous (5)
13. See 14
14-13 The ___ of 15 across is 1620 years (4-4)

Sizewell nuclear power station in Suffolk, England. (see page 187)

A Pershing missile used to carry a nuclear warhead. (see page 190)

This building in Hiroshima, Japan, survived the nuclear blast from a nuclear bomb dropped at the end of the Second World War. But you can see all the windows have been blown out by the shock wave. (see page 190)

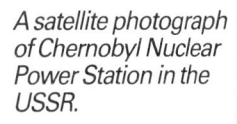

A satellite photograph of Chernobyl Nuclear Power Station in the USSR.

Protective clothing used in a nuclear plant — the reactor core lies beneath. (see page 187)

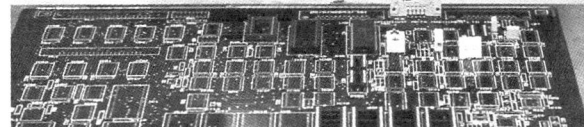

A robot making an electronic circuit board — the robot is fast, accurate and has a simple vision system. (see page 195)

A remote controlled robot in a nuclear plant used to manipulate radioactive material. (see page 187)

Robot welders in a car factory.

201

APPENDIX 1

Measurements in physics

Quantity measured	What it means	Unit and abbreviation
mass	resistance to being moved	kilogram, kg
force	push or pull	newton, N
weight	pull of gravity	newton, N
speed	distance moved every second	metre per second, m/s
velocity	speed in a straight line	metre per second, m/s
acceleration	increase of velocity every second	metre per second per second, m/s^2
work	force used × distance moved	joule, J
energy	the capacity to do work	joule, J
power	work done, or energy used, every second	watt, W

Quantity measured	What it means	Unit and abbreviation
density	the mass of one metre cubed of a material (or one centimetre cubed)	kg/m^3 (or g/cm^3)
pressure	force acting on *one* square metre	newton per square metre, N/m^2 (pascals, Pa)
temperature	level of hotness of an object	degree centigrade or kelvin, °C or K
heat	heat energy lost or gained by an object	joule, J
specific heat capacity	heat needed to raise the temperature of 1 kg of a material by 1°C	joule per kg per °C, J/kg/°C
specific latent heat	heat needed to melt (fusion) or boil (vaporisation) 1 kg of a material	joule per kg, J/kg
electric charge	quantity of electricity (+ or −)	coulomb, C
electric current	quantity of electricity flowing every second	ampere, A
voltage	electro-motive force: the force that pushes electrons round a circuit	volt, V
resistance	decreases the size of the current	ohm, Ω
frequency	number of waves or cycles in one second	hertz, Hz
wavelength	length from one peak to the next	metre, m
amplitude	the largest displacement of a wave	metre, m

APPENDIX 2

Triangles used for calculations

1) Mass M / Volume V / Density D

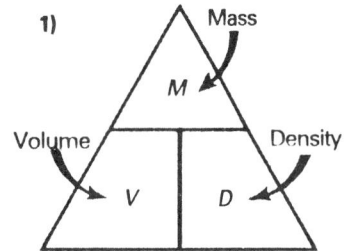

2) Force F / Mass m / Acceleration a

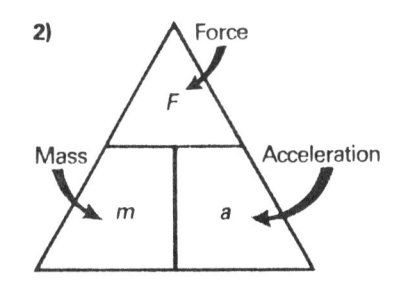

3) Force F / Pressure P / Area A

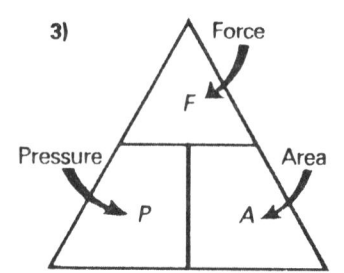

4) Wave speed v / Frequency f / Wavelength λ

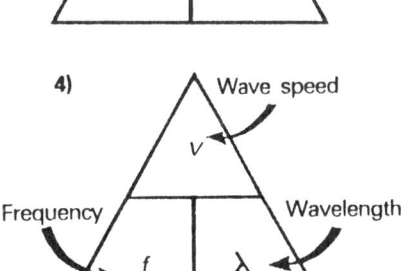

5) Voltage V / Current I / Resistance R

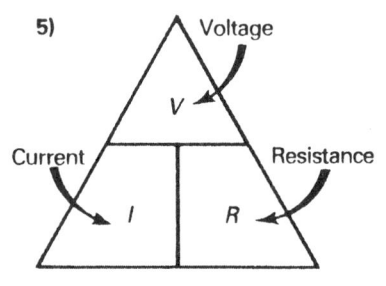

6) Power P / Voltage V / Current I

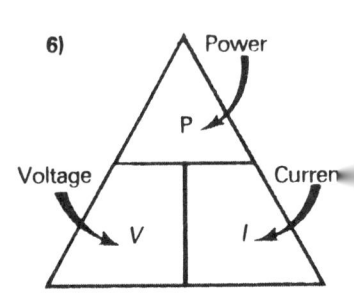

How to use these triangles

- Cover the quantity you want to calculate with your finger:

    e.g. in triangle 1):

    in triangle 2):

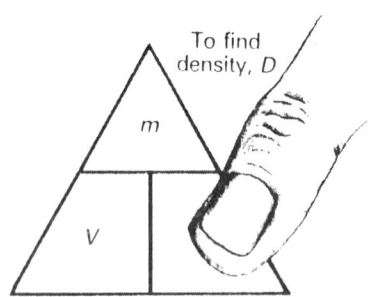

- You will then need to divide one quantity by another or *multiply* them:

    e.g. in 1)   Mass ÷ Volume   or
    e.g. in 2)   Mass × Acceleration

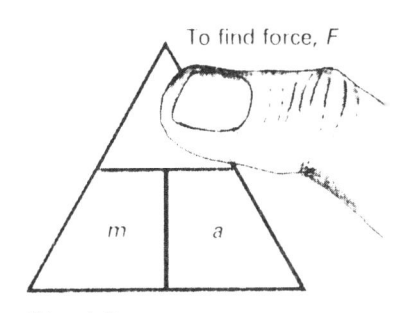

- Put in the numbers and do the division or multiplication:

    e.g. in 1)   if Mass = 60 kg,   Volume = 2m^3
                 Density = 60 ÷ 2 = 30 kg/m^3
    e.g. in 2)   if Mass = 4 kg,   Acceleration = 2m/s^2
                 Force = 4 × 2 = 8 newtons

Triangle 1 — To find density, D

Triangle 2 — To find force, F

204

APPENDIX 3

Meters used in physics

Name of meter	Used to measure
newton-meter	the size of a force in newtons
barometer	atmospheric pressure, in centimetres of mercury or newtons per square metre (two types: aneroid and mercury)
manometer	the pressure of a gas
hydrometer	the density of a liquid
hygrometer	the humidity of the air
thermometer	the temperature of an object
ammeter	the electric current flowing in a circuit
voltmeter	the voltage, potential difference, or e.m.f. 'pushing' the current
Geiger–Müller tube	the radioactivity of a substance

APPENDIX 4

Famous names in physics

■ ■ ■ ■ ■ ■ ■ ■ ■ ■ ■ ■ ■ ■ ■ ■

Robert Van de Graaff	1901–1967	high voltage generator
Enrico Fermi	1901–1954	the first atomic reactor
John Logie Baird	1888–1946	making television
Albert Einstein	1879–1955	relativity and many new theories in physics
Guglielmo Marconi	1874–1937	inventing radio
Ernest Rutherford	1871–1937	founding nuclear physics
Pierre Curie	1867–1934	separating polonium and radium
Marie Curie	1859–1906	experiments with radioactivity
Heinrich Hertz	1857–1894	showing electromagnetic waves
Sir J J Thomson	1856–1940	discovering the electron
Henri Becquerel	1852–1908	discovering radioactivity
Thomas Edison	1847–1931	the gramophone, the light bulb
Wilhelm Röntgen	1845–1923	discovering X-rays
James Dewar	1842–1923	the Dewar, or vacuum flask
James Joule	1818–1889	experiments with heat
Michael Faraday	1791–1867	dynamo, electromagnets, the idea of 'fields'
Georg Ohm	1787–1854	law of electric circuits
Hans Oersted	1777–1851	discovering the magnetism of an electric current
Andre Ampère	1775–1836	studying electric currents
Alessandro Volta	1745–1827	the first electric cell or 'battery'

Luigi Galvani	1737–1798	electricity from frogs' legs
James Watt	1736–1819	improving the steam engine
Anders Celsius	1701–1744	the Celsius or centigrade scale
Daniel Fahrenheit	1686–1736	the first liquid-in-glass thermometers
Thomas Newcomen	1663–1729	inventing the steam engine
Sir Isaac Newton	1642–1726	spectrum, telescope, three new laws of motion
Robert Hooke	1635–1703	Hooke's Law for springs
Johan Kepler	1571–1630	Laws of planetary motion
Galileo	1564–1642	first experiments, and the laws of falling bodies
William Gilbert	1554–1603	studying magnets
Nicolaus Copernicus	1473–1543	picturing the Universe with the Sun at the centre
Ptolemy	2nd century AD	placing Earth at the centre of the Universe
Archimedes	287–212 BC	laws of floating and sinking; the screw
Aristotle	384–322 BC	the first laws of motion
Democritus	470–400 BC	suggesting the 'atom'

APPENDIX 5

Drawing electric circuits

Electric circuits can be easily drawn by using *symbols* to stand for the different parts. Here is a list of symbols that are commonly used. Most of them appear in this book.

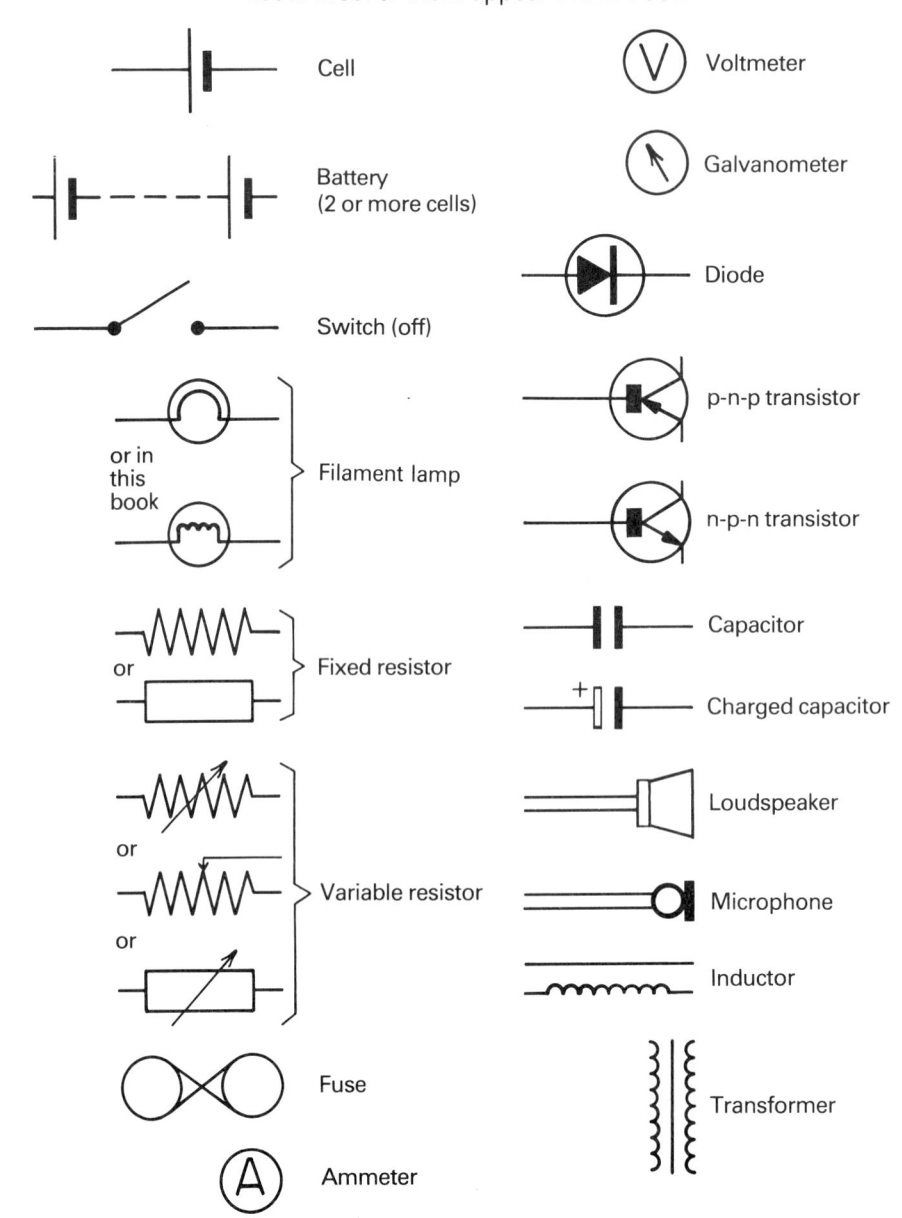

—|⊢—	Cell
—|⊢- - -⊢|—	Battery (2 or more cells)
—• •—	Switch (off)
(filament lamp symbols) or in this book	Filament lamp
—/\/\/\— or ▭	Fixed resistor
—/\/\/\— (with arrow) or ▭ (with arrow)	Variable resistor
∞	Fuse
(A)	Ammeter
(V)	Voltmeter
(arrow in circle)	Galvanometer
—▶|—	Diode
(transistor symbol)	p-n-p transistor
(transistor symbol)	n-p-n transistor
—||—	Capacitor
—+||—	Charged capacitor
(speaker symbol)	Loudspeaker
(microphone symbol)	Microphone
—mmm—	Inductor
(transformer symbol)	Transformer

Index

A

	page
absolute zero	62
acceleration	29
—due to gravity	33
alpha particles	182
alternating current (a.c.)	164
ammeters	148, 164
ampère	148
amplifiers	196
anode	168
Archimedes	48
atmospheric pressure	55
atom	180
atomic bomb	189, 200
atomic mass	180
atomic number	181

B

barometer — aneroid	55
— mercury	55
beta particles	182
bimetallic strip	71
block and tackle	38
boiling	82

C

cameras — lens	111, 137
— pinhole	97
capillary rise	16, 21
cathode	168
— ray oscilloscope	193
cells — dry	140
— lead-acid	141
— simple	140
Celsius (centigrade)	62
centre of gravity	43, 60
chain reaction	187

circuits — parallel	147
— series	147
— symbols	208
cloud chamber	183
colours	116–118
compass	155
conductors — electricity	145
— heat	75
conservation of energy	10, 20, 21
convection	77, 93, 94
converging — lens	107
— mirror	100
critical angle	106
current — electron	145
— conventional	146

D

dam	60
damp course	16, 21
deceleration	29
declination	157
density	17, 49
diode	194
dip, angle of	157
direct current (d.c.)	164
dispersion of light	116
diverging — lens	107
— mirror	100
domain theory, magnetism	158
double glazing	76
dynamo	162, 178

E

earth wire	171
echoes	130
eclipses	97, 137
efficiency	40
effort	39
electric — bell	168
— meters	148
— motor	93, 163
— power	150, 172, 177, 178
electrodes	168

electrolysis	169
electromagnetic — induction	162
— waves	120
electromagnets	161, 177
electromotive force (e.m.f.)	145
electrons	192
electroplating	169
energy, forms of	8
engines — diesel	60, 89
— 4-stroke	88
— jet	90
— rocket	90, 93
— 2-stroke	89
equilibrium	45
evaporation	84
expansion — gases	73
— liquids	72
— solids	70
eye	110

F

fields, magnetic	155, 177
fission	187
floating	48
focal length	107
focus — lens	106
— mirror	101
forces, types of	22, 59
freezing	82
frequency	120–123
friction	22
fulcrum	42
fuses	170
fusion	189

G

galvanometer	164
gamma rays	120, 182
Geiger–Müller tube	183
graphs — distance time	32
— velocity time	32
gravity	22

209

H

half-life	188
heat energy	62, 66
Hooke's Law	26
hot-water system	77
hydraulic jack	53
hydrogen bomb	189, 200
hydrometer	50

I

images — real	97
— virtual	108
incident ray	99
infra-red rays	120
insulators — electrical	142
— heat	75
ions	192
isotopes	182

J

jet	90
joules	12
J P Joule	12

K

Kelvin temperature scale	62
kilogram	4
kilowatt-hour	173
kinetic energy	8

L

latent heat	82
laser	138
lenses — converging	107
— diverging	107
levers	37
lightning	178
load	37
long sight	112
longitudinal waves	121
loudness	131

M

machines	36
magnets	154, 177
magnifying glass	107
manometer	54
mass	3
mass number	181
mechanical advantage	39
melting	82
mirrors — curved	100
— plane	99
molecules	20
moments	42
musical instruments	132, 138

N

National Grid	163
neutral points	156
neutrons	180
Newton, Sir Isaac	2, 207
Newton's Laws	30, 90
normal	99
nucleus	142, 180

O

Oersted, Hans	168
ohm	148
Ohm's Law	149
oscilloscope	193

P

penumbra	97
periscope	100, 106
pinhole camera	97
pitch	131
Plimsoll line	49
plutonium	189
potential — energy	8
— difference	148
power	36
pressure — atmospheric	55
— cooker	83
— in liquids	53
prisms	116
protons	180
pulley systems	38, 60

R

radiation — heat	78
— electromagnetic	120
radio	196
radioactivity	182, 201
ray diagrams	102
reaction	90
reflection — light	99
— total internal	105
— of sound	130
refraction	104
refrigerator	85
relative density	49
resistance, electrical	146
resistors	149
resonance	133
rheostat	146
ring main	170
ripple tank	123
robots	201
rockets	90

S

satellite	137
screw-jack	38
semiconductors	195
shadows	96
short sight	112
Solar System	33, 60
solenoid	154
sound waves	128
specific heat capacity	67
specific latent heat	83
spectacles	112
spectrum — visible	116
— electromagnetic	120
speed	29
stability	45
static electricity	141
surface tension	16, 21

T

telescopes	113, 137
television	194
temperature	62
thermocouple	64
thermometers	63, 64, 94
thermostats	71
transformers	163
transistors	196
transverse waves	121

U

ultra-violet rays	120
umbra	97
upthrust	48
uranium	187

V

vacuum flask	79
velocity	29
velocity ratio	39
vibrations	128
viscosity	22
volt	148
voltmeter	148

W

watt	36, 150
Watt, James	12
waves	120
wavelength	122
weight	3
work	36

X

X-rays	120